★ INVISIBLE ENEMY ★

AMERICA'S RECENT PAST

This new and exciting series charts the most recent historical developments that have shaped America and the world. While the study of history generally concentrates on the distant past, where there are established works and perspectives shaped by several generations of historians, this series tackles new questions and issues. Each book in the series provides a concise and engaging overview of specific events and historical trends of the late twentieth century and beyond. Authors present sustained historical arguments about particular problems in recent American history, to give students an immediate historical grasp of current events and to stimulate general readers interested in contemporary topics and issues.

1 *America's Failing Empire*
Warren I. Cohen
2 *Invisible Enemy*
Greta de Jong

INVISIBLE ENEMY

THE AFRICAN AMERICAN FREEDOM STRUGGLE AFTER 1965

Greta de Jong

A John Wiley & Sons, Ltd., Publication

This edition first published 2010
© Greta de Jong 2010

Blackwell Publishing was acquired by John Wiley & Sons in February 2007. Blackwell's publishing program has been merged with Wiley's global Scientific, Technical, and Medical business to form Wiley-Blackwell.

Registered Office
John Wiley & Sons Ltd, The Atrium, Southern Gate, Chichester, West Sussex, PO19 8SQ, United Kingdom

Editorial Offices
350 Main Street, Malden, MA 02148-5020, USA
9600 Garsington Road, Oxford, OX4 2DQ, UK
The Atrium, Southern Gate, Chichester, West Sussex, PO19 8SQ, UK

For details of our global editorial offices, for customer services, and for information about how to apply for permission to reuse the copyright material in this book please see our website at www.wiley.com/wiley-blackwell.

The right of Greta de Jong to be identified as the author of this work has been asserted in accordance with the UK Copyright, Designs and Patents Act 1988.

Wiley also publishes its books in a variety of electronic formats. Some content that appears in print may not be available in electronic books.

Designations used by companies to distinguish their products are often claimed as trademarks. All brand names and product names used in this book are trade names, service marks, trademarks or registered trademarks of their respective owners. The publisher is not associated with any product or vendor mentioned in this book. This publication is designed to provide accurate and authoritative information in regard to the subject matter covered. It is sold on the understanding that the publisher is not engaged in rendering professional services. If professional advice or other expert assistance is required, the services of a competent professional should be sought.

Library of Congress Cataloging-in-Publication Data

De Jong, Greta.
  Invisible enemy : the African American freedom struggle after 1965 / Greta de Jong.
    p. cm. – (America's recent past)
  Includes bibliographical references and index.
  ISBN 978-1-4051-6717-8 (hardcover : alk. paper) – ISBN 978-1-4051-6718-5 (papback : alk. paper) 1. African Americans–Civil rights–History–20th century. 2. Race discrimination–United States–History–20th century. 3. Civil rights movements–United States–History–20th century. 4. United States–Race relations–History–20th century.
  5. Racism–United States–History–20th century. I. Title.
  E185.615.D436 2010
  323.1196'0730–dc22

                                20090520

A catalogue record for this book is available from the British Library.

Set in 10/12.5 pt Sabon by Toppan Best-set Premedia Limited
Printed and bound in Malaysia by Vivar Printing Sdn Bhd

01   2010

489720806

CONTENTS

Acknowledgments   vi

Introduction   1

1   The Never Ending Story: American Racism from Slavery to
    the Civil Rights Movement   7

2   From the Freedom Movement to Free Markets: Racializing
    the War on Poverty and Colorblinding Jim Crow   30

3   A System without Signs: The Invisible Racism of the
    Post-Civil Rights Era   53

4   Fighting Jim Crow's Shadow: Struggles for Racial Equality
    after 1965   76

5   To See or Not to See: Debates over Affirmative Action   100

6   Is This America? Electoral Politics after the Voting Rights Act   124

7   Fir$t Cla$$ Citizen$hip: Struggles for Economic Justice   147

8   All Around the World: The Freedom Struggle in a
    Global Context   169

Notes   194

Index   230

ACKNOWLEDGMENTS

I am very grateful to Ron Edsforth and Peter Coveney for inviting me to write this book for the America's Recent Past series. The series provides an opportunity for contributing scholars to combine a synthesis of the existing literature with their own analyses and insights, and to present their findings to a larger audience than is usual for most academic studies. It has been both a challenge and a joy to work on this project, and I can only hope that the finished product meets expectations.

Although this study includes some material from my own research on the black freedom movement in the post-civil rights era, it draws significantly from the works of other scholars and reflects the cumulative efforts of historians, sociologists, political scientists, and activists seeking to make sense of developments since the 1960s. Special thanks to Derek Musgrove for offering clarification and sharing insights regarding the experiences of black elected officials as he works to bring his forthcoming book on this topic to publication, and to those who kindly granted permission to use photographs or quotations: Julian Bond, Mazie Butler Ferguson, Nick Cobbing, the Poverty and Race Research Action Council, *Ms.* magazine, the *Nation*, the *New York Times*, and United Press International. The scholarly expertise, talent, and passion on offer in the field of African American studies are truly astounding. I encourage readers who wish to deepen their understanding of the issues discussed in this book to follow up with some of the works cited in the notes to each chapter.

Conversations about race with family, friends, colleagues, and students helped me to sharpen my thinking on many topics and find ways to express my ideas clearly to a broad audience. In particular I would like to thank all members of the de Jong clan; my BFF Greg Locke; graduate students Sue Davis, Whitney Foehl, Geralda Miller, Carla Trounson, Jen Valenzuela, and Chris Zamboni; and my wonderful fellow faculty members (past and present) in the history department at the University of Nevada: Alicia

Barber, Scott Casper, Linda Curcio-Nagy, Richard Davies, Dennis Dworkin, Jerome Edwards, Neal Ferguson, Francis Hartigan, Martha Hildreth, Bruce Moran, Michelle Moran, Andrew Nolan, Elizabeth Raymond, William Rowley, Hugh Shapiro, Kevin Stevens, Charles Tshimanga-Kashama, and Barbara Walker. Thanks also to Jennifer Baryol, departmental administrator extraordinaire, and to the John and Marie Noble Endowment for Historical Research. The history department is extremely fortunate to have both of these sources of support for the scholarly and instructional endeavors of its faculty.

Four anonymous readers reviewed a draft of this book before publication and offered encouragement along with many thoughtful criticisms and suggestions for improvement. Their comments helped me to clarify my arguments, resolve some organizational problems, and eliminate errors, and I am extremely grateful for the careful attention each reader gave to the manuscript. I take full responsibility for any problems or mistakes that remain.

Finally I would like to thank the staff at Wiley-Blackwell who were involved in the production of this book: Galen Smith, whose gentle reminders kept me on track for completing the manuscript; Mervyn Thomas for his careful copyediting; and Scott Graham at Cyandesign for the cover design.

Introduction

"I don't see race," declared political satirist Stephen Colbert during a segment on his television show in 2006. "People tell me I'm white and I believe them, because I belong to an all-white country club."[1] Colbert's fake colorblindness highlighted both the reality of racism in the United States and some key reasons for its persistence after the passage of civil rights legislation in the 1960s. Although the new laws were an essential step toward ensuring racial equality, they were an insufficient remedy for disparities in economic opportunity and political power that were constructed over a period of centuries and could not be eradicated merely by treating everyone equally from now on. Most African Americans lacked the means to join exclusive country clubs even if white administrators could be persuaded to admit them. Participants in the black freedom movement knew that real justice required redistributive policies to address the historical legacies of slavery and Jim Crow. Most other Americans rejected this idea, however, and instead opted for racially neutral approaches that effectively froze existing inequalities in place. In the early twenty-first century African Americans lagged behind white citizens in virtually every measure of social and economic wellbeing. This was not a consequence of obvious forms of discrimination but of mechanisms that continued to allocate wealth and power in racially biased ways after legalized segregation and disfranchisement were abolished. The inequities created by past oppression took on a self-perpetuating life of their own, allowing white Americans to benefit from a racist system even as they professed not to "see race."

The invisible nature of racism in the post-civil rights era posed significant challenges for those who continued the struggle for equality after 1965. Open expressions of hatred and the lethal violence of earlier decades largely disappeared, replaced by rhetoric that emphasized individual liberty and the sanctity of free markets to defend policies that had racially disparate effects. Most frustrating was the erasure of history and refusal to acknowledge the cumulative effects of racist oppression that characterized these arguments. Civil rights leader Julian Bond likened the belief that the nation could move "beyond race" by ignoring everything that had happened before the 1960s to this scenario: "It is the fourth quarter of a football game between the white team and the black team. The white team is ahead 145 to 3. The white team owns the ball, the field, the goalposts, the uniforms and the referees. They have been cheating since the game began. ... Suddenly the white quarterback, who feels badly about things that happened before he entered the game, says, 'Can't we just play fair?'"[2] Playing fair in that context might be a good beginning, but until something was done to even the score, the white team's success rested on unearned advantages that tilted the game in its favor.

Bond's analogy highlighted the systemic nature of racism and its roots in political economy rather than individual prejudice. The power to make laws and set policy (referee the game) is the power to distribute resources (fix the score). In North America from the seventeenth through the twentieth centuries that power rested largely with wealthy white men who used it to advance their own interests. Chapter 1 of this book outlines how a racist social order emerged simultaneously with American capitalism and the connections between the two. Colonial elites sought to secure a stable supply of cheap labor and alleviate social tensions by passing laws that differentiated between European and African settlers, ultimately reducing African Americans to the status of human chattel. Racial slavery established enduring connections between class and race and formed the basis for white Americans' belief in their own superiority. Broad segments of the white population had a stake in this social structure, making it remarkably resistant to challenges. The racial order withstood the Enlightenment revolution that created a new nation based on the principles of liberty and equality, the Civil War and the abolition of slavery, the social reforms initiated during the New Deal and World War II eras, and the civil rights movement of the 1960s. In each period racism changed its form but never disappeared. Instead, new patterns of inequality emerged that perpetuated assumptions of black inferiority.

Civil rights activists understood that racism was deeply ingrained in the economic and political institutions of the United States. In 1967 Stokely Carmichael and Charles Hamilton distinguished between the racist beliefs expressed in white supremacists' resistance to the freedom movement and the broader social forces that restricted black people's lives. "When white terrorists bomb a black church and kill five black children, that is an act of individual racism, widely deplored by most segments of the society," they wrote. "But when in that same city – Birmingham, Alabama – five hundred black babies die each year because of the lack of proper food, shelter and medical facilities ... that is a function of institutional racism."

Institutional racism resulted from laws and practices that purposely restricted African Americans' access to education, housing, employment, and political power in the slavery and Jim Crow eras. All white Americans profited from the system regardless of their particular feelings or actions toward black people. White citizens therefore shared a collective responsibility not just to cease discriminating against African Americans on an individual basis but to actively dismantle the structures that fostered inequality.[3]

Most white people declined to accept this responsibility. As outlined in Chapter 2, efforts to enhance black people's economic opportunities through the war on poverty encountered strong opposition from Americans who argued that these initiatives were unnecessary. Business leaders seeking to halt the trend toward government intervention in the economy, segregationists attempting to maintain white dominance, and upwardly mobile suburbanites who viewed material success as the product of individual effort together crafted a narrative that cast antipoverty initiatives as an unjustified burden on taxpayers that interfered with the natural operation of the free enterprise system. Business-friendly politicians manipulated the latent racism that lay behind these views to construct a powerful electoral majority favoring limited government and economic deregulation after the 1960s. Over the next four decades Republican and Democratic administrations alike promoted a free market agenda that perpetuated the racial disparities created by past discrimination and generated new hardships for many black people.

The political shifts of the late twentieth century occurred simultaneously with global economic transformations that increasingly threatened the jobs and living standards of American workers. Failure to address systemic racism left African Americans concentrated in geographical and occupational areas that were disproportionately affected by these shifts. Chapter 3 examines the hidden Jim Crow system that remained in place after the 1960s and the complex ways in which multiple forms of discrimination interacted to limit black opportunities in the post-civil rights era. Most black families remained confined to inner-city neighborhoods or rural poor communities characterized by high unemployment, deteriorating housing, underfunded schools, and proximity to environmental hazards such as polluting industries and waste dumps. The federal government's waning support for programs to retrain workers or create jobs consigned millions of unemployed people to an impoverished existence on the margins of the postindustrial economy. Policy makers then tried to control the labor that capitalism no longer needed through draconian crime policies that turned black communities into war zones and channeled large numbers of African Americans into prison. Although the underlying mechanics of the post-1960s racial order were largely unseen, their consequences were not. Persistent connections between race, poverty, and crime reinforced racist beliefs and undermined support for policies aimed at addressing the structural inequities that underlay these perceptions.

This did not mean there was no progress in the fight for racial equality. The late twentieth century saw major increases in the proportion of African Americans who completed high school, earned college degrees, secured well-paid jobs, bought homes, and passed the benefits of these advances on to their children. Many Americans viewed the expanding black middle class and the rise of a few black people to prominent positions in business, government, academia, journalism, entertainment, and sports as proof that further action to ensure racial equality was not needed. Some people found reinforcement for these beliefs in November 2008 when voters sent Barack Obama to the White House after a long campaign that repeatedly raised the question of whether the nation's white majority could accept a black president. Commentators Richard Viguerie and Mark Fitzgibbons wrote in the *Washington Times* that the election vindicated their contention that ambition and industry were all it took for anyone to succeed in the United States. "Any individual's potential is boundless," they asserted. "Our system worked."[4]

Such statements suggested that Obama's election was a natural consequence of laws banning discrimination and the evolution of more enlightened racial views. Yet this victory and other advances by black Americans did not happen on their own. They were the result of civil rights and social justice activists' ongoing struggles to realize core goals of the black freedom movement after 1965. Analysts who cited evidence of racial progress to suggest that this work was anachronistic and unnecessary failed to realize that the improvements they noted stemmed from the very activities they criticized. Racist resistance to black equality lasted long after the passage of civil rights legislation and necessitated more lawsuits, more boycotts, more lobbying, and more protests to force violators into complying with the law. Activists also tried to overcome institutional barriers to equality. Chapter 4 details the efforts of national organizations and grassroots groups to fulfill the promise of the legal rights set out in the Civil Rights Act (1964) and combat discrimination in education, housing, environmental policy, and the criminal justice system. Chapter 5 examines efforts to ensure equal employment opportunities for African Americans, the evolution of affirmative action policies aimed at addressing systemic racism, and ensuing debates between defenders of these programs and opponents who viewed them as an immoral deviation from colorblind ideals. Chapter 6 highlights obstacles to black political participation in the decades after passage of the Voting Rights Act (1965) and activists' attempts to overcome them, along with the problems encountered by black elected officials seeking to challenge the prevailing ideological assumptions and improve conditions for poor people.

The civil rights movement was part of a broader struggle for justice that encompassed other goals apart from those embodied in the Civil Rights and Voting Rights Acts. Chapter 7 shows how veterans of voter registration and desegregation efforts followed the legislative victories of the mid-1960s with new projects aimed at ending poverty and ensuring a fairer distribution of the nation's wealth. The welfare rights movement highlighted inequities in the social welfare system and attempted to persuade policy makers to provide adequate incomes for the families of unemployed workers. In a related effort rural poor southerners pooled their resources in cooperative farming and business enterprises that provided jobs and income for displaced plantation laborers. Throughout the nation black community groups and social justice organizations initiated self-help programs that offered valuable services to poor people and tried to compensate for government neglect of citizens' needs in the post-civil rights era.

Chapter 8 places the post-1960s freedom struggle in the context of global responses to the spread of free market capitalism around the world in the late twentieth century. American advocates of economic deregulation and free trade pushed the governments of other countries to remove barriers to the movement of investment capital, goods, and services across national borders. Although these measures created new wealth and enriched some people in some countries, they generated extreme inequality and imposed intolerable hardships on poorer people. Displaced farmers and workers in developing nations organized to challenge the economic policies that disrupted their societies, forging alliances with citizens of wealthier countries who were also concerned about the effects of globalization. In the 1990s the movement for global justice reiterated demands made by participants in the black freedom movement in the United States and asserted the right of all the world's people to meaningful work, a decent standard of living, and a voice in the decisions that affect their lives.

In a 2007 article contemplating the missing white people of African American history – the often unidentified or unnamed citizens whose actions created and maintained systems of oppression – journalist Gary Younge observed, "In removing the instigators, the historians remove the agency and, in the final reckoning, the historical responsibility."[5] A mirror image of this phenomenon occurs when commentators praise the nation's progress toward racial equality in the post-civil rights era without mentioning the part played by those Americans who carried the freedom struggle beyond the 1960s. These activists were people of all ethnicities, ages, and social classes who shared a vision for creating a more equal and more democratic society grounded in economic justice as much as the political and legal rights that traditionally defined citizenship in the United States. They included white as well as black people, veteran activists and younger participants, grassroots organizers and the leaders of national civil rights groups. This book outlines their fight against the invisible racism that persisted after the segregation signs came down and the obstacles posed by racial and economic ideologies that portrayed inequality as the work of unseen market forces rather than the result of political decisions that privileged particular interests.

Note on Terminology

African Americans' centuries-long fight for equality began with the first acts of resistance by enslaved people and continued into the twenty-first century. The "freedom struggle" and "freedom movement" refer to these ongoing efforts and to the broad social justice goals (economic as well as political and legal rights) they encompassed. The "civil rights movement" refers more specifically to that period in the mid-twentieth century when black people and their allies mobilized on a mass scale to challenge the legalized discrimination of the Jim Crow era and succeeded in pressuring Congress to pass the Civil Rights and Voting Rights Acts in the mid-1960s.

The "post-civil rights era" refers to the decades after the passage of these two major pieces of civil rights legislation, when the freedom struggle encountered new challenges stemming from political leaders' declining commitment to racial equality and the erroneous belief among many Americans that racism no longer existed. This term is used synonymously with "after 1965," in the same manner as "post-Civil War" or "post-World War II" indicate the periods after 1865 and 1945, respectively. It is not meant to suggest that the civil rights laws of the 1960s ended racism in the United States.

The terms "institutional racism," "systemic racism," and "structural racism" are used interchangeably in this book to refer to ongoing forms of discrimination that remained ingrained in the nation's political and economic systems in the late twentieth century, mostly as a result of the links between race and class that were created in earlier eras and left largely intact after 1965.

★ 1 ★

The Never Ending Story: American Racism from Slavery to the Civil Rights Movement

Racism is like a Cadillac, they bring out a new model every year.
(Malcolm X, 1964)[1]

In the early 1960s White Citizens' Council leader William J. Simmons explained the reasons why he and other segregationists opposed the civil rights movement. "I was born in Mississippi and the United States and I'm the product of my heredity and education and the society in which I was raised, and I have a vested interest in that society, and I along with a million other white Mississippians will do everything in our power to protect that vested interest," he stated. "It's primarily a struggle for power and I think we would be stupid indeed if we failed to see where the consequences of a supine surrender on our part would lead."[2] Simmons' stark admission of the economic and political motivations driving white Americans' resistance indicated that proponents of racial equality were up against more than just the individual prejudices of a few ignorant rednecks. Ending racism meant ending policies that offered concrete material benefits to white people, and they were not going to relinquish those privileges easily.

Simmons' generation of white supremacists offered the latest round in a series of defenses of a racial system that emerged in the late seventeenth century and withstood multiple challenges over the next 300 years. Blackness first became a significant marker of social identity with the enslavement of large numbers of Africans by Europeans in the colonial period. In the nineteenth century the Jim Crow system replaced slavery as a means of subordinating black people and maintaining the connections between class and race that underlay American racial ideologies. Government policies in the New Deal era both reflected and reinforced those links, building racism into social welfare measures that offered economic assistance to white Americans and excluded most black citizens. In each instance the racial order was modified to adapt to new circumstances and to meet the needs of people who benefited from the system. Understanding the historical processes that created and perpetuated racism, and the vested interests it served, is essential to explaining its persistence into the post-civil rights era.

Capitalism, Slavery, and the Origins of American Racism

The English settlers who colonized North America in the early seventeenth century came from a society that was undergoing significant transformation. Feudal relationships based on mutual obligations between lords and serfs gave way to new arrangements favored by landowners, merchants, bankers, and business owners. These groups promoted the conversion of common lands to private property and encouraged peasants to become free agents selling their labor on the open market. English political leaders along with the rising middle class placed considerable importance on accumulating wealth, and the search for new commodities that could be developed as marketable goods was a key motivation behind the colonizing effort.[3] The production of cash crops such as tobacco and cotton in America promised lucrative opportunities for entrepreneurs, who rushed to acquire large tracts of land and the labor needed to work them.

Some colonists advocated enslaving native people, but attempts to coerce the region's original inhabitants into working for Europeans were not very successful. Native Americans' familiarity with the territory made it easy for them to run away and rejoin their communities. Over time, imported European diseases decimated Indian populations, further limiting their use as a source of labor. Colonial landowners therefore relied on surplus workers from their homeland. The privatization of resources in England enriched some people but left others without any means of support, resulting in widespread poverty and the occasional riot. English political leaders viewed the American colonies as a dumping ground for the nation's unwanted and discontented poor. Sometimes voluntarily, and often involuntarily, these destitute citizens were shipped to America as indentured servants, contracted to work for their colonial employers for terms lasting up to seven years.[4]

English colonists at first showed little interest in another potential source of labor, African slaves. Although slavery had been practiced in various forms in European, Mediterranean, and African societies since ancient times, it had faded from existence in England and other parts of western Europe by the seventeenth century. Access to African labor was also limited because the North American colonies were off the usual route taken by the Dutch ships that monopolized the Atlantic slave trade. With no major market for slaves in existence in Virginia or New England, traders saw little value in taking a detour to those regions on their way to the Spanish colonies in South America.[5]

The small number of Africans who lived in North America in the early seventeenth century occupied a very different position from those who arrived in chains later on. Some were what Ira Berlin terms "Atlantic creoles" – Africans who served as translators, sailors, and servants within the trade networks that traversed the ocean between Europe, Africa, and America. Often of mixed African and European descent, they were fluent in the languages and cultures of both worlds, and their skills were highly valued. Their status in the English colonies was not much different from the other settlers. Europeans and Africans in America were all recent migrants creating new societies in a context that necessitated a willingness to adapt and experiment. Africans had the same opportunities as their European counterparts. Many labored as servants for a set number of years and were then free to work for themselves, buy property, and participate fully in the political and social life of the community. Some African settlers acquired large plantations with many servants and enjoyed the same privileges as English gentlemen.[6]

Initially, then, Africans were incorporated into the English colonies on equal terms. Yet Africans' status as outsiders made them vulnerable. A key difference that set them apart was their ambiguous legal standing. They were not English subjects, and those who were servants often lacked written contracts setting out the terms of their employment. Landowners could easily hold African workers in bondage indefinitely, and by the mid-seventeenth century some black people were essentially enslaved. When an African man named John Punch ran away with two English servants in Virginia in 1640, the courts punished him by forcing him to serve his master for life. The other two servants had their terms extended for a few years. In 1656 the will of deceased landowner Rowland Burnham stipulated that the English workers on his plantation were to serve his family for the remainder of their terms and the African workers "forever." Such differential treatment was inconsistent, however, and the first Africans in America did not experience the systematic discrimination that afflicted later generations. White and black colonists worked and lived alongside each other, formed friendships and intermarried, attended church together, and generally suffered the same punishments for crimes. Occasionally, lower-class English and African settlers joined together to resist mistreatment by colonial elites.[7]

Plantation owners in seventeenth-century America were equal opportunity exploiters. Many of the brutal, dehumanizing practices that characterized slavery were initially inflicted on white and black servants alike. Laborers endured poor housing, inadequate food, and overwork along with beatings, whippings, or maiming if they displeased their masters. Employers could buy or sell workers during the period of indenture, with or without servants' consent. Gamblers sometimes used their servants as stakes. As Edmund Morgan explains in his study of colonial Virginia, "A servant ... became for a number of years a thing, a commodity with a price."[8] Even before the development of racial slavery, a labor system was emerging that reduced human beings to the status of property, and in its early phases it did not distinguish between Europeans and Africans.

Servants resisted these abuses as best they could. Workers who knew that colonial practices regarding indenture violated English law or custom sometimes brought lawsuits against employers who treated them unfairly. Africans whose masters illegally tried to hold them in permanent bondage frequently petitioned the courts for redress. John Baptista, for example, was sold by a Dutch merchant to Thomas Lambert under ambiguous terms, and when he was not freed after four years he appealed to the General Court in Virginia. The judges ruled that Baptista had not been sold for life and ordered Lambert to free him after he had worked for two more years. Some Africans converted to Christianity to secure their freedom in accordance with the English common law prohibition against enslaving fellow Christians. The courts also had to grapple occasionally with the unclear status of children of mixed parentage, as was the case with Elizabeth Key, the daughter of an English planter and his African bondservant. English custom was for the status of the child to follow that of the father. In 1655 Key successfully petitioned for freedom on the grounds that her father was a free man.[9]

Laborers frequently deployed other methods apart from the legal system to express their dissatisfaction, including running away, refusing to work, and theft. In 1663 the eight workers on Richard Preston's Maryland plantation complained that the diet of "Beanes and Bread" he provided was not enough sustenance and refused to perform their duties until they received redress. A group of three English and two African servants employed by John West came up with a different solution to the problem of inadequate rations, habitually stealing hogs from their master to supplement their diet. Instances of interracial cooperation by working people were common in the first half of the seventeenth century. When English servant Sibble Ford ran away from her master in 1645, an African laborer named Phillip helped her to hide for 20 days in a cave on the plantation of his owner. African and European workers often ran away together, and both servants and free laborers were more likely to harbor these fugitives than turn them over to the authorities.[10]

Dealing with what the Virginia Assembly called "the audacious unruliness of many stubborne and incorridgible servants resisting their masters and overseers" was a perpetual problem for colonial rulers. There was also the dilemma of what to do with these people once they became free.

Established planters concerned about increasing competition from newcomers used their influence in the colonial government to enact legislation solidifying their control over resources and making it difficult for others to gain access to land, credit, and transportation. Those laborers who survived their terms of indenture entered an economy that offered shrinking opportunities for advancement. Widespread discontent with the situation created new challenges for colonial rulers in the mid-seventeenth century. In 1661 and 1663 authorities in Virginia uncovered and suppressed servant conspiracies in two different counties that aimed to protest deteriorating living conditions and demand freedom for workers. Small farmers trying to eke a living from marginal land in the frontier regions were also restless and angry. Government corruption alienated some wealthier planters as well. In 1676 landowner Nathaniel Bacon led an open rebellion against the colonial leadership, promising freedom to any bound laborers who joined him. Several thousand of these workers participated in the rebellion; among the last of the rebels to be subdued after English forces arrived to crush the uprising was an interracial group of 80 African and 20 English laborers.[11]

A royal commission investigated the causes of the trouble and colonial leaders passed some moderate reforms as a result, but neither they nor authorities in England wanted to do anything that interfered with the profits generated by the existing system. In 1681 observers reported that the colony was "poorer and more populous than ever" and that "extreme poverty may cause the servants to plunder the stores and ships." Two decades later the fear of lower-class rebellion still weighed on Virginia authorities who rejected a proposal to arm servants to protect the colony from enemy attacks. "If they were armed ... we have just reason to fear they may rise upon us," colonial leaders explained. Similarly, Maryland governor Francis Nicholas expressed fears that African and English laborers in his colony might join together to foment "great disturbances, if not a rebellion."[12] Such concerns influenced efforts to construct a new social order that alleviated the burdens of one set of workers and heightened oppression of the other. In the second half of the seventeenth century the fates of African and other laborers began to diverge, leading to a system that ensured freedom for white workers and made most of their black counterparts slaves for life.

Political motivations coincided with economic factors that encouraged a shift toward greater reliance on enslaved African labor. After the 1660s the expanding English economy and the need for soldiers to fight in European wars absorbed more workers than had been possible earlier in the century, alleviating the unemployment problem and causing a decline in migration to the colonies. Planters in North America gained easier access to African workers after English victory in a war with the Dutch passed control of the

Atlantic slave trade to the Royal African Company. Falling tobacco prices intensified landowners' efforts to keep labor costs as low as possible, and the shortage of English workers made African labor the less expensive option. Virginia's colonial secretary Nicholas Spencer asserted in 1683 that the "low price of Tobacco requires it should bee made as cheap as possible, and that Blacks can make it cheaper than Whites." Noting the handsome revenues that England's rulers earned from the import taxes on tobacco, the colony's governor urged the Royal African Company to keep slave prices within reasonable limits. "I conceive it is for his Majesty's Interest full as much as the Countrys, or rather much more, to have Blacks as cheap as possible in Virginia," he stated.[13]

Colonial authorities also took measures of their own to ensure that they reaped maximum benefits from the employment of African labor. The Virginia legislature passed a series of laws in the late seventeenth century that effectively cut off avenues to freedom and made Africans coming into the colony, along with their children, slaves for life. In the 1660s the government negated established English custom by deciding that conversion to Christianity did not alter a person's enslaved status and declaring children's servitude status to follow that of the mother instead of the father. Planters could thus increase their fortunes by impregnating their female servants, secure in the knowledge that the resulting progeny could not sue for freedom as Elizabeth Key had done in 1655. A measure enacted in 1691 made it illegal for masters to free their African slaves. Finally, legislation passed in 1705 defined enslaved people as property inheritable like other belongings from one generation of slaveholders to the next.[14]

These laws secured for plantation owners the permanently enslaved, cheap labor supply they sought. Other initiatives implemented in these decades aimed to draw clear distinctions between the social status of European and African colonists. In 1668 the legislature declared free black women liable to pay taxes, explaining that "though permitted to enjoy their freedome ... [they] ought not in all respects be admitted to a full fruition of the exemptions and impunities of the English." A law aimed at preventing "abominable mixture" and "spurious issue" imposed fines on white women who bore children with black men and banned interracial marriage. Other laws passed in the late seventeenth and early eighteenth centuries prohibited free African Americans from owning European servants, holding political office, owning guns, or serving in the militia. In 1723 the Virginia Assembly denied voting rights to free black people. Asked to explain the reasons for the act by officials in England who could not see why "one freeman should be used worse than another, merely upon account of his complexion," Governor William Gooch revealed the deliberate intent that lay behind discriminatory policies when he replied that the new law aimed "to fix a perpetual Brand upon Free Negros & Mulattos" and "to make the Free Negros sensible that a distinction ought to be made between their offspring and the descendants of an Englishman."[15]

As Africans faced declining opportunities for advancement, Europeans gained new legal protections that shielded them from abuse. In 1660 Virginia's leaders repealed an act passed in 1655 that required Irish immigrants to serve longer terms than their English counterparts, amending the law to equalize terms of service for all colonists from "Christian" nations. In 1705 the legislature stipulated that masters must provide adequate food and shelter for "christian white servants" and refrain from harsh physical punishments such as whipping them naked. White servants were allowed to own property, a right that was denied to enslaved people under the act. The same law that transformed black workers into chattel ordered the livestock and other belongings they had acquired to be confiscated, sold, and the proceeds used to help poor white people. Colonial leaders ensured that the new racial order benefited lower-class European Americans in other ways as well. South Carolina and Georgia both passed legislation in the eighteenth century that required the employment of one or more white men to oversee every four to six slaves and barred the use of enslaved people for skilled work except on their owners' plantations. These measures increased job opportunities for white workers and protected them from black competition. Over time, working-class white Americans came to view the privileges they gained from racism as rights and actively participated in maintaining the system. Instances of interracial cooperation by working people became less common once skin color superseded class as the most important indicator of social position.[16]

The racial system taught Americans to associate blackness with slavery and to accept this as the "natural" place of African Americans. Meanwhile, whiteness connoted free status and exemption from the worst jobs and harshest abuses associated with the economic system. These developments spawned the ideology of white supremacy that played such a central role in the history of the United States. As Anthony Benezet wrote in 1762, observing black people "constantly employed in servile Labour, and the abject Condition in which we see them, from our Childhood, has a natural Tendency to create in us an Idea of a Superiority over them, which induces most People to look upon them as an ignorant and contemptible Part of Mankind."[17]

White supremacy was more than just a belief held by individuals. It was an entire social structure designed through law and policy to subordinate African Americans and channel an unequal share of colonial wealth to European Americans. The freedom and opportunities that white Americans perceived as their birthright were the direct result of denying those rights to black people. White colonists in the seventeenth century were fully aware that their rising fortunes depended on African slavery. Noting the tendency of English servants to "desire freedome to plant for themselves, and not stay but for verie great wages," New England settler Emanuel Downing asserted in 1645: "I doe not see how wee can thrive until wee get into a stock of slaves sufficient to do all our business." Similarly, migrants to Georgia in the early eighteenth century quickly perceived the disadvantages they suffered as a consequence of the colony's initial ban on slavery. Contrasting their own poverty with the prosperity of slaveholding neighbors in South Carolina, they drew the obvious conclusion and began smuggling slaves into Georgia. Under pressure from the colonists, Georgia's rulers eventually ended the prohibition against slave labor, and plantation owners' profits increased accordingly.[18]

Racial Exclusion in the Early Republic

Few slaveholders held any moral qualms about holding people in bondage or felt the need to defend their actions in the early colonial period. Slavery was just one form of coerced labor that had existed among many others in the course of human history, and its role in the achievements of ancient civilizations in Rome and Greece enhanced its legitimacy. The rise of Enlightenment philosophies in the eighteenth century presented the first real challenge to the system. The proposition that all men were born with certain natural rights, including the right to freedom, implied that slavery was morally wrong. Complicating matters, however, were the tangled connections between property and liberty posited by Enlightenment theorists. Property ownership was the basis for the enjoyment of liberty, because people who had the means to provide for themselves could not be forced to submit to the will of others. Since the system of human bondage in America defined enslaved people as property, ending slavery endangered the property rights, and therefore the liberty, of slaveholders.[19]

The presence of enslaved workers deeply affected colonists' interpretations of Enlightenment principles and the revolutionary ideals that created the United States. White Americans in the eighteenth century were economically better off and enjoyed more political rights than their counterparts in Europe. The contrasting treatment accorded to African Americans provided stark examples of what could happen to people whose liberty was revoked. Colonists' ideas about the benefits of freedom and the dangers of its absence were thus based on observed realities, not abstract theories. Nor was it possible to overlook the links between white and black experiences. As Edmund Morgan points out, the greatest proponents of liberty in the revolutionary era were also slaveholders. Thomas Jefferson, George Washington, and others who promoted independence "inherited both their slaves and their attachment to freedom from an earlier generation, and they knew that the two were not unconnected." The founders of the United States understood that freedom for white Americans was built on the enslavement of black Americans. Their wealth and that of the nation as a whole depended on the production of tobacco, cotton, sugar, and other commodities with slave labor. In debates over whether slavery should be tolerated in a society based on Enlightenment ideals, therefore, the rights of enslaved people to liberty were repeatedly sacrificed to protect the property rights of their owners.[20]

When the framers of the Constitution met in 1787 to devise new regulations guiding the relationships between the federal government, the states, and the people who made up the nation, they included several measures that protected slavery. Delegates rejected a proposal to halt the importation of slaves and allowed the slave trade to continue for another two decades. Article IV of the Constitution mandated the return of fugitive slaves to their owners and promised federal assistance to states threatened by slave rebellions. The compromise three-fifths clause allowed states to include three-fifths of their enslaved residents in the population counts that determined representation in the House of Representatives. This clause accorded slaveholders disproportionate influence over the national government and enabled them to block efforts to interfere with the slave system. The same goal was served by reserving important powers for the state governments and limiting the federal government's authority over local institutions. In later decades the defense of "states' rights" served as a crucial mechanism for preserving slavery, segregation, and other racist structures in the United States.

Many people who believed slavery was incompatible with the ideals of the Revolution were nonetheless doubtful that African Americans could be incorporated into the nation as full citizens. According to the prevailing political ideologies of the time, only economically independent property owners could be trusted to make wise political decisions. People who depended on others for their support, including women and poor white laborers as well as enslaved workers, could too easily be influenced by those who held power over them. Associations between black skin and dependence that grew out of slavery affected the treatment of free African Americans in the early republic. The gradual demise of slavery in the northern states after the Revolution was accompanied by restrictions on black people's rights, including curfews, limitations on travel, disfranchising measures, and denial of the right to testify in court or serve on juries.[21] As working-class white men successfully struggled for the extension of voting rights to themselves in the late eighteenth and early nineteenth centuries, the ability of free black people to participate in politics was curtailed.

White workers were key participants in defining the place of African Americans in the United States in the nineteenth century. The transition to industrial capitalism undermined the ability of many young men to follow the expected path to economic success: starting out as an apprentice in some trade, acquiring enough skill to become a journeyman at higher wages, and eventually earning enough money to establish a business and work for oneself. Instead, the factory system and mass production techniques trapped many workers in unskilled, dead-end jobs with few opportunities for advancement. In 1836 a handbill distributed by a group of tailors who were trying to organize a union in New York asserted: "Freemen of the North are now on a level with the slaves of the South."[22] Such comparisons might have encouraged some identification with enslaved workers and led to efforts to free both groups from exploitation. That approach, however, risked reminding other Americans that working people's status as dependent laborers did not meet the ideal of republican citizenship. White workers therefore distinguished between treatment that was appropriate for black people and treatment befitting other citizens, emphasizing their whiteness to demand protection from capitalist abuses. Early craft unions excluded free black people from membership, and white laborers participated in violent campaigns aimed at driving African Americans out of skilled occupations. As the southern labor system came under attack from antislavery forces that coalesced into the Republican Party in the mid-nineteenth century, working-class white northerners who feared competition from emancipated black labor joined with wealthy plantation owners in the Democratic Party in a fight to preserve slavery and uphold white supremacy.[23]

The coalition of elite and poor white factions within the antebellum Democratic Party reflected the multiple functions of racism and the diverse class interests it served. Defining black people as inferior beings that could be subjected to all kinds of dehumanizing treatment secured for plantation owners the cheap, reliable workforce they wanted. Exempting white Americans from such treatment encouraged even the poorest among them to believe they had more in common with wealthy landowners and business people than with African Americans whose economic status more closely resembled their own. This helped to suppress class conflicts among white Americans and discourage interracial uprisings by the poor. At the same time, white workers gained material and psychological benefits from the system. Racial discrimination enabled them to reserve the best jobs and access to other resources for themselves. Even after the exclusion of black workers, the fruits of white people's labor often proved meager. Nonetheless, no matter how poor they might be they were comfortable in the knowledge that at least they were not black. Racism was central in the formation of the American working class and in shaping white workers' identity, and they along with more powerful white people had a stake in its preservation.[24]

Given the advantages that white Americans accrued from the existing racial order, advocates for a more egalitarian society faced formidable obstacles in their efforts to overthrow slavery. Increasing antislavery sentiment in the nineteenth century was met by more strident defenses of the institution from its practitioners. Proponents of slavery drew on a burgeoning body of scientific "evidence" that made European dominance over other people seem natural and inevitable. Samuel Morton, for example, conducted a series of deeply flawed experiments that involved measuring skulls collected from various parts of the world and concluded that Europeans had bigger brains and greater intelligence than the native inhabitants of Asia, Africa, and America. When Morton died in 1851, Robert W. Gibbes praised his role in scientifically bolstering white supremacy in the *Charleston Medical Journal.* "We of the South should consider him as our benefactor," Gibbes explained, "for aiding most materially in giving to the negro his true position as an inferior race."[25]

Far from being the result of impartial inquiry that proved the "true position" of any people, race scientists' conclusions were shaped by a global social context in which Europeans were busy subordinating darker skinned peoples to serve their own economic interests. As Audrey Smedley points out, support for these ideas was drawn from "the writings, descriptions, commentaries, speculations, musings, opinions, and beliefs of travelers, explorers, traders, missionaries, plantation owners, and the like" who were involved in a variety of projects where Europeans interacted with others on less than equal terms.[26] Scientific racism grew out of and reinforced these relationships, giving them an aura of legitimacy that for many Americans erased any doubts regarding the proper place of black people in their society. Race scientists linked behavioral differences to physical characteristics, making them seem biological and inherent rather than cultural and changeable. Evidence that African Americans could be prominent property owners and responsible citizens was ignored or discarded in favor of a rigid racial hierarchy that denied nonwhite people the capacity for economic advancement or democratic participation.

After Slavery: Labor Control and White Supremacy in the Jim Crow Era

The abolition of slavery as a result of the Civil War provided opportunities to challenge racist assumptions. Emancipation altered the context for interaction between white and black people who had previously known each other only as masters and slaves, opening possibilities for new ideas about race to emerge. The Civil Rights Act of 1866 and the Fourteenth Amendment to the Constitution granted citizenship to black people and accorded them the same political and legal rights as white Americans. The Fifteenth Amendment prohibited states from denying voting rights on the basis of race. In the 1860s and 1870s black men voted in large numbers and held political offices at the local, state, and national levels. The influence of African Americans within the interracial, Republican governments elected in the southern states during these decades led to some modest projects that benefited poorer people, including tax reform, the establishment of public schools, and legislation protecting the rights of workers. Freed people enjoyed a modest amount of bargaining power that enabled them to resist planters' attempts to restore the gang labor system that existed under slavery, resulting in a compromise solution that allowed families to work small plots of land as tenants and sharecroppers instead.[27]

Freed people and abolitionists also advocated more sweeping economic reforms to break the power of plantation owners and redistribute land to poor white and black southerners. These activists argued that true citizenship meant more than just voting rights and equal treatment under the law. Former slaves needed access to land, equipment, and skills to successfully navigate the capitalist economy and participate fully in American society. Redistributive policies were too radical for the northern business leaders who dominated the Republican Party to accept, however. Like their landowning counterparts in the South, these men believed large-scale agricultural production was more efficient than small farms and considered maintaining the southern plantation system essential to the future prosperity of the nation. They expected African Americans to continue to work for white employers as free laborers, not aspire to become independent landowners. (The same expectation consigned increasing numbers of white workers to the status of permanent wage labor in the late nineteenth century.) Failure to grant economic rights to black people in the 1860s left them dependent on white employers and powerless to prevent the erosion of their political rights. Over the next decade southern Democrats in collusion with the Ku Klux Klan and other paramilitary groups employed economic reprisals, intimidation, fraud, and violence to discourage black voting and restore white dominance.[28]

Despite the return of white racists to power in the late 1870s, the southern racial order remained remarkably fluid for several decades after the end of Reconstruction. Mass black political participation declined but some African Americans continued to vote and hold office in the South until the turn of the century. A growing black middle class emerged whose members increasingly asserted their right to be treated the same as white people of their social status. Black people with money patronized the same stores, restaurants, and theaters as their white counterparts.[29] In 1878 an English visitor to the South observed white and black people sharing public facilities "on terms of perfect equality, and without the smallest symptom of malice or dislike on either side." Seven years later black Bostonian T. McCants Stewart took a tour through the southern states and reported from South Carolina: "I feel about as safe here as in Providence, R.I. I can ride in first-class cars on the railroads and in the streets. I can go into saloons and get refreshments even as in New York. I can stop in and drink a glass of soda and be more politely waited upon than in some parts of New England." In 1897 a white newspaper editor in Charleston opposed a proposed law to segregate trains on the grounds that it was unnecessary and "a needless affront to our respectable and well behaved colored people."[30] As C. Vann Woodward notes in his study of the gradual and unsteady rise of the Jim Crow system, the first few decades after the Civil War were "a time of experiment, testing, and uncertainty – quite different from the time of repression and rigid uniformity that was to come toward the end of the century. Alternatives were still open and real choices had to be made."[31]

As had been the case in the transition to racial slavery in the seventeenth century, the choice between allowing black equality and reinstituting legal structures aimed at holding African Americans in positions of inferiority was influenced by the rise of an interracial movement of poor people that threatened the interests of the wealthy white men who dominated southern politics. Small farmers and workers had not benefited much from economic policies that granted tax breaks to corporations, altered crop lien laws to favor large landowners and banks, slashed funding for public services, and undercut union organizing in the late nineteenth century. Dissatisfied constituencies joined together in the People's Party in the 1880s, attacking inequities in the economic system and the ways that white supremacist ideologies divided the nation's working class. In an article calling for unity among white and black farmers in 1892, Georgia Populist Tom Watson explained the role that racism played in facilitating the exploitation of both groups. "You are kept apart that you may be separately fleeced of your earnings," he wrote. "You are made to hate each other because upon that hatred is rested the keystone of the arch of financial despotism which enslaves you both. You are deceived and blinded that you may not see how this race antagonism perpetuates a monetary system which beggars both."[32]

Populist successes in state and national elections in the 1890s frightened the business-oriented leaders of the southern Democratic Party. Their approach to boosting regional prosperity relied on promoting low property taxes, an abundance of natural resources, and the availability of cheap labor to lure northern capital to their states. The Populists' plans for higher taxes on the wealthy, more government regulation of the economy, and better wages and conditions for workers threatened the interests of large landowners and corporations. Convinced that these reforms were a recipe for stifling investment and economic development, Democrats employed the same tactics they had used to overthrow Reconstruction to prevent further victories by the People's Party. Appeals to white supremacy played a major role in this campaign. The fragile coalition that Populist leaders had been working to build across racial lines split apart as white southerners of all classes joined together to preserve the benefits they gained from racism.[33]

In the late nineteenth and early twentieth centuries southern legislators constructed a new racial order that blocked opportunities for economic advancement and confined most black southerners to agricultural labor or other unskilled, low-wage jobs. Segregation laws consigned African Americans to separate and inferior schools and other public services. Labor legislation empowered plantation owners to restrict black workers' mobility and cheat them out of their earnings, ensnaring many sharecropping families in a system of perpetual debt peonage. Additional qualifications for voting limited political participation by the poor and ill-educated, a category that included most black southerners. Relegation to the status of non-citizens made African Americans vulnerable to extreme acts of individual and mob violence aimed at keeping them "in their place." Between 1882 and 1946 more than 4,700 black people were lynched in the South, for reasons that ranged from suspicion of murder to insulting a white person. White southerners defined black "crimes" that warranted such brutal punishment broadly to include virtually any action that challenged the racial hierarchy, including attempting to vote, using facilities designated for white people, or simply asking to be paid.[34]

The Jim Crow system was not the inevitable result of white prejudices held over from slavery. It was designed to cut off the alternatives that existed in the first few decades after the Civil War, when African Americans enjoyed expanding opportunities and racism could have been mitigated or even eliminated through continued interracial interaction on the basis of equality. South Carolina resident Mamie Garvin Fields remembered that black and white families on her street lived amiably together, played together, and shared food and other resources with each other in the decades before the state legislature began mandating segregation. "The Jim Crow law made friends into enemies overnight," she stated. Children began calling each other "nigger" and "cracker" and fighting each other in the streets. "The law made the children do this," Fields explained. "The law made it that we weren't really neighbors any more."[35]

Segregation was literally and figuratively a system of signs that aimed to teach a new generation of southerners who had no experience with slavery the meaning of race. When the word "White" designated drinking fountains, train cars, or schools that were luxurious and clean compared with the filthy, decrepit facilities reserved for "Colored" citizens, the association between blackness and inferiority was recreated in people's minds. Although proponents argued that the new laws were necessary to minimize racial friction and safeguard public health, these rationales conflicted with evidence that white people considered close interaction with black people problematic only in certain circumstances. The same white citizens who refused to share public facilities with "dirty" or "diseased" African Americans had no such qualms about hiring black domestic workers to cook and clean for them. Policy makers separated white and black school children and restricted African Americans' access to quality education for economic rather than social purposes. "What I want here is Negroes who can make cotton, and they don't need education to help them make cotton," one landowner explained. "I could not use educated Negroes on my place." Employers believed education "spoiled" black people by making them unwilling to work in the occupations designated for them in the racial order. "White people want to 'keep the negro in his place,' and educated people have a way of making their own places and their own terms," observed white Mississippian Thomas Pearce Bailey in the early twentieth century. Like slavery, Jim Crow was a system of labor control that kept black people working for white people and prevented African Americans from competing with white Americans for the best jobs.[36]

Racism served political functions in this period as well. Disfranchising measures such as poll taxes and literacy tests were aimed mostly at African Americans but they also discouraged many poor white people from participating in the political process. Voting restrictions effectively removed two potentially troublesome constituencies whose interests were not well served by the business-friendly policies favored by wealthier citizens. Additionally, the presence of a large pool of economically desperate black workers undermined white workers' ability to demand higher wages. Employers frequently responded to union organizing efforts by threatening to replace white laborers with African Americans. As during slavery, racism hindered efforts by black and white workers to form interracial coalitions based on their common economic interests in the twentieth century. Political analyst V. O. Key Jr. observed in 1949: "When a glimmer of informed political self-interest begins to well up from the masses, the issue of white supremacy may be raised to whip them back into line."[37]

Segregation and the racist beliefs it fostered were not purely southern phenomena. Federal officials who allowed blatant violations of black southerners' constitutional rights were complicit in the construction and maintenance of the system. The Supreme Court sanctioned racial discrimination by ruling in *Plessy v. Ferguson* (1896) that requiring white and black people to use "separate but equal" facilities was within the law. In the northern states, government policies as well as informal practices confined black residents to substandard housing and schools, shut them out of higher paying skilled jobs, and excluded them or offered second-class treatment in hotels, stores, and restaurants. Negative depictions of African Americans in a newly emerging mass culture comprised of popular magazines and literature, vaudeville acts, music, and films also perpetuated racist stereo-types on a national scale. In the first half of the twentieth century white Americans rarely encountered any real or fictional black people who were not poorly educated menial laborers. The Jim Crow system thus perpetu-ated the same assumptions of black inferiority that had helped to justify racial oppression in earlier centuries.[38]

New Deal Reforms and Institutional Racism

Racial ideologies deflected attention from deficiencies in the capitalist eco-nomic system that prevented many Americans from enjoying possibilities for property ownership and wealth accumulation that were presumed to be available to everyone. Industrialization and the growth of large corpora-tions concentrated wealth in the hands of a relatively small number of people and generated increasing economic inequality at the turn of the twentieth century. If poverty was understood as the result of black people's inherent inferiority instead of social structures that limited poor people's economic options, citizens could assume there was nothing wrong with the nation's core institutions. Such beliefs fit well with the laissez-faire eco-nomic policies promoted by business owners and absolved political leaders from trying to solve social problems.

The crisis of capitalism sparked by the Great Depression in the 1930s shook the confidence of even the strongest opponents of government inter-vention in the economy. Millions of middle-class Americans lost their jobs, savings, and homes, exposing them to the same hardships that poorer people already endured. Overwhelming evidence that the economic system had failed opened possibilities for experimentation and a shift in direction. Democratic president Franklin D. Roosevelt's New Deal policies gained enthusiastic support from social reformers as well as poor white and black people who benefited from efforts to enhance economic security and encour-age labor union organizing. Thousands of black Republicans shifted their allegiance to the Democratic Party in the 1930s, forcing party leaders to reassess the organization's commitment to maintaining white supremacy. At the same time, challenges to scientific racism from anthropologists who debunked biological determinism undermined previous rationales for excluding black people from economic opportunities and political participa-tion. Confident that class, not race, was the underlying source of black people's problems, the architects of the New Deal expected equal access to government programs to raise African Americans' social status and elimi-nate racial inequality in the United States.[39]

Racist resistance from other Americans and the policies pursued by key government agencies meant that these hopes were not realized. Unwilling to upset powerful southern Democrats whose support was necessary to implement reforms, Roosevelt left control over relief programs to state and local officials. The president's sensitivity to states' rights allowed administrators to discriminate against black residents in the allocation of jobs and other government assistance. Pressure from large landowners in the South and West convinced Congress to exclude agricultural and domestic workers from the unemployment insurance and old age pension programs created by the Social Security Act of 1935. Sixty percent of the nation's black labor force and 75 percent of those who lived in the South were employed in occupations not covered by the act, causing black lawyer Charles Houston to label it "a sieve with the holes just big enough for the majority of Negroes to fall through." Most African Americans, therefore, had no access to important social services that greatly improved the lives of working-class white families over the next few decades. White Americans who saw their Social Security taxes deducted from their paychecks each week viewed these benefits as rights that they had earned through years of hard work. In contrast, most poor black families relied on public assistance programs ("welfare") that were funded by the states with help from federal grants. These were widely perceived and stigmatized as unearned government handouts to people who were "too lazy" to work. Racism was thus built into and perpetuated by a two-tiered social welfare system that offered more generous assistance to white people than to black Americans.[40]

Federal programs aimed at facilitating home ownership also buttressed racial inequality. The development of housing policy in the United States illustrates how individual and institutional racism acted in mutually reinforcing ways to generate interconnected forms of discrimination that restricted African Americans' opportunities for economic advancement in the twentieth century. Contrary to assumptions that racially segregated neighborhoods reflected people's natural preference for living among those who look like themselves, the spatial structure that characterized many American communities in the 1930s was a relatively new phenomenon. In the nineteenth century housing was integrated in both the North and the South. White employers needed their black workers close by and scattering African Americans throughout cities instead of concentrating them in one area helped to minimize the threat of slave rebellions. Black people's accommodations were often substandard but they lived among wealthier people in economically mixed neighborhoods. Middle-class African Americans lived in houses alongside white families of similar status, sharing the same services and sometimes attending the same churches and social events. A white man who grew up in New Orleans' Lower Ninth Ward in the early twentieth century recalled, "Everybody helped everybody else. Every Saturday night, the blacks across the street would have a fish fry, and they would always bring a batch over to my mother. There was never any hatred between us; we all lived together and that's the way things were."[41]

With the emergence of the Jim Crow system came local ordinances that sought to confine black residents to separate neighborhoods in some cities, but the Supreme Court struck these down in 1917 in response to a lawsuit filed by the National Association for the Advancement of Colored People (NAACP). Consequently, homeowners and policy makers who favored segregation had to resort to other methods. White perceptions of black people as undesirable neighbors were based on actual disadvantages that resulted from racist discrimination (such as poverty and lower education levels) as well as fabricated stereotypes disseminated by mass media (such as African Americans' purported propensity for crime). Segregationists fearing competition for jobs, lowered standards in schools, higher crime rates, and declining property values deployed a variety of methods to exclude black people from their communities. African Americans seeking to buy or rent homes in white neighborhoods frequently encountered threats, intimidation, physical attacks, or offers of money to look elsewhere. In the 1920s white homeowners' associations formed in many cities with the goal of forcing existing black residents to leave and preventing new ones from moving in. These organizations lobbied local governments to pass zoning ordinances prohibiting undesirable uses of properties (such as leasing them to African Americans), boycotted stores and businesses that catered to black people, and raised money to pay unwanted neighbors to move away. They also promoted and enforced restrictive covenants – private agreements that prohibited homeowners from renting or selling their properties to black families.[42]

Exclusion from white neighborhoods restricted black families' housing options and created all-black sections of cities characterized by overcrowding, exorbitant rents and home prices, and strained resources. Local officials allowed services in black areas to decline and diverted city funds to white constituents instead. Black communities often lacked paved roads, street lights, recreational facilities, sanitary sewer systems, and garbage collection services. African Americans who overpaid for their homes were left with little money to pay for repairs or upkeep, and landlords assured of a ready market for rentals had few incentives to maintain their properties. All of these factors strengthened the association of blackness with slum conditions in the minds of white homeowners and reinforced their determination to keep African Americans out of their neighborhoods.[43] In 1924 the National Association of Real Estate Brokers adopted housing segregation as standard practice, writing into its code of ethics: "A Realtor should never be instrumental in introducing into a neighborhood ... members of any race or nationality ... whose presence will clearly be detrimental to property values in that neighborhood."

The belief that the presence of African Americans *in itself* lowered property values influenced the policies of federal agencies that were created during the New Deal era to encourage home ownership. The Home Owners Loan Corporation and later the Federal Housing Administration (FHA) established the 30-year, fixed-payment mortgage as the industry standard, making housing purchases affordable for millions of families and greatly expanding the American middle class. In their efforts to ensure some consistency in home valuation practices, however, government officials incorporated racist assumptions that had long been a feature of the profession into federal guidelines. Criteria used to determine neighborhood desirability included the ethnicity of residents along with the age and type of housing, demand for homes, and local amenities. Homogenous, upscale, white neighborhoods received the highest ranking (colored green on "residential security" maps), while those with mixed or nonwhite populations were given the lowest ranking (colored red). Lenders then used these designations to determine whether to make loans. The FHA discouraged banks from loaning money to people who lived in "red" areas, deeming them too risky to qualify for federal mortgage guarantees. "Redlining" referred to banks' practice of refusing to make loans for home purchases or repairs in those (mostly nonwhite) neighborhoods. The FHA also urged homeowners to protect the value of their property through the use of restrictive covenants. Residential segregation increased throughout the United States in the wake of these developments, the result of government policy as much as individual bigotry.[44]

African Americans were also largely left out of programs that were designed to help returning World War II veterans in the 1940s and 1950s. The Servicemen's Readjustment Act of 1944 (more commonly known as the GI Bill) rewarded those who had fought in the war with generous benefits that included stipends while they looked for work, preference for civil service jobs, money to attend college, and low-interest loans to buy homes, farms, or businesses. Eighty percent of American men born in the 1920s received some kind of assistance under these programs, accepting more than $95 billion in government benefits between 1944 and 1971. As white veterans secured college degrees and high-paying professional jobs, bought suburban homes, and passed those advantages on to their children, however, many African Americans found access to the programs blocked. Local officials often discriminated against black veterans and discouraged them from seeking higher education or skilled positions. The Veterans Administration also thwarted African Americans' aspirations by following the FHA's practices of denying home loans to black families and preventing them from integrating white housing developments.[45]

From the 1930s through the 1960s the federal government financed the geographical and social mobility of white Americans while making it virtually impossible for black families to leave declining inner-city neighbor-hoods. African Americans Jim and Ann Braithewaite faced repeated obstruc-tions from realtors when they began looking for a suburban home in Philadelphia in 1957. Agents claimed they had nothing available or that houses the couple expressed interest in had already been sold. One realtor simply stated, "You're colored, aren't you? I can't do anything for you." Finally, in 1959, the Braithewaites bought a vacant lot and quietly built their dream home, visiting the site only at night to avoid drawing the atten-tion of neighbors. A black engineer who recalled a similarly prolonged and humiliating search stated, "In all my life I have never felt so completely shut out."[46]

Obstacles to black suburbanization as well as the increasing migration of rural poor people to the nation's cities exacerbated the problems of deteriorating urban areas. In the 1950s Congress made an effort to address these problems by providing federal funding for slum clearance projects and redevelopment of blighted neighborhoods. Rather than improving condi-tions, however, urban renewal disrupted black communities and worsened conditions for many families. City officials often targeted African American neighborhoods that threatened to spread into white enclaves for destruc-tion, razing homes and relocating residents to poorly constructed high-rise public housing projects erected in other black areas. Stacking people on top of each other instead of allowing black neighborhoods to expand was the way many cities chose to contain growing populations of African Americans (see Figure 1.1).[47]

The nation's racialized class structure meant that concentrations of black people were also concentrations of poverty. Many African Americans who migrated to urban areas during and after World War II were former share-croppers who had received little or no education within the segregated southern school system. Consequently they lacked the expertise necessary to succeed in an economy that increasingly demanded high school or college qualifications. Fewer positions were available in older manufacturing enter-prises such as steel and auto making that had once offered black workers stable employment, and new jobs opening up in high tech industries were out of reach for most African Americans. As more highly educated white workers moved to the suburbs, industries and businesses followed. Plant closings resulted in a shrinking job market that made it difficult for inner-city residents to find work. Lower incomes meant fewer purchases, causing stores and businesses in poor communities to close and eliminating even more jobs. Residents' poverty left local governments without the tax base needed to provide adequate schools, roads, parks, public transportation, or other services. These factors in turn discouraged new industries and businesses from locating in black communities, perpetuating the spiral of decline.[48]

Figure 1.1 Black children playing outside the Ida B. Wells public housing project in Chicago, 1973
Source: John H. White/National Archives and Records Administration 412-DA-13707

Jim Crow and its Shadow: Dual Challenges for the Black Freedom Movement

Disparities in the types of housing, schools, and jobs available to black people compared with white Americans in the mid-twentieth century reinforced the racial lessons of past eras. Being white meant having access to quality housing, good schools, higher education, and work that paid enough to enable participation in the nation's burgeoning consumer culture. In contrast, black Americans remained confined to low-wage jobs, deteriorating housing, and inferior schools that did not prepare them well to participate in the postwar economy. Most white Americans did not perceive the privileges they enjoyed under this system as unearned advantages. They attributed their success to hard work and individual effort, ignoring the role that New Deal social programs and government subsidization of suburban development played in lifting them into the middle class. Federal officials encouraged such beliefs by portraying the emergence of all-white suburbs as the result of private choices within the free enterprise system even as they regulated housing markets in ways that limited black people's residential options. As David Freund notes, "In addition to creating wealth for some while helping to marginalize others, federal intervention also helped create and popularize a unique postwar political narrative that obscured the origins of race and class inequality in the modern metropolis."[49]

Racial oppression in the mid-twentieth century United States was multi-faceted, encompassing both the overt discrimination of the southern Jim Crow system and the less visible racism built into government policies and private industry practices that enhanced white Americans' fortunes while excluding large numbers of black people from opportunities for upward mobility. At the same time, social conditions had never been more condu-cive to overturning the blatant forms of discrimination practiced in the South. Nazi atrocities in Germany during World War II discredited white supremacist ideologies and encouraged more racially egalitarian beliefs among large numbers of Americans. Mass migrations of black southerners to cities in the North and West opened new opportunities for economic advancement and political activism. Southern plantation owners responded by mechanizing their operations, reducing their need for black workers and the repressive methods they had used to control the labor force. Two decades of unprecedented prosperity after the war suggested possibilities for a more equitable distribution of resources between white and black Americans. The Cold War with the Soviet Union made ending racial dis-crimination a matter of national security as the United States courted allies among newly decolonized nations in Africa and Asia. These developments provided African Americans with their best opportunity since Reconstruction to push their demands for equality.

The NAACP intensified its efforts to challenge racist beliefs and policies, culminating in the Supreme Court's decision declaring segregated public schools unconstitutional in *Brown v. Board of Education of Topeka, Kansas* (1954). The ruling had implications for other discriminatory practices and offered further encouragement to local protest activities across the nation. Members of the Congress of Racial Equality (CORE) deployed nonviolent tactics such as sit-ins and boycotts to assert black Americans' right to equal treatment in the 1950s. In Montgomery, Alabama, African Americans engaged in a year-long boycott of the city's segregated buses that gained national media attention and elevated Martin Luther King Jr. to prominence as a leading spokesman for the civil rights movement. King and other activ-ists formed the Southern Christian Leadership Conference (SCLC) in 1957 to facilitate communication and the development of unified strategies among local movements in the region. Another new organization emerged in the early 1960s as college students who were impatient with the slow pace of change came together in the Student Nonviolent Coordinating Committee (SNCC) with the goal of engaging in direct action against racism. Older groups including the NAACP and the National Urban League (NUL), an organization formed in 1911 to assist rural black migrants to northern cities, in turn adopted more confrontational approaches as they competed for members and funding in an era when most African Americans favored bold action.[50]

Civil rights activists deployed lawsuits, boycotts, sit-ins, mass demonstrations, and voter registration drives to make the case for black equality and force action from political leaders. Violent reactions from white supremacists, including many southern Democrats, embarrassed the national government and presented President John F. Kennedy with some politically difficult choices. Kennedy sympathized with black aspirations but did not want to upset the southern wing of his party by siding too strongly with the freedom movement. Persistent protests, the clear injustices of the Jim Crow system, and concerns that American global leadership was being undermined ultimately convinced Kennedy to propose comprehensive civil rights legislation banning racial discrimination in public accommodations, education, and employment. After Kennedy's assassination in 1963 his successor Lyndon B. Johnson strongly supported passage of the bill, and Congress finally outlawed overtly racist practices with the Civil Rights Act in 1964. Legislators provided protections for black political participation in the Voting Rights Act passed the following year.

Black people's struggles did not end with these victories. Activists' initial focus on segregation and disfranchisement in the South was the first round in a fight that many participants knew must ultimately address the structural inequities that lay behind black unemployment, poverty, and political powerlessness in communities throughout the nation. These complexities notwithstanding, most white Americans interpreted the civil rights movement as a simple and morally persuasive demand that African Americans be treated the same as other citizens. After passage of the Civil Rights and Voting Rights Acts, many people expected African Americans to stop protesting and rely on the new opportunities now open to them to improve the conditions of their lives. The belief that civil rights legislation magically transformed the United States into a colorblind nation posed significant problems for activists seeking more comprehensive reforms in the late twentieth century.

From the Freedom Movement to Free Markets: Racializing the War on Poverty and Colorblinding Jim Crow

There's a connection between politics and economics. If we ever wake up the Archie Bunkers of this country to what's going down in the multi-national corporations and the rich individuals of this country, they will soon learn that busing is not the issue and that blacks are not the enemy. (Congressman Walter Fauntroy, 1976)[1]

Less than a week after President Lyndon Johnson signed the Voting Rights Act into law, one of the largest urban uprisings in the nation's history broke out in the poor black neighborhood of Watts in Los Angeles. The desperate conditions that ignited residents' frustrations in Watts were typical of segregated African American communities across the nation: high unemployment; dilapidated housing; inadequate schools and services; and frequent acts of police brutality aimed at keeping black people in line. On August 11, 1965 an altercation between some law enforcement officers and a crowd of onlookers who gathered after a black man was pulled over for speeding escalated into four days of violent attacks on people and property that caused 34 deaths, hundreds of injuries, and millions of dollars in damage to buildings and businesses.[2]

Watts was a reminder that the legislative victories of the mid-1960s did not signal the end of the black freedom struggle or the national responsibility for ending racism. Merely removing segregation signs did not address the more deeply rooted inequities that resulted from centuries of unequal access to the benefits of American capitalism. California assemblyman Mervyn Dymally acknowledged, "We've got a big job to do and we must do it better. We've been pushing for civil rights, but we've missed the point completely in Watts."[3] Participants in the freedom movement and their supporters believed that solving the nation's racial problems required the federal government to intervene in the economy on the same scale that it had intervened politically with the Civil Rights and Voting Rights Acts.

Americans who believed that enhancing black people's economic opportunities was essential to ensuring racial equality pushed for sustained government efforts to improve education, housing, employment, and social services in poor communities, goals that were partially realized with federal antipoverty initiatives in the late 1960s. As in earlier periods when possibilities were opened to end racism in the United States, however, the vested interests of powerful constituencies conspired to obstruct further progress. The same white supremacists who opposed civil rights legislation attacked the war on poverty with equal ferocity. Middle-class homeowners seeking to preserve their ability to exclude African Americans from their communities reacted strongly against the Johnson administration's attempts to enforce civil rights laws. Business leaders concerned about declining profits in the face of increasing international competition also favored a more limited role for government. The convergence of racial and economic resentments provided the Republican Party with a chance to break up the progressive coalition that Democrats had forged in the 1930s and replace the reform agenda of earlier decades with policies aimed at rolling back federal power in the late twentieth century. The free market ideologies that prevailed after the 1960s simultaneously preserved existing racial hierarchies and attributed them to natural economic forces rather than deliberate discrimination, thus exempting white Americans from responsibility for addressing persistent injustices.

Continuing the Freedom Struggle through the War on Poverty

Black joblessness and poverty were among the many injustices that civil rights activists sought to highlight in the 1960s. The unemployment rate for nonwhite workers increased from 6 percent to 11 percent between 1940 and 1962 while the rate for white workers remained steady at roughly 5 percent in the same period. The roots of the crisis lay in the modernization of southern agriculture in the mid-twentieth century. This process began with New Deal agricultural policies that encouraged plantation owners to cut production and invest in machines, accelerated during World War II as many black laborers left to go and work in defense industries, and received a final push with intensified civil rights activism and the threat of voting rights legislation in the 1950s and 1960s. In those decades economic and political considerations drove plantation owners to get rid of their remaining black laborers as fast as possible, leading to mass job losses that left thousands of families without any means of support. At the same time, the automation of many manufacturing tasks and decline of industries that employed large numbers of people in the North meant that the employment prospects for southern migrants to northern cities grew bleaker as the decades progressed. Civil rights leaders argued that these dislocations necessitated coordinated efforts to help displaced workers, white and black. In a memorandum outlining the purpose of the March on Washington for Jobs and Freedom in 1963, Bayard Rustin wrote, "Clearly there is no need for Negroes to demand jobs that do not exist. Nor do Negroes seek to displace white workers as both are being displaced by machines. Negroes seek instead, *as an integral part of their own struggle as a people*, the creation of more jobs for all Americans."[4]

National leaders were also concerned about persistent poverty. Some thought it shameful that the richest nation on earth could not find a way to ensure adequate incomes for all its people and considered antipoverty efforts a moral imperative. Others argued that poor people represented an untapped resource that the United States could not afford to ignore. Maintaining the nation's status as a world superpower depended on developing the skills of all citizens to their highest capacity. In an economy based on consumerism it made sense to ensure stable jobs at good wages for workers so that they could buy the products made by American manufacturers. Excluding large numbers of people from participation in the consumer society deprived businesses of an important market and undermined the economic health of the nation. All of these factors lay behind President Johnson's declaration of an "unconditional war on poverty" in January 1964. The president's first State of the Union address outlined plans to expand economic development efforts in depressed areas, initiate youth employment programs, strengthen the social safety net, and provide affordable housing for low-income families. Johnson knew that including all Americans on the basis of equality was essential to success. "Let me make one principle of this Administration abundantly clear," he stated. "All of these increased opportunities in employment and education, in housing and in every field must be open to Americans of every color."[5]

For the next two months a task force comprised of representatives from several government agencies discussed various initiatives and sought advice from business and labor leaders, philanthropic foundations, and civil rights organizations to determine how best to implement the president's proposals. Draft legislation for a comprehensive Economic Opportunity Act presented to Congress in March included some promising forms of assistance for poor people but did not incorporate civil rights leaders' suggestions for ensuring employment for all workers. The emphasis was on providing training and services rather than job creation, and the amount of money allocated was less than one-tenth of what most analysts thought was needed. Black leaders nonetheless supported the bill as a necessary corollary to ending legalized segregation. Whitney Young of the NUL told a House subcommittee in April that passage of the legislation was needed to demonstrate to African Americans that the nation was truly committed to racial equality. Young recounted the violent opposition that met efforts to overturn the southern Jim Crow system and also highlighted "the years of want, poor housing and rats biting their children" that black people endured in the urban North. Emphasizing that the nation urgently needed antipoverty as well as civil rights initiatives, he stated, "We are afraid that we might end up here with a mouthful of civil rights and an empty stomach, living in a hovel."[6]

Congress passed the legislation over the opposition of 145 Republicans and 40 southern Democrats in 1964. The act provided $800 million in the first year of the war on poverty for job training programs, economic development efforts, and improving social services for poor people (see Figure 2.1). An innovative provision granting federal funds to civic organizations as well as local governments to create Community Action Programs (CAPs) aimed to involve poor people directly in antipoverty efforts. The legislation also established an Office of Economic Opportunity (OEO) within the

Figure 2.1 Poster advertising the Office of Economic Opportunity's Head Start program, 1960s
Source: Unknown/National Archives and Records Administration 381-PX-65

executive branch of the government to provide national coordination and oversight. Strengthening the federal government's role in addressing poverty was crucial to overcoming obstacles presented by racist state and local officials who opposed economic assistance for African Americans. In contrast to the New Deal, which left the administration of programs in the hands of political leaders, hundreds of local community groups received funds directly from the OEO to operate CAPs in the 1960s.[7]

The war on poverty fostered some creative and highly successful initiatives in communities across the nation. Adult education programs, job training and placement, legal services, health clinics, small business development, credit unions, and outreach programs were just a few of the services that CAPs provided. In Mississippi, poor black people were actively involved in the Child Development Group of Mississippi (CDGM), an early childhood education program that was hailed as a model by outside observers. The group received an OEO grant of $1.5 million to operate a summer Head Start program that served 6,000 children in 24 counties. The program provided nutritious meals, health care, and preschool education to the children and employed many of their parents along with other local people in operating the centers. Both the advances made by the children and the new sense of hope among the adults impressed government officials and child development experts who evaluated its efforts. According to child psychiatrist Robert Coles, the CDGM's achievements and the benefits it brought to the community were "truly extraordinary."[8]

Not every program was as successful. Some CAPs were poorly administered and mismanaged their funds. Often these problems reflected the inexperience of staff members who lacked accounting expertise or inadvertently used money for inappropriate purposes. In other cases there was deliberate fraud. Many of these instances resulted from the business-as-usual approach of corrupt politicians who used antipoverty programs to enhance their own wealth and power instead of helping poor people. The best CAPs were those that channeled federal funds directly to grassroots organizations with no interference from local officials. Programs controlled by the traditional political leadership, in contrast, often misallocated resources to people who neither deserved nor needed them. Such problems occurred in the North as well as the South. In Newark, New Jersey, black activists complained that the city officials who controlled United Community Corporation (UCC) misused antipoverty funds and denied poor people jobs in the CAP. A struggle for control of the program ensued between civil rights groups and leaders of the Democratic political machine that dominated the city.[9] Similar scenarios played out in other cities, undermining antipoverty efforts and generating disunity within the Democratic coalition.

Racist Attacks on Antipoverty Efforts

Some Americans actively opposed the war on poverty. The entire Mississippi congressional delegation voted against the Economic Opportunity Act in 1964, and the *Jackson Daily News* portrayed Head Start as a totalitarian plot to "mongrelize" the nation. Segregationists were convinced the initiative was just another attempt by the federal government to force integration on them. Southern governments were slow to request antipoverty funds for their communities, preferring to forego federal money rather than adhere to the requirement that black as well as white citizens must be involved as planners and beneficiaries of the programs.[10]

Another concern was that antipoverty programs encouraged poor black southerners to remain in the region instead of migrating. Wealthy white southerners who owed their fortunes to cheap black labor and whose actions had generated widespread poverty and homelessness refused to bear the costs of addressing these problems. Journalist Robert Sherrill quoted one planter in Mississippi as saying that field hands were now as "as useless as a mule" and reported that many white residents thought the best solution to the state's economic troubles was for black people to disappear. "The same people who were considered 'good ol' darkies' a few years ago are now considered deadwood, hardly worth keeping alive," he wrote. "They and their shotgun shanties only clutter the landscape, chafing the consciences and the pocketbooks of the region." White southerners understood that black political empowerment was likely to lead to redistributive policies aimed at raising the economic status of their African American neighbors and that these measures could come at some expense to themselves. Ellett Lawrence of the Association of Citizens' Councils of Mississippi acknowledged as much when he warned that property owners could face a "100%, 200%, or more tax increase" if more white residents did not join the organization in its fight to prevent black people from voting.[11] The convergence of political and economic threats embodied in civil rights and antipoverty initiatives represented the realization of such fears.

Opponents of the war on poverty countered arguments in favor of government intervention by suggesting that the problems afflicting black communities stemmed from uncontrollable laws of economics rather than decisions made by human beings who could be held accountable. Alabama newspaper editor Hamner Cobbs explained, "We like our Nigras but we can't afford to keep 'em around. The county's economy can't take it." Similar arguments were presented to OEO staff who visited Coahoma County, Mississippi, to find out why a group of leading white residents refused to cooperate on antipoverty projects. Local lawyer Semmes Luckett opposed the war on poverty because it attempted to meddle with natural forces that encouraged African Americans to leave. The OEO officials reported: "[Luckett] thinks that the real purpose of the OEO in Coahoma County is to interfere with the normal laws of supply and demand and to negate the outmigration of Negroes from the Delta."[12] Invoking the primacy of market forces was a convenient way for plantation owners and political elites to avoid dealing with a social crisis that they had created through the various oppressions they inflicted on black southerners in the Jim Crow era and actions taken in the 1960s for the purpose of maximizing profits and preserving their power.

State and local governments' reluctance to initiate antipoverty projects left the field open for black community groups, whose organizing achievements in the civil rights struggle ideally situated them for applying for OEO funds. Many CAPs combined antipoverty work with political consciousness raising among the poor people they served. Mississippi activist Unita Blackwell reported that in the CDGM, "People learned coming off the plantations that they could make some decisions. This brought dignity to the people; ... they learned that they could argue with one another and try to reason and found out they could make some decisions for themselves." Participation as board members and administrative staff of antipoverty programs offered lessons in how power relationships influenced the distribution of economic resources and enhanced black people's ability to negotiate the system. As a *New York Times* article noted in 1973, "The war on poverty ... nourished a generation of talented blacks in managerial skills that until then had been the prerogatives of whites."[13]

Black people's increasing assertiveness sparked complaints from some quarters that the federal government was using taxpayers' money to fund civil rights agitation. Mississippi governor Paul Johnson accused the CDGM of working to "create division and dissension between the races" and Senator John Stennis used his position as a member of the Senate Appropriations Committee to undermine the program. Stennis sent staff members to Mississippi to investigate the CDGM, uncovered some minor irregularities in financial operations, and used these anomalies to charge misuse of federal funds. Reforms mandated by the OEO failed to appease the senator. Stennis' relentless bullying finally led federal officials to ask a biracial group of moderate Mississippians to form a rival CAP as a less politicized alternative to the CDGM in August 1966. The OEO thus capitulated to the state's white supremacist leadership and destroyed one of the most successful antipoverty programs in Mississippi.[14]

Similar developments occurred in the North. Addressing the urban crisis was a major focus of the war on poverty, and city governments initially welcomed the infusion of federal funds into their communities. Within a few years, however, the political mobilization of marginalized groups inspired by antipoverty programs unnerved local officials. Northerners accustomed to thinking of racism as a southern problem were shocked when black people in their own neighborhoods began to use sit-ins and mass demonstrations to draw attention to social ills. Baltimore mayor Theodore McKeldin asserted that activists who encouraged the residents of poor neighborhoods to demand better public services did "not understand the problems and requirements of local governments." In Newark, a committee appointed by the city council to investigate the UCC after civil rights leaders increased their influence over the program accused it of being more of a "political action group" than an antipoverty agency and suggested replacing it with a commission that allowed municipal officials more control. In the wake of a Watts-style uprising that devastated the city in July 1967 Mayor Hugh Addonizio blamed the CAP for increasing racial tensions, violence, and crime. White people in many other cities also associated antipoverty programs with increasing black militancy and social strife that threatened rather than helped their communities.[15]

Segregationist opponents of antipoverty initiatives agitated such concerns in their attacks on the programs. The White Citizens' Council's *Citizen* magazine frequently maligned government efforts to assist poor people as political bribes that only encouraged bad behavior. A 1967 article by South Carolina senator Strom Thurmond contended, "Instead of organizing an individual's assets to do battle with the hard facts of life, the programs organize the recipients into pressure groups prepared to blackmail the government and society itself." When the National Advisory Commission on Civil Disorders issued a report that traced urban unrest to racial injustice and urged an expansion of social programs, the magazine's editors responded with scorn. "The propaganda machines in this nation have for years drummed into the Negro's head that he is, and has been, mistreated by white people," they stated, and went on to deride the government for rewarding rioters with "all manner of giveaway programs" instead of putting them in jail.[16]

Another thread in the segregationist narrative cast white Americans as victims of federal policies that transferred their hard-earned money to lazy, undeserving black people. When a group of African Americans in Louisiana received OEO funds to operate a cooperative bakery, the local Citizens' Council newsletter ridiculed the project by publishing a recipe for a "Poverty Fruit Cake" that included among the ingredients "Dough from Taxpayers," "Sugar from Politicians," "1 Gullible Public," and "1/2 baked ideas." South Carolina industrialist William Lowndes believed antipoverty efforts created a new kind of "forgotten man" in the United States – the "law-abiding, respectable, hardworking individual ... who is allowed a $600 yearly tax deduction to raise and educate his child while an unwed mother on relief gets many times that amount in welfare checks to support her burgeoning brood." Similarly, a story in the November 1972 issue of the *Citizen* claimed that the federal government was helping poor people to purchase modern new houses with intercom systems that piped music to every room while many middle-class families were struggling to pay mortgages on their modest homes. "Think about this, fellow citizens, the next time you stand in line at the supermarket while the woman ahead of you uses food stamps to pay for enough groceries to load the back seat and trunk of her Cadillac!" the author urged.[17]

Antipoverty workers faced violent as well as verbal attacks on their activities. In Lowndes County, Alabama, opponents of the local CAP burned down a church that was used for board meetings and poisoned some cattle belonging to a county official who supported the program. Participants in a job training project in Mississippi experienced similar harassment. Vigilantes bombed a church and burned crosses on the lawns of trainees, and one social worker lost her home to arson. In many communities white parents who enrolled their children in Head Start received threatening phone calls or visits from the Ku Klux Klan.[18] Poor white people along with African Americans stood to benefit from the war on poverty, but many were discouraged from taking advantage of the programs by fears of how their neighbors might respond. White Americans' reluctance to participate and the high incidence of poverty in the black population meant that African Americans made up a disproportionate number of people receiving assistance. The resulting assumption that the initiatives mostly served non-white people fueled perceptions that the nation's (white) taxpayers were unfairly burdened with the costs of solving the nation's (black) poverty problem.

"Colorblind" Resistance to Civil Rights Enforcement

The federal government's efforts to overcome resistance to civil rights enforcement also generated angry reactions. White Americans who associated black people with deteriorating neighborhoods, inferior schools, and crime used every available means to prevent African Americans from gaining access to spaces and facilities previously reserved for their own use. After the mid-1960s opponents of integration often explained their position in language that denied any racist motivations, focusing instead on the need to protect private property rights, local control over schools, and individual liberties against threats to these values resulting from the exercise of state authority to achieve equality. They were not seeking to preserve segregation, they explained, but merely asserting their rights as homeowners, parents, and citizens.[19] However well intended, these arguments served to maintain racism as surely as the compromises with slavery made by the nation's founders in the revolutionary era. Like earlier generations of white

Americans who were reluctant to relinquish the benefits they derived from the system, "colorblind" defenders of the status quo resolved the conflict between their rights and those of African Americans in ways that preserved their racial privileges.

Efforts to equalize educational opportunities encountered some of the most intense opposition. In the first decade after the Supreme Court's decision in *Brown v. Board of Education* many school districts circumvented the ruling by engaging in protracted legal battles to avoid obeying the law or relying on "freedom of choice" plans that placed the burden of integrating schools on black Americans. Economic reprisals, physical attacks, and other forms of intimidation discouraged black families from sending their children to white schools, and progress toward ending segregation was minimal. Local officials also relied on residential segregation, gerrymandered zoning, and individual school assignments to avoid integration.[20]

In 1964 the Civil Rights Act strengthened national administrators' enforcement powers by allowing the Department of Health, Education and Welfare (HEW) to deny federal funds to school districts that continued to engage in racial discrimination. Four years later, in *Green v. County School Board of New Kent County* (1968), the Supreme Court attempted to speed the pace of desegregation and move beyond ineffective freedom of choice plans by ordering districts to integrate every aspect of their school systems, including facilities, teachers, administrative staff, and transportation as well as students. These "Green factors" became the standard used by federal officials to determine whether districts had achieved "unitary" school systems that offered white and black students the same quality of education. In two decisions in the early 1970s the Court approved the use of busing to overcome the obstacles posed by residential segregation and ruled that districts were responsible for addressing the effects of other policies that indirectly resulted in school segregation.[21]

The federal government's new assertiveness drew violent responses from some citizens. Segregationists in Chicago protested a busing plan that was implemented in their city in 1968 by fire bombing a white school the day it began receiving black students. Saboteurs in one Texas town blew up 36 buses in July 1970, just before busing to integrate the schools was to take effect. In Bensonhurst, New York, groups of white men wielding baseball bats, chains, and tire irons threatened the lives of black children walking between the train station and an integrated school. Antibusing activists in Boston also engaged in harassment and physical attacks on African Americans and supporters of integration.[22]

Other opponents of busing denounced the overt racism expressed in such Klan-like tactics and presented their own objections as a legitimate response to excessive bureaucratic meddling that placed their children's future at risk. A woman in Louisiana expressed concern that enabling black children to attend suburban schools forced middle-class white children to sit in classes with the offspring of "people on welfare, degenerates, etc." She stated, "I have been all for them having the right to an education. But please, sir, not at the expense of my children." Similarly, Boston antibusing leader Louise Day Hicks stated, "I believe in integrated school systems, but I do not believe in forceable busing of children for the purpose of racially balancing schools."[23]

The most common reasons cited for opposition to busing were the long hours students spent traveling to and from school, disruptions to families, and resentment over being told which schools children must attend rather than personal antipathy toward African Americans. Yet providing transportation for school children had been the practice in every state since the early twentieth century and never stirred controversy until it was associated with integration. As the United States Commission on Civil Rights pointed out, "For decades black and white children alike in the South were bused as much as 50 miles or more each day to assure perfect racial segregation. No complaints then were heard from whites of any harmful effects." Supporters of school integration in Boston noted that before the 1970s school officials bused white students into the black neighborhood of Roxbury to attend an elite school located there and transported other children out of racially mixed communities so they could attend all-white schools elsewhere, with none of the histrionics about "forced busing" that accompanied efforts to end segregation. One white man stated, "I took buses to go to school and no one ever called it busing. These people just don't want their Johnny or Mary to go to school with Black kids, or have their kids make friends with Blacks. It really is a racist movement."[24]

Many white families responded to integration efforts by abandoning the public school system in favor of private schools that accepted few or no black children. Segregationists encouraged this movement by warning of an impending crisis in public education now that white and black children attended the same schools. A 1966 article in the *Citizen* claimed, "Negro education is inferior because Negro family standards are inferior" and that African Americans were "less adequately endowed with native intelligence." The author urged white parents who were concerned about their children's future to turn to private schooling instead. In November 1971 the Southern Independent School Association reported that it had 396 member schools located throughout the region with a combined enrollment of 176,000. Its executives cited integration of the public schools as the main reason for the organization's rapid growth and stated that white people's unwillingness to associate with African Americans was a "fundamental, God-given law of nature that the doctrinaire liberals violate." Private schoolers who were uncomfortable with openly racist rationales could cite their opposition to federal interference in the education system or a desire to include Christian values in their children's training after the Supreme Court banned compulsory religious activities in the public schools in 1963. Such explanations were not entirely convincing. In Starkville, Mississippi, both white and black public school attendees referred to the local private academy as "Bigot High."[25]

Attempts to open white schools and other facilities to black people accelerated "white flight" to racially homogenous suburbs in the decades after the 1960s. This movement was more than just the logical outcome of government policies that encouraged urban sprawl in the decades after World War II. What historian Kevin Kruse terms "suburban secession" reflected the conscious desire of many white homeowners to preserve the spatial and social distance that the Jim Crow system placed between themselves and black people. As African Americans gained access to schools, parks, buses, and other public spaces, white Americans resisted integration by retreating to private facilities that they could control. They drove cars instead of using public transportation, built their own swimming pools in their back yards, played golf at exclusive country clubs, and sent their children to private schools.[26]

White citizens who had no need for public amenities resented paying taxes to support facilities that were mostly used by black people, giving rise to individualistic, antigovernment sentiments that impelled dramatic reductions in social spending after the 1960s. In California, after education reformers secured a ruling from the state Supreme Court requiring legislators to devise a system of "fair taxation" and share education revenues evenly among wealthy and poor districts, antitax activists succeeded in persuading voters to pass Proposition 13 in 1978, fixing property taxes at one percent and prohibiting any new tax increases. Over the next few decades California's public education system dropped from among the top ten to the bottom ten states for per-pupil expenditures. Similar measures to reduce and cap taxes were proposed in eighteen other states over the next four years and in many instances became law.[27]

Hostility to racial and economic integration was expressed in other ways as well. Suburban communities frequently adopted ordinances aimed at keeping poor and black people out, such as minimum sizes for house lots or prohibitions on public housing, and fought to control their own tax revenues so that they could spend the money locally instead of sharing it with larger metropolitan areas. The growth of self-contained suburbs with their own amenities and governments insulated middle-class white families from the crises they left behind in poorer communities and enabled the deficiencies evident in African American neighborhoods to be defined as "black" problems that they felt no responsibility for solving. In a letter to Louisiana senator Russell Long, constituent Roger Samson expressed the views of many other people who were oblivious to the interconnected forms of oppression that limited black Americans' economic prospects. Black people, he claimed, "don't want to work. They want everything handed out to them on a silver platter, not caring to know the whites worked hard to get what they have."[28]

In the minds of Samson and many other Americans, middle-class status was earned through individual effort and hard work, and those who achieved it were entitled to demand that others apply themselves with equal tenacity rather than relying on government assistance. Economic inequality was not the result of mechanisms that distributed resources unevenly but the natural product of market forces that rewarded talent, initiative, and industry. Such analyses ignored the extent to which many white families' success rested on taxpayer-funded programs such as Social Security, the GI Bill, and federally subsidized suburban development, not to mention the racist practices that eliminated most African Americans from competition for these resources. As Matthew Lassiter notes, this " 'color-blind' discourse of suburban innocence [and] meritocratic individualism" served to justify actions that preserved racism in the post-civil rights era while convincing many citizens of their righteousness.[29]

The White Man's Party

Political leaders seeking to win support from these voters encouraged their resistance to civil rights enforcement and validated their rationalizations. George Wallace's campaign for the Democratic Party's presidential nomination in 1964 revealed how subtle appeals to racism couched in the language of individual liberty could be used to draw support from broad segments of the white population. As governor of Alabama Wallace famously pledged to defend "Segregation now! Segregation tomorrow! Segregation forever!" in the early 1960s. When the passage of civil rights legislation and increasing black voter registration made such overtly racist positions less tenable, Wallace shifted his focus to attacking federal "tyranny" and administrators' attempts to impose their unpopular social ideals on other Americans. Wallace emphasized his support for limited government, protection of property rights, and traditional religious values – issues that seemingly had nothing to do with race. In a decade that had seen segregationists defend their position by citing these same ideals, however, the connections between racism and Wallace's antigovernment stance were clear. One Alabaman stated, "He can use all the other issues – law and order, running your own schools, protecting property rights – and never mention race. But people will know he's telling them, 'A nigger's trying to get your job, trying to move into your neighborhood.' "[30]

Republican Party leaders also understood the power of such appeals and used them to build a powerful new coalition comprised of business leaders, middle-class suburbanites, and social conservatives in the late twentieth century. According to political strategist Kevin Phillips, Republicans' nomination of Arizona senator Barry Goldwater for the presidency in 1964 was the point when the Grand Old Party "decided to break with its formative antecedents and make an ideological bid for the anti-civil rights South." The Goldwater campaign mirrored Wallace's approach with its emphasis on colorblind ideals that served to maintain white advantages. Goldwater explained his opposition to the Civil Rights Act in racially neutral terms, stating that he supported integration but not the use of federal power to achieve it. Like Wallace, however, Goldwater manipulated the racial fears of white Americans in his speeches. To highlight the problem of increasing criminal activity in the nation's cities, for example, Goldwater cited predominantly black cities that had strong civil rights movements instead of whiter cities that had higher rates of crime. Journalist Richard Rovere noted that such tactics proved highly appealing to the all-white crowds who flocked to hear the senator speak during a tour of the South in September and concluded the Goldwater movement was "a racist movement and very little else."[31]

Other concerns such as threats to free market capitalism and national security also motivated participants, but there is no question that the Goldwater campaign drew many white racists into the Republican Party. At the Young Republicans convention in 1963, *Wall Street Journal* columnist Robert Novak observed that a majority of the delegates shared an enthusiasm for Goldwater and "an unabashed hostility toward the Negro rights movement." Many party leaders "envisioned substantial political gold to be mined in the racial crisis by becoming in fact, though not in name, the White Man's Party," he wrote. In September 1964 Strom Thurmond announced that he was leaving the Democratic Party to support Goldwater, and in the November election large numbers of rank-and-file Democrats followed the senator's lead. Goldwater lost to Lyndon Johnson but won more than 26 million votes and carried the five Deep South states that most strongly resisted the civil rights movement – Alabama, Georgia, Louisiana, Mississippi, and South Carolina. Roy Harris of the White Citizens' Council took encouragement from the election results. Writing in the *Citizen*, Harris declared that segregationists had made "great progress" in the struggle to turn the tide against civil rights efforts and force the nation's politicians "back to our position that segregation is best for both races!" A cartoon reinforcing Harris' analysis depicted an elephant labeled "G.O.P." galloping across the page bearing a Confederate flag (see Figure 2.2). Other observers noted the implications of Goldwater's success with somewhat less enthusiasm. In an address to the Mississippi Council on Human Relations in February 1966, Illinois Republican Charles Percy stated that he was anxious to see more southern support for the party but "not for the reasons that it was there on election day, 1964." Many people

Figure 2.2   Cartoon that appeared in the November 1964 issue of the *Citizen* after Republican candidate Barry Goldwater won the five Deep South states in that year's presidential election
Source: Unknown/The Citizens' Council

voted Republican to protest the Johnson administration's civil rights initiatives and expected the party to "take a far weaker stand, or perhaps even squelch the Negro revolution," he acknowledged. Percy emphasized: "I am not proud of these votes."[32]

The Goldwater campaign increased the influence of anti-civil rights forces within the Republican Party. Convention rules that allocated delegates to states based on their performance in the last election enhanced the power of southerners at the national convention in Miami in 1968, where Richard Nixon vied with racial moderate Nelson Rockefeller and Goldwater heir Ronald Reagan for the presidential nomination. Nixon knew that southern delegates' votes were crucial and courted their support by promising to ease up on integration efforts. He criticized federal judges for ordering school districts to adopt busing plans to achieve desegregation and stated that these actions went beyond the proper role of the courts. In response to a question regarding likely appointees to the Supreme Court, Nixon said he would choose judges "who will interpret the Constitution strictly" rather than trying to broaden its application to ensure racial equality. Nixon's pledge to roll back federal power and return responsibility for enforcing laws to state and local governments reassured the southern delegates and helped him to secure the nomination.[33]

Nixon's bid for the presidency consciously used racism for political purposes. The Republican nominee accepted his assistants' advice to emulate Goldwater's "southern strategy" in an effort to draw more white voters away from the Democratic Party and destroy the New Deal coalition. As campaign staffer Pat Buchanan explained, the growing discord over civil rights was a "dividing line" that could be used to "really tear up the pea patch ... and cut the Democratic Party and country in half." Like Wallace and Goldwater before him, Nixon used covert appeals to racism that signaled to white voters that he was on their side. His speeches highlighted social problems such as crime and welfare dependency that many Americans associated with black people. He promised to appoint more restrained judges to the Supreme Court and restore local control over schools. In the process, Nixon reassured white Americans that their individualistic analysis of economic inequality was correct and that they were not responsible for the problems that afflicted black communities. "There is no reason to feel guilty about wanting to enjoy what you get and get what you earn, about wanting your children in good schools close to home," he told supporters.[34]

This approach secured Nixon's election in 1968 and initiated federal officials' gradual disengagement from efforts to ensure that African Americans enjoyed equal access to education, housing, political power, and economic opportunity in the late twentieth century. Nixon honored his promises to southern Republicans by instructing the staff of government agencies responsible for protecting civil rights to do the minimum required by law and no more. On the issue of the economy, Nixon sought to replace government action to reduce poverty with policies that encouraged greater self-reliance. The new administration cut funding for antipoverty programs and gradually dismantled the OEO by parceling out most of its functions to other government agencies. The innovative aspects of the war on poverty were lost as more traditional government bureaucracies took over operation of OEO programs. The president also decreased federal oversight over the use of antipoverty funds by replacing categorical grants marked for specific purposes with block grants that could be used any way state and local governments saw fit. Restoring control over the money to political leaders gave them the ability to choose which programs were funded and which ones shut down. Community action programs that worked to empower poor black people found it difficult to secure grants to continue these efforts in the post civil-rights era as regional elites reverted to their usual approach of distributing resources in ways that favored their own interests.[35]

Global Economic Transformations

Economic developments in addition to racist reactions against the black freedom movement transformed national politics and society in this period. In the late 1960s American capitalism encountered new challenges that undermined the uniquely powerful position the United States occupied in the global economy after World War II. Manufacturers faced growing competition from their counterparts in Europe and Asia as those regions' economies recovered from the devastation caused by the war. An oil embargo imposed by the Organization of Petroleum Exporting Countries (OPEC) in 1973 added to these problems by further raising production costs and prices for American-made products relative to cheaper foreign imports. Huge increases in the price of oil, heavy borrowing by businesses, and government spending on social programs and the Vietnam War generated rising inflation in the 1970s. Corporate profits fell from 14 percent in 1965 to 8 percent annually in the next decade, causing business and political leaders to search for new ways to maintain the prosperity of the postwar era.[36]

The next few decades saw a gradual abandonment of New Deal-era policies that sustained domestic demand and generated profits for American companies by enhancing people's ability to buy consumer items. Corporate leaders and their political allies instead promoted an agenda of economic deregulation, tax cuts, reduced social spending, and international free trade agreements to generate wealth. The growing availability of global markets and global sources of labor dramatically altered the relationship between businesses and workers. In a world where corporations could make and sell their products virtually anywhere, it was no longer so important to employ Americans and pay them well.[37] Rather than acceding to union demands that wages keep up with inflation in the 1970s, manufacturers cut costs by closing factories in the United States and relocating operations in countries were labor was cheaper, taxes were lower, and government regulations less stringent.

The decline in domestic manufacturing was partly offset by an expanding service sector, but many communities experienced a net loss of jobs in the 1970s and 1980s. Except for a few specialized occupations requiring high levels of expertise, most jobs in growth areas such as retail, office work, finance, insurance, and real estate did not offer the same level of pay or benefits as those in older industries. In all sectors the stable, secure employment demanded by unionized factory workers in previous decades conflicted with employers' preference for a leaner and more flexible workforce in the late twentieth century. Corporate leaders cited the need to remain competitive in a globalized economy to justify laying off workers and cutting pay or benefits for those who remained. Economic restructuring consigned increasing numbers of Americans to low-wage, part-time or temporary work that restricted their chances for upward mobility. Other workers were not needed in the new economy at all. Average weekly earnings (in constant dollars) declined from $187 to $170 between 1970 and 1985, and the nation's unemployment rate increased sharply during the same period.[38]

Unlike previous periods of economic growth that spread the benefits to broad spectrums of the society, that of the post-civil rights era was more selective. In the 1960s the average pay for corporate chief executive officers (CEOs) was 41 times that of the average factory worker. By 1996 CEOs were earning 212 times more than working-class Americans. College educated people secured the best jobs, enjoyed comfortable incomes, and adapted more easily to changes that required them to acquire new skills. Those with high school qualifications or less found good jobs harder to find and often experienced long periods of unemployment or underemployment.[39]

The Uses of Racism in the Late Twentieth Century

Proponents of free market policies both facilitated these developments and explained them in ways that obscured their complex causes. Rather than highlighting global capitalist transformations or the actions of corporate elites, they emphasized federal spending on antipoverty programs and burdensome regulations on American businesses. In 1974 Ronald Reagan asserted, "There is one reason for inflation in America and that is simply that government for too long has been spending too much money." Reagan considered most federal regulatory agencies unnecessary and argued that "too much government, too much red tape, too many taxes, and too many regulations" were "robbing our people of the prosperity that is rightfully theirs."[40]

Like other politicians, Reagan knew how to deploy racism to win support for his economic agenda. In a televised address in 1976 he cited "forced school busing" as an example of excessive government. During a speech in Florida the same year, Reagan sympathized with the anger many citizens felt over having to tighten their grocery budgets when a "strapping young buck" could use food stamps to buy T-bone steaks. Another story he told repeatedly during his several bids for the Republican Party's presidential nomination involved a black "welfare queen" who allegedly defrauded the government of $150,000 by using "80 names, 30 addresses, 12 Social Security cards and ... collecting veterans' benefits on four nonexisting deceased husbands." Reagan's information was based on sensationalized newspaper accounts that exaggerated the misdeeds of Linda Taylor, a welfare recipient in Chicago. During prosecution of the case the charges against her were greatly reduced, and she was eventually convicted of wrongly appropriating $8,000 in public assistance checks.[41]

Reagan's portrayal of social programs as a misuse of taxpayer funds for the benefit of lazy, cheating African Americans paralleled the narratives presented by southern segregationists seeking to undermine antipoverty efforts and limit federal power. The similarities were not entirely accidental.

Lee Atwater, a South Carolinian who began his political career working on Strom Thurmond's 1970 senatorial campaign and helped Reagan to devise his own version of the Republican southern strategy, outlined the merging of racial and economic messages as follows: "You start out in 1954 by saying 'Nigger, nigger, nigger.' By 1968 you can't say 'nigger' – that hurts you. Backfires. So you say stuff like forced busing, states' rights, and all that stuff. You're getting so abstract now [that] you're talking about cutting taxes, and all these things you're talking about are totally economic things and a by-product of them is [that] blacks get hurt worse than whites." In the mid-1980s Republican operative Hastings Wyman Jr. reflected with some shame on the methods his party used to win support for its candidates after the 1960s. "I want to say: But those were insignificant details!" he wrote. "Our real pitch was for freedom – free enterprise, freedom from government interference in the rights of states, of communities, of business. ... But I can't buy my own line." Recalling tactics such as denouncing busing and mailing leaflets to white voters highlighting Democratic candidates' support for integration, Wyman acknowledged that Republican electoral successes rested largely on a racist reaction against the civil rights movement that was "consciously encouraged – no, fanned – by the GOP itself."[42]

The strategy helped to secure Reagan's victories in the presidential elections of 1980 and 1984 and cemented the political realignment begun in the 1960s. Throughout his presidency Reagan and other opponents of government intervention in the economy reiterated suggestions that billions of dollars in taxpayers' money were being wasted on antipoverty efforts that unjustly appropriated white wealth for the benefit of African Americans. In reality, the public assistance programs targeted in these attacks represented a tiny portion of the federal budget. Most social spending was on programs such as Social Security and Medicare that disproportionately benefited the white middle class.[43] By focusing on "black" programs such as welfare, food stamps, and public housing, free market proponents convinced millions of white Americans who owed their economic success to New Deal social welfare measures that the government was their enemy, not the solution to their problems.

At a time when companies were trimming their workforces and reducing employee benefits, an expansion of services such as unemployment compensation, retraining programs, subsidized health care, and affordable housing could have alleviated the economic anxieties of millions of white as well as black families. By the mid-1980s, however, many white Americans so closely associated government programs with African Americans that they could not see how they might benefit from such policies themselves. "Unfortunately, most of the people who need help ... are black and most of the people who are doing the helping are white," Chicago resident Dan

Donahue asserted. "We are tired of paying for the Chicago Housing Authority, and for public housing and public transportation that we don't use." A study of the shifting political views of white citizens in Macomb County, Michigan, who had voted solidly Democratic in the 1960s and switched to supporting to Republicans in the 1970s and 1980s, revealed that many of them blamed African Americans for everything that was wrong in their lives. "These white Democratic defectors express a profound distaste for blacks, a sentiment that pervades almost everything they think about government and politics," the report stated. "Virtually all progressive symbols and themes have been redefined in racial and pejorative terms."[44] As in the slavery and Jim Crow eras, the nation divided along racial instead of class lines, enabling political leaders to pursue policies that benefited a wealthy minority and did not do much to improve the lives of the majority of Americans.

Free Market Fallout

The version of capitalism that prevailed in the Reagan era represented a revival of classical, laissez-faire economic theories that considered the pursuit of profit by individuals, unencumbered by regulations or efforts to redistribute resources, the best way to organize societies and ensure the most benefit to the most people. Proponents of these ideas believed that some of the wealth generated by profitable activities eventually made its way from rich to poor people through normal market mechanisms, leading to rising living standards for everyone. In this model, the needs of business owners and investors took precedence above other concerns because those people created the prosperity that was necessary to improve the lives of the less fortunate.[45]

Reagan's strategy was to starve federal bureaucracies of funds and transfer money back into the private sector where he believed it belonged. Corporations and wealthy individuals received roughly $750 billion in tax cuts in the 1980s while almost every federal program that offered assistance to poor people was scaled back or eliminated altogether. Funding for public assistance programs, food stamps, school lunches, health services, and housing declined by a total of $40 billion. The construction of low-income housing projects was halted, leading to a severe shortage of affordable homes and an increase in homelessness in many communities. Reagan reduced federal aid to cities by 46 percent and cut the block grants that state and local governments relied on to provide social services by one-third. These measures generated fiscal crises in many places that political leaders chose to resolve by cutting programs rather than taking the more unpopular path of raising taxes. As scholars Thomas Byrne Edsall and Mary Edsall observed in 1992, Reagan's tax policies and budget cuts "produced one of the most dramatic redistributions of income in the nation's history." Between 1980 and 1990 the average after-tax income of the poorest one tenth of Americans fell by 10 percent, from $4,785 to $4,295. In the same period average after-tax incomes for the richest 1 percent increased by 87 percent, from $231,416 to $399,697.[46]

The free market agenda imposed particular hardships on African Americans. One-third of the nation's black citizens lived below the poverty line in the 1980s and they suffered greatly from the weakening of the social safety net. Many middle-class black people worked in the public sector where their jobs were susceptible to budget cuts. Acting on his belief that government could perform few functions "as well or as economically as the private sector of the economy," Reagan ordered federal agencies to contract as much work as possible to private companies. Food services, building maintenance, and data processing were among the many positions that were privatized. Federal workers in these areas frequently saw their full-time, year-round jobs transformed into temporary and part-time positions that offered no health insurance or pensions.[47] The drive for increased efficiency and flexibility in government as well as the private sector thus came at the expense of workers' job security and economic wellbeing.

Democrats along with Republicans contributed to these developments. Democratic candidates responded to Republican electoral victories by distancing themselves from ideas and programs that were associated with African Americans. The two Democratic presidents elected between 1968 and 2008, Jimmy Carter (1976) and Bill Clinton (1992), were both racially moderate southerners who rejected the segregationist rhetoric of past decades but did not revive the forceful commitment to black equality the party had demonstrated in the 1960s. Budget constraints and growing antitax sentiment among voters during the Carter administration precluded any efforts to address poverty that entailed significant government spending. The president avoided talking about race issues and pursued an economic agenda that focused on helping businesses to create jobs and spur economic recovery. His efforts failed to solve the problems of high unemployment and high inflation that plagued the nation in the late 1970s, however, and he lost to Ronald Reagan in the 1980 election.[48]

Reagan's landslide reelection in 1984 inspired a group of Democratic politicians from the South and West to form the Democratic Leadership Council (DLC) in an effort to push their party in new directions. Senator Sam Nunn of Georgia asserted, "There is a perception our party has moved away from mainstream America." In response to DLC members' concerns, Democratic National Committee chair Paul Kirk Jr. promised to reduce the influence of "single-issue groups" within the party and work to expand its base in states where Republicans had been making significant gains.[49]

Rather than explaining to voters how government initiatives to create jobs or improve conditions for poor people could help everyone, Democratic leaders tacitly accepted their opponents' portrayals of such policies as programs that benefited "special interests" (meaning black people) at other Americans' expense.

The DLC did not just work to influence policy but succeeded in changing party rules in ways that strengthened its preferred candidates' chances in the presidential primaries. These efforts bore fruit with the nomination of Arkansas governor and DLC chair Bill Clinton as the party's presidential candidate in the 1992 election. Clinton's campaign mimicked many of the themes that Nixon and Reagan had used to court white voters, including support for tough measures to combat crime and criticisms of excessive federal intervention in the economy.[50] The party platform expressed the DLC's view that "big government" solutions to social problems had failed and asserted a need to place more emphasis on "work, family and individual responsibility."[51] These tactics reflected the Democratic Party's retreat from its earlier support for the black freedom movement and its leaders' tendency to legitimize more than challenge the racial and economic ideologies promoted by their Republican opponents in the late twentieth century.

Growing inequality characterized the Clinton presidency as it did previous administrations. Huge budget deficits resulting from tax cuts and increases in military spending in the 1980s prevented Clinton from reviving costly antipoverty initiatives even if he had wanted to. Strong economic growth in the 1990s stemming from the invention of new computer technologies, relaxed credit markets, and increasing international trade suggested there was no need for interventionist policies that redistributed wealth downward. Unemployment fell to its lowest level since the 1970s, and low-wage workers as well as those with more skills saw modest increases in their incomes. Much of this growth was based on speculative trading in internet company stocks, however, and when the bubble burst in 2001 the economy went into recession.

The terrorist attacks of September 11, 2001 and the policies pursued by Clinton's successor George W. Bush worsened economic conditions for many Americans. Bush pushed supply-side policies that focused on helping the nation's wealthiest citizens to new extremes by further cutting taxes, reducing social investments, increasing military spending, and encouraging privatization of services previously supplied by the government. Bush also undermined the effectiveness of many regulatory agencies by staffing them with people whose ideologies and qualifications were antithetical to the missions they were supposed to carry out. Civil rights enforcement, protections for workers and the environment, and oversight of powerful financial institutions were greatly weakened during his two terms in office.[52] Toward the end of Bush's presidency the consequences of his laissez-faire approach were exposed in a massive economic collapse that rivaled the Great Depression in its impact on middle- and working-class Americans. Voters expressed their anger by ejecting Republicans from power in 2008, but blame for the crisis really lay with the leaders of both political parties and other Americans who promoted policies that concentrated wealth at the top of the income pyramid, generated extreme inequality, and eroded the middle class after the 1960s.

Part of the responsibility lay with those citizens whose resistance to the war on poverty and civil rights enforcement rejected notions of mutual responsibility and reserved the right to enjoy decent housing, education, and other services to those who could afford to pay for them. These beliefs facilitated a reordering of national priorities that sacrificed the inclusive social reforms embodied in the black freedom movement for the pursuit of private wealth within the context of free markets. Neither the benefits nor the burdens of the new order were evenly shared. Failure to address institutional racism in the late twentieth century left the shadow cast by Jim Crow in place, quietly perpetuating inequities that made black people more vulnerable than most other Americans to the downside of capitalist restructuring.

A System without Signs: The Invisible Racism of the Post-Civil Rights Era

To later generations these wrongs – and the need for collective efforts to right them – will be as clear as the wrongs of slavery were to those born after 1865, or of segregation to those born after 1964. (Thomas C. Holt, 2000)[1]

One night in December 1995 three white soldiers stationed at Fort Bragg, North Carolina, ventured into nearby Fayetteville looking for African Americans to harass. Within a short time they came across black residents Jackie Burden and Michael James taking an evening walk. An argument ensued that ended with the soldiers executing Burden and James. The resulting murder investigation revealed that two of the soldiers, James Burmeister and Malcolm Wright, were among a small group of skinheads at Fort Bragg who admired Adolf Hitler and openly espoused racist views. News accounts and citizen reactions to the incident treated the pair of neo-Nazis as ignorant, irrational people whose racial beliefs were far out of the mainstream. "I never thought we had that kind of hatred still in our midst" and "I thought it was over" were typical comments gathered from local residents in the wake of the Fayetteville murders. A newspaper reporter found it hard to explain the soldiers' actions, informing readers that "there seemed to be nothing in their pasts to account for their hatred."[2] No one considered whether there might be something in the current configuration of American society that could cause some people to conclude that African Americans were second-class citizens unworthy of enjoying the same rights as other people.

Three decades after the passage of civil rights legislation the social order was still structured in ways that encouraged assumptions of black inferiority, and people who held the types of racist views expressed by Burmeister and Wright had only to look around them to find evidence that appeared to confirm their beliefs. Individual racism and institutional barriers continued to affect black people's chances of acquiring decent housing and adequate education, in turn shaping their economic prospects. The crisis conditions in the nation's inner cities and rural black communities only worsened as policy makers cut back on antipoverty initiatives. National leaders replaced the war on poverty with a war on crime that channeled surplus laborers into prison instead of jobs. The racial biases that lay behind these processes were invisible to most citizens, causing many observers to conclude that black people's problems could not be the result of racism. Most white Americans attributed conditions in African American communities to cultural deficiencies that prevented residents from advancing economically rather than political decisions that perpetuated black disadvantages and left displaced workers without the resources they needed to adjust to the postindustrial economy.

Persistent Racial Disparities

The racial order of the post-civil rights era was not as rigidly oppressive as those of earlier times. Educational and economic opportunities were more widely available than in the past and many black people experienced significant social mobility as a result. The high school graduation rate for black students increased dramatically, from 20 percent in 1960 to 81 percent in 2006. In the same period the proportion of African Americans who held college degrees grew from 3 percent to 19 percent. The 3 percent of black households with annual incomes over $75,000 in 1970 increased to 17 percent by 2006. Meanwhile, the black poverty rate was cut in half, declining from 51 percent to 25 percent. Forty out every 1,000 black infants born in 1965 died before reaching one year old compared with only 14 in 2005. Life expectancy for African Americans increased from 64 to 73 years in the same period.[3]

Despite these advances African Americans' experiences continued to differ substantially from those of white people. In the four decades after 1965 the black unemployment rate consistently remained more than double the rate for white workers. In 2005, one-fourth of African Americans were poor compared to just 11 percent of white Americans, and the median income of white families was $24,000 more than that of black families. More than one-third of white households had incomes over $75,000 per year compared with less than one-fifth of black households. When other financial assets as well as earnings were included, the economic divide was even greater. White Americans had a median net worth of $140,700, more than five times the $24,800 reported for African Americans. Black people were less likely than white Americans to complete college degrees and more likely to lack health insurance. The black infant mortality rate was still more than twice the rate for white babies.[4]

Both the lingering effects of past discrimination and the policies pursued after the 1960s contributed to the disparities. Even without the overt racism of earlier times, the nation's black citizens suffered more than white people in the new economy that emerged in the late twentieth century. African Americans were disproportionately represented among the unskilled and poorly educated and their economic prospects suffered accordingly. Many black people worked in the public sector or in industries that were vulnerable to layoffs, and their recent entry into occupations that had previously been reserved for white Americans meant they lacked the seniority to withstand waves of downsizing. In the early 1980s, when the unemployment rate for white workers climbed to 9 percent (up from 5 percent in 1970), the black unemployment rate reached 20 percent. After renewed job growth brought white unemployment back down to 5 percent toward the end of the decade, black unemployment remained in double digits at 12 percent. Although younger black people enjoyed greater educational opportunities than previous generations, geographical isolation in declining urban areas limited their access to jobs. In 1988 the unemployment rate for college-educated black workers was 17 percent, compared with 6 percent for their white counterparts. For African Americans aged between 16 and 24 who lacked college qualifications, the unemployment rate was 34 percent, more than twice as high as the 14 percent recorded for similarly educated white Americans.[5] In an era that generated intense economic hardship for many citizens, already disadvantaged black communities received an unequal share of the pain.

The federal government's turn away from rigorous enforcement of civil rights laws also bore some responsibility for the disparities. African Americans lost some key allies in the Department of Justice as new appointees took over from the lawyers who directed policy in the Johnson administration. When Nixon's attorney general John Mitchell spoke of "vigorous" efforts to preserve law and order, he meant getting tough with protesters who engaged in civil disobedience, not racists who discriminated against black people. President Reagan also weakened enforcement efforts by cutting the budgets and staff of government agencies that were responsible for ensuring equal treatment for nonwhite people. The president and his appointees believed racism was no longer a problem and attributed persistent segregation to individual choices that were beyond the purview of federal authorities. Assistant Attorney General for Civil Rights William Bradford Reynolds stated that there was nothing inherently wrong with white and black people living in separate neighborhoods and that the government should not be involved in forcing integration. Rather than aggressively seeking to uncover and punish violations of antidiscrimination regulations, the Reagan administration relied on voluntary compliance by local governments, federal agencies, and private citizens. Justice Department lawyers brought cases only when they could prove discriminatory intent by individuals, leaving covert practices that generated patterns of inequality unchallenged.[6]

Nixon and Reagan also exerted a lasting influence on civil rights enforcement through their appointments to the federal courts. Nixon's picks for the Supreme Court – Warren Burger, Harry Blackmun, Lewis Powell, and William Rehnquist – reflected the limited role he expected of judges. The president expressed confidence that, unlike the "judicial activists" responsible for many of the rulings that pushed the nation in a more racially egalitarian direction after World War II, his appointees would not try to "twist" the Constitution to advance their "personal, political, or social views." After the mid-1970s the Court was much less likely to be persuaded by lawyers who argued that forceful measures were necessary to overcome institutional racism. Reagan's appointment of Supreme Court justices Sandra Day O'Connor, Antonin Scalia, and Anthony Kennedy, along with 368 lower court judges, solidified the tendency to accept inadequate, colorblind solutions to racial problems.[7] Unfavorable rulings in civil rights cases discouraged participants in the freedom struggle and emboldened their opponents in the later part of the century.

Separate and Unequal Communities: Housing Segregation and Environmental Racism

These shifts ensured that the racist social structure created during the Jim Crow era remained in place, only without the segregation signs. At the end of the twentieth century most African American families still lived in predominantly black neighborhoods. The consequences of this extended beyond the minimal social interaction between white and black Americans that resulted. As Douglas Massey and Nancy Denton observed in their study of the separate and unequal geographical spaces that Americans occupied in the 1990s, "Barriers to spatial mobility are barriers to social mobility, and where one lives determines a variety of salient factors that affect individual well-being: the quality of schooling, the value of housing, exposure to crime, the quality of public services, and the character of children's peers."[8] Failure to address the problem of segregated housing was a major factor in the persistence of racial inequality in the post-civil rights era.

In the early 1960s the Kennedy and Johnson administrations made some attempts to expand black people's housing options by banning discrimination in federally funded housing projects and in the government's mortgage guarantee programs. Opposition to open housing policies from homeowners, real estate industry leaders, and congressional representatives made it difficult to extend antidiscrimination measures to the private sector, however. Southern Democrats and their Republican allies in Congress deployed the rhetoric of individual freedom and private property rights to block fair housing legislation proposed by President Johnson in the late 1960s. Many northern Democrats who feared negative reactions from their white constituents offered only lukewarm support and allowed amendments to the original proposal that greatly weakened its enforcement provisions. These changes were still not enough to ensure passage of the legislation, and it remained stalled in the House of Representatives when James Earl Ray assassinated Martin Luther King Jr. on April 4, 1968. The murder sparked violent protests in cities throughout the nation. Massive social unrest convinced Congress to act, and on April 11 Johnson signed the Fair Housing Act into law.[9]

The legislation made it illegal to discriminate by race in advertising properties, renting or selling homes, and offering loan terms to prospective home buyers. Limited enforcement mechanisms made it difficult to prosecute offenders and undermined the effectiveness of the law, however. Subtle methods of denying housing options to black people such as withholding information or steering home seekers toward particular neighborhoods often went undetected. Even clear cases of discrimination were difficult to punish. Staff of the Department of Housing and Urban Development (HUD) who were responsible for implementing the new regulations could only act after receiving individual complaints of racism and then were limited to negotiating with offending parties to persuade them to stop discriminating. Administrators could refer cases to the Justice Department for prosecution if they identified a consistent pattern of violating the law. Uncovering such activity was rare, though, because it required systematic testing and comparison of the treatment given to white and black applicants. Plaintiffs' responsibility for paying legal fees and limits on the damages they could claim discouraged many victims of discrimination from bringing lawsuits.[10]

Administrators' antipathy toward civil rights enforcement further undermined efforts to ensure fair housing practices after the late 1960s. The FHA and private lenders continued to redline central cities on the assumption that, as HUD secretary George Romney put it, areas "occupied largely by minority groups had an unfavorable economic future." When Romney tried to open up the suburbs by threatening to withhold federal infrastructure funds from communities that relied on exclusionary zoning to keep poor people out, President Nixon ordered him to stop. Nixon maintained that there was a difference between intentional racial discrimination and the economic segregation that was presumed to result naturally from market forces. In a policy statement issued in June 1971, the president promised not to subject middle-class neighborhoods to "a flood of low-income families."[11]

Greater reliance on the private sector to allocate housing resources in the 1970s and 1980s led to increased segregation. Rather than financing the construction of low-income housing, the federal government shifted to subsidizing rents and mortgages for people who could not afford to pay market rates. If the housing industry had not been deeply contaminated with racism these programs might have helped to scatter poor people throughout cities and alleviate some of the problems caused by the concentration of poverty in public housing projects. Instead, persistent discrimination in home rentals, sales, and mortgage financing enabled poor white people to escape to the suburbs and intensified the isolation of African Americans in the nation's inner cities. Fear of violence or other means of making them feel unwelcome discouraged many black families from looking for apartments or houses in white neighborhoods. Real estate agents continued to engage in differential treatment of white and black home seekers, often showing African Americans who inquired about homes fewer units, quoting them higher prices, neglecting to discuss financial aid options, or treating them rudely. Discrimination continued in the banking industry as well. Studies conducted in the 1990s showed that black applicants were twice as likely to be rejected for home loans compared with white people who had identical qualifications. The greater difficulty African Americans encountered in securing conventional home loans made them easy targets for subprime lenders who offered more lenient acceptance criteria but higher interest rates.[12] As in the Jim Crow era, black families found decent housing difficult to acquire and paid more for it than white families.

The costs of being black were also evident in the frequency with which local governments zoned African American communities for land uses that white homeowners found intolerable. Past racist practices meant that black neighborhoods and housing projects were located in the most undesirable parts of cities, often near landfills, highways, or industrial activities that regularly spewed smoke and toxins into the air. In the late twentieth century black communities continued to act as dumping grounds for waste processing facilities and high pollution industries that white suburbanites blocked from being built near their own homes. In Houston, Texas, out of 13 incinerators and landfills operated by the city from the late 1920s through the late 1970s, only one was located in a white neighborhood. One was in a Latino area and the rest were in black communities. In 1982 political leaders in North Carolina chose predominantly black Warren County as the site for holding 32,000 cubic yards of toxic soil, even though the area's geology made it very likely that the poisons would eventually seep into residents' drinking water. An official at the Environmental Protection Agency (EPA) noted the lack of "science, truth, knowledge or facts" that went into such site selections and stated that they were "purely political" decisions. An investigation into the geography of dumping in the South by the federal government's General Accounting Office (GAO) in 1983 found a strong correlation between the racial make up of communities and the location of toxic waste sites. A nationwide study by the United Church of Christ's Commission for Racial Justice (CRJ) identified a similar pattern and estimated the chances of this being coincidental as "less than 1 in 10,000."[13]

Poor black counties and towns were often targeted as places where decisions to locate undesirable land uses were unlikely to encounter resistance. In the rural South, especially, residents of communities that were desperate for new job-creating industries were easily persuaded that the economic benefits outweighed the environmental dangers. In the second half of the twentieth century the Gulf Coast region of Alabama, Louisiana, Mississippi, and Texas became packed with chemical plants, paper mills, and waste disposal and treatment facilities (see Figure 3.1). By the 1990s one-fourth of the nation's petrochemicals were being produced along an 85 mile long corridor between Baton Rouge and New Orleans that local people called "Cancer Alley" because of the many carcinogens that contaminated the air,

Figure 3.1 Petrochemical installation built over the remains of Madewood Plantation in Louisiana, 1973
Source: John Messina/National Archives and Records Administration 412-DA-3495

soil, and water. In Louisiana's St. James Parish alone, the mostly black population was exposed to 4,500 pounds of toxic releases by nearby industrial plants every year, compared with the national average of 10 pounds per year.[14]

Louisiana activist and scholar Beverly Wright viewed the petrochemical industry as the latest incarnation of an economic structure that had long exploited the region's people and resources for the benefit of wealthy white elites. "A colonial mentality exists in the South, where local governments and big business take advantage of people who are politically and economically powerless," she wrote in 2005. The powerful Louisiana Association of Business and Industry exerted enormous influence over state legislators, often recruiting and supporting candidates for office. Like their nineteenth-century predecessors, political leaders assumed that facilitating private enterprise was the best way to ensure economic growth and consistently placed corporate interests ahead of other residents' needs. The state offered generous property tax exemptions for new industries that cost $2.5 billion in lost revenue between 1988 and 1998 alone. As a result, local governments were left without adequate funds to pay for schools, roads, recreation facilities, and other services for residents. "This tax exemption program could best be described as a corporate welfare program paid for by the poor of Louisiana," Wright asserted. Yet when community organizations attempted to persuade legislators to repeal the program or at least exclude education taxes from the exemptions, corporate lobbyists derided the effort as a job-killing initiative promoted by "anti-business special interest groups."[15]

In many cases the jobs and other economic benefits promised to rural poor communities failed to materialize. When Chemical Waste Management secured a permit to open a hazardous waste treatment plant near Emelle, Alabama, the local newspaper reported that a "unique new industry" and additional employment opportunities were coming to the area. Most of the newly created jobs went to people who lived outside the county, however. Local resident Wendell Paris stated, "We were promised jobs, but what we got was a giant hazardous-waste headache." Similarly, the construction of a Union Carbide plant in the all-black town of Institute, West Virginia, looked like economic salvation to many residents, but only 10 percent of positions at the factory went to local people. After a poisonous gas leak at one of the company's plants in Bophal, India, killed 3,400 people, the citizens of Institute questioned whether the risks they had taken for the sake of industrial development were worth it.[16]

The presence of polluters often worsened economic conditions instead of improving them. In Emelle, Mayor James Dailey watched the value of his home decline from $50,000 to $15,000 after the arrival of Chemical Waste Management's toxic waste landfill. As for jobs, Dailey reported,

"We've been losing businesses, not gaining them. The only thing that a toxic waste dump attracts is toxic waste." Declining property values and tax revenues added to the difficulties poor communities faced in providing basic services for residents. Meanwhile, corporations often did not increase the tax base because of the exemptions granted by states that were eager to attract new industries. Even when the companies did contribute funds to the larger community, residents doubted that this compensated for the damage they caused. As one black man in Houston pointed out, "We need all the money we can get to upgrade our school system. But we shouldn't have to be poisoned to get improvements for our children."[17]

Environmental racism had serious consequences for black people's health. Greater exposure to poor quality air meant that African Americans suffered from respiratory diseases such as bronchitis and asthma at higher rates than white Americans. Similarly, the concentration of many poor black families in older housing meant their children were at greater risk of lead poisoning than white children living in modern suburban homes. A 1988 study found that among families earning less than $6,000 per year in the United States, 68 percent of black children were afflicted with lead poisoning compared with 36 percent of the children in white families. More health problems meant more time lost from work and more money spent on doctors and medications, imposing significant financial burdens on families that could least afford them.[18]

Separate and Unequal Education: Resegregation and Neglect of Public Schools

Black children growing up in communities plagued by unemployment, poverty, underfunded public services, and environmental hazards did not start out with the same opportunities as children in most white families. These initial disadvantages were compounded by a return to segregated schools and the poor quality of education offered to many African Americans in the late twentieth century. In July 1969 Justice Department and HEW officials signaled the beginning of a gradual shift away from attempts to realize the promise of *Brown v. Board of Education* when they announced that rigid deadlines for school desegregation imposed too much hardship on some communities and pledged to take a more flexible approach from now on. Senator Russell Long wrote optimistically to a constituent in Louisiana: "It is a little early to think in terms of repealing any of the so-called Civil Rights bills, but I feel that the pendulum is finally beginning to swing in our direction."[19]

The Nixon administration's equivocation on civil rights enforcement emboldened segregationists in the 1970s. Former HEW staffer Barney

Sellers accused Nixon of creating "confusion where, after years of legal battles, the basic victories had been won," thus encouraging opponents of black equality to continue their resistance. Throughout the decade racist intransigence obstructed integration efforts in many communities. Public policy scholar Charles Clotfelter's account of the response to a court-ordered desegregation plan in Louisville, Kentucky, in 1975 provides a vivid example: "Following two years of legal orders, appeals, and postpone-ments, the plan's eventual implementation was accompanied by protest rallies, a boycott by whites, the burning of buses, physical violence, and the use of tear gas by National Guard troops." White public school enrollment dropped by an average of 6 percent per year between 1974 and 1982, level-ing off at around 50,000 by the end of the century (down from 120,000 in 1970). In Charlotte, North Carolina, maintaining integrated schools in the face of a similar white exodus necessitated reassigning several thousand students every year after the mid-1970s. Black students in Boston who braved the rocks and bottles thrown at the buses that transported them to white schools were often no safer inside their new classrooms than they were on the streets. "Harassment and name calling and shoving is con-stant," reported observers at South Boston High School in 1975. Some white students expressed their feelings about attending classes with black people by chanting, "Two, four, six, eight, assassinate the nigger apes."[20]

Not all the voices raised against school integration were those of white racists. Some opposition came from African Americans as well. Black parents worried about the safety of children who were being transported every day into communities where they were clearly not welcome. School boards' reluctance to transfer white children to previously black schools meant that busing was often a one-way street that imposed more disrup-tions on black families than white ones. African American children fre-quently spent more time traveling and less time studying than their white counterparts, a situation that was hardly conducive to equalizing their educational opportunities. Racist teachers, administrators, and classmates often mistreated black students who attended integrated schools and hin-dered their learning. Fifteen-year-old Sheryl Threadgill suffered through some kind of insult or physical assault every day she attended Wilcox County High School in Alabama. Third grader Dolores Ray encountered a similarly hostile environment at the school she attended. "The teacher wasn't nice to me," she said. "I had to let my books stay in school, 'cos I was colored. So I did my assignments in the daytime. I got Ds and Fs."[21]

Some black activists questioned whether the single-minded pursuit of integration was worth the costs they saw in African American neighbor-hoods: school closings, job losses for black teachers, a weakened sense of community, and disruptions to their children's education. "Black power" advocates who sought to foster the development of black institutions that could operate independently of white control believed integrationist projects merely perpetuated racist assumptions. Stokely Carmichael and Charles Hamilton argued that these efforts were "based on complete acceptance of the fact that in order to have a decent house or education, black people must move into a white neighborhood or send their children to a white school. This reinforces, among both black and white, the idea that 'white' is automatically superior and 'black' is by definition inferior." Rather than spending thousands of dollars to ensure that equal numbers of white and black students attended each school, some African Americans suggested, school districts should focus on enhancing the quality of education offered within institutions, regardless of their racial composition.[22] These arguments meshed well with those of white opponents of desegregation and with political leaders' desire to limit the federal government's role in education. Over the next two decades declining support for integration and the growing influence of judges who interpreted the law "strictly" in the federal courts resulted in policy shifts that halted the transition to unitary systems and allowed schools to resegregate.

Within a few years of ordering school districts to adopt measures aimed at overcoming structural obstacles to integration, the Supreme Court reversed course in a series of decisions that exempted education officials from this responsibility. In *Milliken v. Bradley* (1974) the Court sided with suburban districts in Detroit that refused to take part in a metropolitan busing plan and allowed the city's schools to remain segregated. A follow up decision in 1977 (*Milliken v. Bradley II*) authorized states to pay for compensatory programs in minority schools to address the inequalities that resulted from past racist practices. The *Milliken* decisions essentially nullified *Brown v. Board of Education* and returned to the "separate but equal" doctrine of the Jim Crow era. As before, "equal" in theory meant unequal in practice. Administrators implemented remedial programs with little planning, no clear goals, and no means of evaluating their effects. One observer's assessment of a program in Little Rock, Arkansas, that filled classrooms with new equipment but failed to improve student achievement concluded that "the enhancements were really to [say] 'we're making you go to these segregated schools, so we're going to give you a lot of neat things to do while you're there.'"[23]

School districts that had vigorously fought desegregation in the 1950s and 1960s and moved toward integrated systems only under federal duress in the 1970s gradually resegregated when the government's commitment to racial equality weakened in the 1980s and 1990s. The case of Norfolk, Virginia, demonstrates the trajectory. Officials there took no action to desegregate the schools until a lawsuit placed them under court order in 1958. The state's governor responded by closing the public schools. Further legal action forced the school board to adopt a desegregation plan in 1970 but the zoning system was designed to ensure only token integration. A busing plan implemented after 1972 finally brought the system to unitary status in 1975. In 1983, encouraged by the opposition to busing expressed by President Reagan and his appointees to the Department of Justice, the school board voted to approve a new student assignment plan that resulted in almost entirely black enrollment at ten of the city's schools. Federal courts upheld the plan after Justice officials filed a brief favoring the school board's position. Assistant Attorney General William Bradford Reynolds argued that achieving unitary status entitled the school district to be treated as though it had never discriminated against African Americans. Federal officials thus granted Norfolk permission to resegregate its schools.[24]

In the 1990s the Supreme Court solidified the return to separate and unequal education in a set of decisions that, like Reynolds, assumed that desegregating a community's schools for a few years could wipe out the effects of past discrimination and ensure fair treatment for African Americans in future. In *Board of Education of Oklahoma v. Dowell* (1991) the Court decided that attainment of a unitary system ended a district's obligation to maintain integration and allowed Oklahoma to return to segregated neighborhood schools. A year later in *Freeman v. Pitts* the criteria for defining unitary status were relaxed so that school districts no longer had to meet all of the Green factors before being allowed to resegregate. *Missouri v. Jenkins* (1995) permitted school boards to limit the duration of compensatory programs for minority schools and to abandon them without having to demonstrate that they had solved the problems they were supposed to address.[25] Education scholar Gary Orfield observed, "In the 1990s, power was turned back to the local school districts in spite of the fact that almost every city and many states had strongly resisted desegregation and many were actively planning to resegregate. ... The courts and many political leaders decided that the same state and local governments that had historically engaged in blatant discrimination would now be fair, and that race-related issues could safely be settled at the local level."[26]

Proponents of resegregation did not openly express racist intentions. Many sincerely believed that the return to separate and (this time) truly equal schools was best for children, their families, and communities. Supporters often presented the measures as educational reforms aimed at ending the disruptions caused by desegregation efforts and providing better quality of education for all children. In some cases school districts spent millions of dollars on curricular innovations, upgrading facilities, and creating "magnet" schools in an attempt to entice private schoolers back to public education. None of this addressed the inequities caused by the economic disparities that still separated white and black Americans in the post-civil rights era. "Neighborhood schools" in the mostly black, mostly poor inner cities meant schools that had to deal with the effects of concentrated poverty associated with residential segregation. Students often came from homes where low incomes generated multiple problems that interfered with the ability to learn, such as inadequate nutrition, crowded and noisy living conditions, frequent evictions and moving, illness, domestic violence, and substance abuse. Resources that schools had to expend on overcoming these disadvantages in order to develop basic skills in reading, math, and science meant less money was left for "luxuries" such as music, art, or college preparation classes. In contrast, suburban schools free from the burdens of addressing the social problems in the cities offered more comprehensive curricula, better equipment and facilities, and higher quality instruction.[27]

Reliance on local property tax revenues for most school funding meant that children living in wealthier districts had inherent advantages over those in poorer communities. It also meant that the antitax ethos of the post-civil rights era had some damaging consequences for public education. Segregated schools made it hard to persuade some citizens to support taxes and bond issues aimed at raising money for facilities they did not use. In Kansas City, Missouri, 1969 was the last year a majority of children in the city's public schools were white and also the last year voters approved a bond measure for education. By 1994 the schools were 75 percent black and 19 attempts to raise money to improve educational services had been defeated at the polls. An Alabama woman who wrote to congressman Bill Nichols in 1982 to ask him to support a bill granting a tax credit to people who relied on private education typified the thinking of many parents. "I along with others am paying taxes for public school even though I choose to send my child to a private school," she pointed out. "I feel we should receive a Tax-Credit afterall we are paying for something we cannot benefit from. The Tax-Credit is the only fair thing to do."[28] It did not occur to voters who refused to help fund schools for other people's children that education was a social investment that benefited the whole community. Their focus on ensuring quality instruction for their own children and failure to acknowledge any wider social responsibilities meant that African Americans continued to receive and suffer the consequences of inferior education even after the deliberately racist practices of the Jim Crow era ended.

Criminal Injustice: The Prison-Industrial Complex and Surplus Labor Control

Unequal education further limited black people's employment options and contributed to high levels of crime in African American communities. As political leaders cut funding for job training programs and other antipoverty efforts in the late twentieth century, some people turned to stealing or drug dealing to get by. In an essay recounting his childhood in New Haven, Connecticut, Antoine Reddick described the harsh economic circumstances that drove people to such measures. His unemployed father could not support the family and eventually left so that the others could qualify for public assistance. His mother was overwhelmed by the task of caring for 16 children by herself. "There was never enough food, money, clothes, or even love," Reddick recalled. The older children "found escape in the streets … in the drug houses and back alleys, where narcotics ran free and were easy to buy or sell." The contrast between his poor black neighborhood and the suburban homes of the white children he befriended in school generated awareness of the role that racial injustice played in his life. Crime became a way to strike back at the system as well as to acquire the basic necessities and consumer items the family could not afford to buy. Reddick regretted his past misdeeds and did not seek to excuse criminals for their actions. At the same time, he asserted, "poverty, frustration, and hate for a society that refused black children equality as human beings were the creators of the crimes we committed."[29]

Analyses that linked criminal activity to social circumstances fell out of favor after the 1960s. Policy makers' efforts to crack down on crime generated exponential increases in the prison population in the post-civil rights era. The number of people held in correctional facilities nationwide rose from 326,000 in 1972 to 2.1 million in 2003, an increase of 552 percent in a country where the population grew by only 37 percent in the same period. By 2008 the United States had the highest incarceration rate in the world. In January that year a Pew Center study counted 1,596,127 inmates held in federal and state prisons and another 723,131 in local jails, bringing the total number of people behind bars to 2,319,258 – one in every 100 American adults. The rate for African Americans was much higher, at one in 29, and for black men aged 20–34 it was one in nine.[30]

Multiple factors contributed to the expansion of the prison system and the increasing numbers of African Americans who were ensnared by it in the decades following the civil rights movement. The social turmoil of the 1960s convinced many Americans that the nation was threatened by increasing lawlessness and disrespect for authority. Proponents of stronger measures to combat crime often did not distinguish between legitimate political protest and actual criminal activity, framing peaceful civil rights demonstrations, urban uprisings, and student protests against the Vietnam War as part of a general breakdown of the social fabric. George Wallace's campaign speeches frequently linked blackness, civil rights activism, and crime by attacking Supreme Court decisions that protected the rights of suspected criminals along with the rulings in favor of black equality. In 1966 Richard Nixon blamed the growing unrest in the nation's cities on "the spread of the corrosive doctrine that every citizen possesses an inherent right to decide for himself which laws to obey and when to disobey them," a reference to the civil disobedience tactics used in the struggle for racial justice. During his campaign for the presidency in 1968, Nixon dismissed research that suggested factors such as lack of education or unemployment were key sources of crime. "Doubling the conviction rate in this country would do far more to cure crime in America than quadrupling the funds for [the] war on poverty," he asserted.[31]

The association between African Americans and criminality helped to increase public support for policies that aimed to harshly punish offenders instead of rehabilitating them. The wave of violent protests that swept through Watts, Newark, and dozens of other cities in the late 1960s inspired calls for strong measures to prevent further disturbances, including a proposed crime bill for the District of Columbia that allowed police to preemptively detain people and increased the minimum prison sentence for robbery from six months to five years. The same representatives in Congress who sought to limit funding for antipoverty initiatives allocated millions of dollars for programs to strengthen law enforcement in the Omnibus Crime Control and Safe Streets Act of 1968. State legislators also passed laws that imposed mandatory minimum sentences and made prison terms rather than alternatives such as counseling or supervision the default punishment for many crimes. By 1987 46 states had adopted mandatory sentencing laws. The same year, federal sentencing guidelines drawn up under the Sentencing Reform Act of 1984 went into effect, ordering jail time for most offenses and restricting judges' ability to take mitigating circumstances into account. The guidelines specifically prohibited giving reduced sentences for "circumstances indicating a disadvantaged upbringing," reflecting an emphasis on individual responsibility for criminal acts rather than economic hardships that encouraged people to break the law.[32] Changes in sentencing practices that resulted from legislators' unforgiving stance on crime significantly increased the number of offenders who ended up in jail.

Federal efforts to combat substance abuse by declaring a "war on drugs" also contributed to the rising prison population. Funding for drug law enforcement increased from $800 million to $2.5 billion between 1981 and 1988, and prosecutions for drug related crimes rose by 99 percent. A surge in drug use stemming in part from the development of cheaper crack cocaine led Congress to pass the Anti-Drug Abuse Act of 1986. The legislation imposed mandatory prison terms for drug dealers and ordered especially long sentences for those whose activities caused injuries to others. "The American people want their government to get tough and go on the offensive," President Reagan stated at the signing ceremony.[33] Antidrug crusaders did not demonstrate equal levels of commitment to combating all forms of substance abuse, however. Alcohol and tobacco killed far more people every year than the narcotics singled out by the new drug laws and yet they were not outlawed. Drunk drivers typically received punishments of a few days in jail and community service rather than the years in prison meted out to people who abused other drugs. As scholar Andrew Barlow noted in 2003, the war on drugs was "highly selective," targeting only the drugs that were "used by the most marginalized and impoverished and racially oppressed segments of the United States."[34]

The main achievement of federal drug policy was that it filled the nation's jails with addicts whose actions had not directly harmed anyone other than themselves. People who purchased small quantities of drugs for their own use were criminalized along with the dealers and pushers. The millions of dollars the federal government provided for enforcement encouraged police departments to devote more resources to the drug war and to actively seek out people who were involved in the trade. Arrests almost tripled between 1980 and 2000, increasing from 581,000 to 1,579,566. Mandatory sentencing meant that those who were convicted were virtually certain to serve time. By 2004, drug offenders made up 55 percent of American prisoners, double the percentage they had been in 1980.[35]

Poor black people in the inner cities were especially vulnerable to getting caught in the dragnet. Despite evidence indicating that most drug addicts and dealers were white, racial profiling by police who believed that African Americans were more likely to engage in criminal behavior than other citizens meant officers paid closer attention to black people as they cruised neighborhoods looking for suspicious activity. In 1985, a directive to state highway patrol officers in Florida specifically instructed them to focus on "ethnic groups associated with the drug trade." Videotapes of police activity later revealed that African Americans comprised 85 percent of drivers stopped by officers in their hunt for drug traffickers. Across the nation police often pulled over African American drivers or questioned black youths they encountered in the streets for no real cause. One study of law enforcement practices in New York City in 1998 and 1999 found that although African Americans made up 25 percent of the population, they were 50 percent of those stopped by police. Police officers' tendency to single out black people for harassment meant African Americans were more likely than white people to be caught breaking the law. Individuals with prior infractions on record were in turn more likely to be sentenced to prison if they were later found guilty of more serious crimes. The disproportionate numbers of African Americans who were convicted and jailed as a result had the effect of reinforcing the connection between blackness and criminality, encouraging more racial profiling by law enforcement agencies.[36]

Racialized class inequalities as well as racist policing contributed to inequities in the criminal justice system. Middle-class professionals and white suburban teenagers who developed drug addictions relied on social networks and private sales behind closed doors to obtain illicit substances. In contrast, the drug trade in poor black communities was carried out in the open, on street corners and in other public spaces where the chances of getting caught were higher. Laws that increased the penalties for drug selling near schools or public housing projects also had a disparate effect. In Illinois, for example, a teenaged black public housing resident caught dealing at home would be tried as an adult and most likely serve jail time, while a white youth engaging in the same activity in suburbia would be treated as a juvenile and receive counseling instead of being sent to prison. Harsher penalties for the possession of crack cocaine versus powder cocaine were notorious for their racist effects. Possession of just five grams of the crack cocaine commonly used by poorer people carried a prison term of five years. Wealthier users who could afford the more expensive powder cocaine had to be caught with 500 grams to incur the same sentence. White addicts also typically had greater resources to draw on that could help them stay out of jail, such as health insurance, access to treatment programs, money to pay lawyers, and family support.[37]

By the turn of the twenty-first century more than 900,000 African Americans were imprisoned, making up almost half of the nation's jailed population. One in three black men aged 20–29 was caught up in the criminal justice system in some way, either on probation, in prison, or on parole. The number of black women who spent part of their lives in prison was also increasing, rising by 267 percent between 1985 and 2000. Incarceration had long-term consequences that went beyond the loss of freedom, lost earnings, and separation from family members that prisoners experienced during the time they spent in jail. Exposure to diseases and the psychological stresses of prison life often had lasting effects on people's health. Upon release, most ex-offenders found it difficult to find employment, and they were no longer eligible for social services such as welfare, public housing, or student loan programs. The factors that led many poor people to break the law in first place – inadequate education, joblessness, and lack of money – were all magnified by even a brief stint in jail.[38]

The effects of the nation's crime policies were equally devastating at the community level. Legislation that barred prisoners and former felons from voting in many states represented a new form of mass disfranchisement that undercut black political power in the late twentieth century. Families that were already strained economically and emotionally became even more so when parents or children were imprisoned, particularly if they were the central breadwinners. Without adequate income other family members might resort to stealing food and other necessities or selling drugs to survive. The loss of large numbers of adults from black communities disrupted social institutions and left children without guidance, increasing the likelihood of criminal activity. Serving time seemed like such a routine part of being black and poor in the United States that the thought of going to prison no longer deterred many African Americans from lawbreaking. Tougher sentencing policies often increased instead of reducing crime in black neighborhoods by further destabilizing disadvantaged and vulnerable communities.[39]

As in more conventional wars, authorities responded to the lack of results by escalating the violence. Police departments in many cities turned into small armies equipped with semi-automatic weapons, armored vehicles, and helicopters. Officers trained in paramilitary techniques engaged in actions that seemed designed to terrorize entire communities as much as to apprehend individual criminals. Analysts of the racism and brutality that permeated the criminal justice system frequently drew comparisons to the slave patrols and lynching parties of earlier eras. Sociologist Loïc Wacquant called anticrime initiatives the latest in a "historical sequence of 'peculiar institutions' that have shouldered the task of defining and confining African Americans, alongside slavery, the Jim Crow regime, and the ghetto." Similarly, writer and activist Jennifer E. Smith labeled mass incarceration "second only to slavery in its devastating impact on African Americans."[40]

Despite mounting evidence that the punitive approach to crime had failed, political leaders continued to favor measures that made it easier to send people to prison over other options. Between 1980 and 1993 federal spending on training and employment programs declined by 35 percent while spending on corrections increased by 521 percent. In the 1990s President Bill Clinton expressed support for community policing and drug treatment programs, but legislation passed during his two terms devoted far more resources to punishment than prevention. A telling indication of political priorities came in the wake of a major uprising by poor people in South Central Los Angeles in 1992 after a jury acquitted four police officers who had brutally beaten black motorist Rodney King while arresting him for speeding. Fifty-three people died amidst the violence and the property damage reached one billion dollars. These events highlighted the ongoing injustices that existed in urban neighborhoods, and in 1993 the Clinton administration proposed spending $30 billion on job creation and economic development in the nation's neglected inner cities. Opponents argued that the plan was unaffordable and pared it back to an allocation of $5 billion to enhance unemployment insurance and a few other social programs. One year later, Congress approved $30 billion to fund the Omnibus Crime Act of 1994. The measure included $8 billion for new prison construction, more mandatory minimum sentences, and other punitive measures designed to enhance legislators' "tough on crime" credentials.[41]

Expansion of the prison system created powerful constituencies that had an interest in maintaining the punitive measures that were helping to fill the nation's jails. Construction companies, prison administrators and guards, and contractors who provided services to correctional facilities all benefited from draconian crime policies. In 1996 the World Research Group invited entrepreneurs who were interested in profiting from rising incarceration rates to a conference where they could learn how to "get in on the ground floor of this booming industry now." Corporations such as Microsoft and Boeing employed incarcerated people as inexpensive workers in joint venture operations developed in collaboration with state governments. The communities where prisons were located also benefited economically. Crescent City, a dying small town in California, saw a revival of its fortunes in the 1990s after it became home to a new state prison and 1,500 new jobs. Residents of many other small towns and rural areas hit hard by the disappearance of manufacturing enterprises viewed prisons as welcome replacements for the industries that had been lost.[42] The policies that funneled thousands of poor people into jail in the late twentieth century thus cushioned the effects of deindustrialization and globalization for other poor people who found new employment opportunities as prison guards.

The New Face of White Supremacy

As in earlier periods of American history, the racial order was modified to fit new circumstances in the late twentieth century. Capitalist transformations rendered large numbers of workers obsolete and generated mass joblessness among African Americans in the 1970s and 1980s. Rather than acknowledging deficiencies in the economic system that required government action to address the crisis, the nation's leaders chose to control unneeded workers through mass incarceration policies that only added to black people's problems. These decisions ensured that African Americans shouldered the heaviest burdens imposed by economic restructuring and shielded most white Americans from the harshest consequences of the new order.

When black communities collapsed under the weight of rampant unemployment, deteriorating infrastructure, the loss of social services, and repressive policing, many citizens accepted explanations that located the source of the problems in black people's behavior rather than in the larger social world. A form of cultural racism – the belief that African Americans lacked the commitment to mainstream values such as education and hard work that was presumed to be the basis for middle-class success – replaced the biological determinism that legitimized racial oppression in the slavery and Jim Crow eras. Many people understood the disproportionate representation of African Americans among the unemployed, poor, inadequately educated, unhealthy, and imprisoned not as the product of law and policy, but as evidence of behavioral deficiencies that explained the failure of many black people to improve their economic status after the passage of civil rights legislation.[43]

An assortment of scholars and intellectuals, including some African Americans, performed a similar function as nineteenth-century race scientists in reinforcing these ideas. Analysts such as Charles Murray, Abigail and Stephan Thernstrom, and Dinesh D'Souza denied that racism remained a significant barrier to black advancement and suggested that government social programs harmed more than they helped poor people. Murray's *Losing Ground* (1984) linked black poverty to disincentives to employment provided by public assistance programs and provided intellectual cover for Reagan-era cuts in services for poor people. In *The End of Racism* (1995), D'Souza disparaged efforts to expose "disguised and hidden forms of white racism" and suggested that proponents of racial equality focus on addressing African Americans' "destructive and pathological cultural patterns" instead. Similarly, African Americans Shelby Steele and Ward Connerly urged black people to stop blaming white people for their problems and acknowledge the opportunities available to all who were willing to study, work hard, save their money, and adhere to traditional moral values. "The major obstacle facing the average black person in America is not race; it is the attitude and approach of black people toward their role in American society," Connerly asserted.[44]

Such theories had widespread appeal among white Americans who failed to perceive their own complicity in perpetuating the racist structures that disadvantaged black people. Eliminating racial disparities required participation by all Americans and a more equitable sharing of resources, yet throughout the late twentieth century efforts to include white communities in plans to improve conditions for poor black people generally met intense opposition. White citizens' refusal to take part in metropolitan solutions to problems in the inner cities, resistance to paying taxes to support public services, and retreat to private facilities all reflected the latent racism that lay beneath professions of colorblindness. Occasionally, these sentiments bubbled to the surface. In the 1980s and 1990s residents of counties on the outskirts of Atlanta vigorously fought attempts to annex them to the city and blocked the extension of mass transit systems to the suburbs, fearing that it would allow African Americans access to jobs, residences, and schools in their all-white communities. Civil rights activists and city officials involved in the negotiations were disturbed by the sentiments expressed by many suburbanites who rejected the project. One legislator from Gwinnet County stated that most of his constituents could "come up with 12 different ways of saying they are not racist in public. ... But you get them alone, behind a closed door and you see this old blatant racism that we have had here for quite some time."[45]

Even people who harbored no personal prejudices toward African Americans often felt constrained to act in ways that reinforced the system. Citizens pondered options on where to live, where to send their children to school, or whether to visit certain neighborhoods within a racialized social context that made some choices more appealing than others. As public education was slowly strangled and poor black neighborhoods were left to deteriorate, many middle-class African Americans and racially liberal white people made decisions rooted in practical realities that perpetuated the cycle of racism and decline initiated in earlier decades.

Minimal effort was required on the part of those who benefited from the shadow Jim Crow system to maintain it. Simply leaving things alone ensured that it continued to allocate a greater share of the nation's wealth to white people than to African Americans. Since most white people did not see themselves as directly causing the problems they saw in black communities, few felt any responsibility for solving them. The absence of any overtly discriminatory laws convinced many Americans that racism no longer existed, and arguments to the contrary seemed anachronistic now that the nation had moved "beyond race." As black activist Dorothy Height explained, "During the civil rights movement, when Bull Connor put his foot on the neck of a woman lying on the ground, or when dogs and fire hoses swept away innocent children, a kind of righteous indignation gripped the country. But now ... that sense of outrage was gone. Now whites wondered what our problem was."[46]

Waking Up to Racism in the Twenty-First Century

It took a major natural disaster that laid bare persistent injustices to shake the nation out of its post-racial dream. On August 29, 2005 Hurricane Katrina devastated the Gulf Coast of Alabama, Louisiana, and Mississippi, sweeping away homes and causing massive storm surges that burst through aging levees in New Orleans and placed 80 percent of the city under water. More than 1,400 people, mostly poor and black, were killed. Thousands more who lacked the resources to evacuate before the storm hit were stranded for days on rooftops, highway overpasses, and in buildings such as the Superdome football stadium that were located on higher ground. Americans across the nation were shocked by the failures of government at all levels revealed by the hurricane. Political leaders had known for years that the levees were deteriorating but neglected to allocate adequate funds for repairing them. Disaster preparedness plans included no provisions for evacuating the 40,000 residents of New Orleans who did not own cars. Relief agencies took far too long to get food, water, and medical assistance to citizens after the wind and rain subsided. Dozens of people who lived through the storm perished before help arrived in the days that followed. Television and newspaper coverage reported incidents of official incompetence and callousness more akin to Americans' images of "third world" countries than their own nation.[47] In testimony before a congressional committee in December, hurricane survivor Leah Hodges offered a blunt summary of what happened: "The people of New Orleans were stranded in a flood and were allowed to die."[48]

The images of people standing on rooftops surrounded by water, abandoned by their government, represented the logical consequence and enduring symbol of the political and economic ideologies that prevailed in the United States after 1965. George W. Bush's tax cuts, misplaced spending priorities, and evisceration of government agencies responsible for dealing with such emergencies took these measures to new levels and were rightly blamed for directly contributing to the disaster, but they were just the latest manifestation of policies that favored individualism and the pursuit of private wealth over the mutual responsibility of citizens to care for each other. The results of this approach for the nation's poorest and most vulnerable people were starkly exposed in August 2005. Barbara Arnwine of the Lawyers' Committee for Civil Rights Under Law (Lawyers' Committee) noted that for many Americans, "Katrina provided their first look at the face of poverty and race in this country. The storm and its devastating aftermath forced Americans to witness first-hand a deadly combination of racism, racial disparities, racial insensitivity, poverty, and governmental incompetence."[49]

The hurricane revealed all of the complex ways in which racism remained embedded in American society. New Orleans was a segregated city with a population that was 68 percent black and 23 percent poor. The median household income of $31,369 was almost $15,000 lower than the national average. Within the city low-income people lived in modest homes and public housing projects in the areas most susceptible to flooding while middle- and upper-class residents occupied more desirable neighborhoods on higher ground. When the mayor issued a mandatory evacuation order on August 28 most residents who were able to packed their cars and drove hundreds of miles to stay in hotels where they were safe. These people were largely white. Poorer citizens who did not own vehicles or lacked money for gas, bus fares, and accommodation remained behind. Most of these people were black. The spatial and income disparities that existed in New Orleans meant that African Americans made up the largest number of people who could not get out and were subsequently drowned or stranded.[50]

Widely held perceptions of black people as unintelligent, dependent, and criminal affected relief efforts and media coverage after the storm. Some commentators attributed victims' failure to evacuate to black people's inherent lack of initiative or self-reliance. Journalists reported unsubstantiated rumors that drug use, violence, and rape were rampant in the buildings where people took shelter. (Many of these reports later proved to be false.) Cable news networks repeatedly ran footage of "the same picture of the same few people carrying gym shoes, clothing, food, and in one case a T.V. from a few stores," as attorney Ishmael Muhammad put it. "To the major media, black people seeking and finding food from abandoned stores were looters, while whites doing the same were identified as having found food." Aid workers fearing violence refused to go into black neighborhoods to rescue people. Law enforcement officers and national guard units were directed to patrol white neighborhoods with orders to "shoot to kill" looters instead of helping people in the flooded areas. Police and residents in some of the city's white suburbs barricaded their communities and prevented black people seeking refuge from entering. At an open-air camp located on an interstate highway, soldiers held thousands of people under armed guard while they waited for buses to take them out of the city. According to Leah Hodges, the soldiers allowed white people to leave first, did nothing to help the sick or the elderly, and threatened to shoot people who requested medical assistance. "They were all about detention, as if it were Iraq, like we were foreigners and they were fighting a war," she stated. "As a hurricane survivor, I and my family were detained, not rescued."[51]

Buried under reports of official ineptitude and social disintegration that dominated the news were incidents demonstrating the resilience of black communities in the face of calamity. Hodges began her testimony to the congressional committee by revealing a background that contradicted prevailing assumptions regarding the lawbreaking, welfare-dependent, dysfunctional people presumed to inhabit the black neighborhoods of cities like New Orleans. "I come from a family of musicians," she stated. "Before Hurricane Katrina ... I had taken time off from pursuing my law degree to care for my sick granddad. I was also in the process of working with community leaders on setting up music and art workshops for youths." Traditions of family and community responsibility helped people through the storm just as they had helped people endure the hardships of earlier times. Neighbors shared food and other provisions with each other and young people helped older victims while they awaited rescue. In New Orleans and throughout the Gulf Coast area black churches and community organizations provided food, shelter, transportation, and medical assistance that helped to bridge the gap between citizens' needs and the government's lame response.[52] Along with racism, African Americans' ongoing struggles against injustice continued in the decades after the 1960s, often as invisible to other Americans as the system that necessitated such activity.

* 4 *

FIGHTING JIM CROW'S SHADOW: STRUGGLES FOR RACIAL EQUALITY AFTER 1965

Freedom is never given to anybody. ... Privileged classes never give up their privileges without strong resistance. (Martin Luther King Jr., 1957)[1]

In the popular imagination the black freedom movement began with the Montgomery bus boycott in 1955 and ended with the assassination of Martin Luther King Jr. in 1968. As Fred Powledge observed in 1991, for many Americans "the Reverend Dr. Martin Luther King, Jr., *was* the civil rights movement. Thought it up, led it, produced its victories, became its sole martyr."[2] Media coverage helped to create that perception by focusing on King's inspiring leadership and his ability to express black Americans' aspirations in terms that appealed to many white citizens as well. In later decades annual commemorations of King's legacy and the creation of a national holiday in his honor solidified the tendency to conflate the movement with the man. These memorials often overlooked the millions of ordinary people who were active in the freedom struggle before King's rise to prominence and who continued to fight for equality after his death.

Having secured the passage of civil rights legislation, activists worked to preserve the rights they had won and pushed for more fundamental changes that were necessary to ensure justice. This ongoing pressure was essential to realizing the most basic objectives of the struggle for equality. Attempts to force individuals, businesses, local governments, and federal agencies simply to uphold the law consumed large amounts of energy and grew more difficult as political leaders and the courts abandoned the cause. African Americans and their allies needed to use every means at their disposal to prevent the achievements of the civil rights movement from being negated by official indifference and colorblind denial. Legal action, boycotts, and street protests were all deployed on battlefields old and new as activists confronted continued discrimination in housing, environmental policy, education, and the criminal justice system.

Realizing the Dream

Although violent retaliation and other means of suppressing black protest diminished after 1965, the invisible racism of the post-civil rights era posed its own problems. Many Americans saw no need for further action on racial equality now that legalized disfranchisement and segregation had ended. Some observers questioned whether continued struggle was necessary and accused black leaders of being more concerned with enhancing their own material interests than improving conditions for African Americans. "These activists have found a way to turn racial victimization, which was their historical condition, into a successful career," Dinesh D'Souza wrote in 1995. Proponents of colorblind policies countered suggestions that eliminating racism required more than just equal treatment by citing a few lines from King's most famous speech, delivered at the March on Washington in August 1963: "I have a dream that my four little children will one day live in a nation where they will not be judged by the color of their skin but by the content of their character." D'Souza and others believed demands for "special treatment" for black Americans violated the original ideals of the civil rights movement. They argued that the keys to further progress lay within the black community, in programs that promoted individualism and self-reliance, rather than in continued protests over nonexistent injustices.[3]

Yet Martin Luther King Jr. and other participants in the freedom movement never viewed the passage of civil rights legislation as their ultimate goal or the end of their fight against white supremacy. In a book published the year before his death, King outlined the hard work that remained to be done by Americans who were committed to racial equality and warned that it could not be achieved without some sacrifice on the part of the nation's white citizens – many of whom, he noted, were now abandoning the struggle in recognition of that fact. Desegregating public spaces and allowing black southerners to vote required no new taxes or expenditures, but the same could not be said of expanding other opportunities for African Americans. "The real cost lies ahead," King wrote. "The discount education given Negroes will in the future have to be purchased at full price if quality education is to be realized. Jobs are harder and costlier to create than voting rolls."

King explicitly rejected the view that black people's unequal economic status could be explained by "the myth of the Negro's innate incapacities, or by the more sophisticated rationalization of his acquired infirmities (family disorganization, poor education, etc.)." Instead, he argued that black disadvantage was "a structural part of the economic system" that resulted from the reliance of key industries on cheap black labor. Given that history, he suggested, colorblind approaches to overcoming racial inequality were inadequate. King urged white Americans to accept that "a society that has done something special *against* the Negro for hundreds of years must now do something special *for* him, in order to equip him to compete on a just and equal basis." He also recognized that waiting passively for racism's beneficiaries to voluntarily end practices that perpetuated injustice was unlikely to be effective. Ensuring equality necessitated "persistent pressure and agitation" to enforce existing laws and encourage more comprehensive reforms.[4]

"Rumors of my death ..."

Activists' continued vigilance after the 1960s was appropriate and in keeping with King's legacy. Most of the major civil rights groups that were prominent in the fight to end legalized discrimination in the 1960s carried their work into the twenty-first century. The NAACP remained the nation's largest and best known civil rights organization in this period as before. Its lobbying efforts kept black concerns in the nation's consciousness and held the line against attempts to roll back civil rights legislation. The NAACP Legal Defense and Education Fund (LDF) and the Lawyers' Committee both played major roles in ensuring enforcement of antidiscrimination laws and pushing for expansive interpretations to combat institutional racism after 1965.[5] The SCLC also maintained a national presence. Under the guidance of Ralph Abernathy, Joseph Lowery, and others who took over after King's death, the SCLC continued the mission its fallen leader began to set out for it toward the end of his life, pushing the struggle into broader areas of social justice such as poverty, war, and international human rights. For many African Americans local branches of the NAACP and SCLC remained the first place to turn for help when they experienced discrimination. These organizations' hundreds of thousands of members were the foot soldiers in efforts to combat racism in all of its forms, from Klan violence and police brutality to policies that disproportionately burdened black communities with high unemployment and its distressing social consequences.[6] Meanwhile, the NUL maintained its focus on addressing the urban crisis. The NUL's relative conservatism compared with other civil rights groups and its emphasis on fostering economic self-reliance appealed to political leaders and enabled it to secure government contracts to operate job training programs and other services in black communities. Toward the end of the century the NUL combined efforts to address issues such as crime, teenage pregnancy, and single-parent families with calls for more government action to combat the underlying causes of social problems.[7]

Unlike the other civil rights groups, neither CORE nor SNCC emerged from the 1960s with a coherent mission and their original structure intact.

Ideological divisions sparked by the emergence of the black power movement disrupted both organizations, leading to the loss of members and declining contributions from white supporters who helped finance their activities in the civil rights era. SNCC disintegrated completely by the end of the decade, and CORE struggled to implement programs focused on black self-determination with minimal resources after the mid-1960s. CORE director Floyd McKissick came under fire from some members for accepting funding from white foundations and was replaced by Roy Innis in 1968. Innis' authoritarian leadership style and unpopular stances on some issues (such as his support for segregated schools) alienated many members and supporters. In the 1980s Innis embraced the Reagan administration's free market ideology and earned the patronage of powerful conservatives by speaking out against affirmative action, black crime, and welfare dependency. CORE maintained few programs in the 1990s and concerned itself mostly with raising funds through annual dinners and telephone solicitations. In 2002 *New York Times* columnist Maureen Dowd described Innis as "the head of a shell organization called CORE [who] routinely rents himself out as Black Friend to Disgraced Whites."[8]

Many former members of SNCC and CORE found other ways of pursuing the goal of an integrated, more socially just society in the post-civil rights era. The first generation of black political leaders elected after the 1960s included dozens of veterans of civil rights organizations, among them Julian Bond and John Lewis (SNCC), Andrew Young (SCLC), and Richard Hatcher (NAACP). Others found employment as teachers, journalists, lawyers, social workers, community organizers, business people, law enforcement officers, and government officials. Entering mainstream professions such as these ran the risk of being coopted and deradicalized, but it also offered the chance to influence important institutions and make them more responsive to black people's needs. Barack Obama's ability to rally support from millions of white Americans in the presidential election of 2008 undoubtedly owed much to the normalization of core tenets of the black freedom movement throughout American society in the decades after 1965.

Some activists created new organizations to carry on the fight when older civil rights groups no longer reflected their own values. In 1966 a group of disaffected CORE members formed the Scholarship, Education and Defense Fund for Racial Equality (SEDFRE) to continue the nonviolent, integrationist approach to racial justice that first inspired them to join CORE. SEDFRE provided college scholarships to young people who participated in the civil rights movement and trained thousands of grassroots leaders to run for political office in the years following passage of the Voting Rights Act. George Wiley also left CORE when black nationalists gained control over the organization. After losing his bid to become national director of CORE to Floyd McKissick, Wiley set up the Poverty/Rights Action Center and became a leading figure in the welfare rights movement of the late 1960s and early 1970s. That movement in turn spun off the Association of Community Organizations for Reform Now (ACORN), an interracial coalition that worked on a range of social justice issues including poverty, homelessness, and voting rights. Similarly, Jesse Jackson broke with the SCLC to establish Operation PUSH (People United to Serve Humanity) in 1971 and organized the Rainbow Coalition to support his campaigns for the Democratic presidential nomination in 1984 and 1988. The two groups later merged as the Rainbow/PUSH Coalition and combined projects aimed at enhancing black political power with efforts to increase employment and business opportunities for African Americans. In the rural South, activists who worked on voter registration and community organizing projects initiated by the SCLC, CORE, and SNCC in the early 1960s joined together in the Federation of Southern Cooperatives (FSC) in the later part of the decade to encourage the development of farmers' cooperatives and black-owned business enterprises that provided alternatives to migration for displaced agricultural workers.[9]

Much of the action initiated by these and other organizations took place at the local level, out of the media spotlight that centered attention on the mass demonstrations and protests led by national civil rights groups in the 1960s. In many ways the late twentieth-century freedom struggle resembled what was happening before the Montgomery bus boycott and Martin Luther King Jr.'s rise to fame: ordinary people working together in their own neighborhoods to challenge racist practices and improve conditions for African Americans. In 1997 Manning Marable reported dozens of examples of such activity in every region of the country, ranging from attempts to pressure the construction industry in Chicago to employ more black workers to church-run youth programs aimed at providing alternatives to drugs and crime. "Rumors of the death of the black freedom movement have been greatly exaggerated," he proclaimed. "Resistance is flourishing in hundreds of black communities across the nation."[10]

The Environmental Justice Movement

The struggle for environmental justice began with such activities by local grassroots organizations and grew into a movement that united people across the lines of race, class, and nationality at the turn of the century.[11] In the late 1970s and early 1980s residents of poor black communities that were dumping grounds for consumer waste and polluting industries began drawing attention to the unequal burden these siting decisions placed on African Americans and other nonwhite citizens. Participants in these efforts connected the right to a safe and healthy environment to other struggles for equality in politics, education, and economic opportunity. Black people's political powerlessness lay behind zoning decisions that allowed undesirable land uses in their neighborhoods. The pollutants generated by these activities contributed to health problems that interfered with children's education and adults' ability to hold jobs. The location of waste dumps and factories near their homes depressed housing values and discouraged the establishment of cleaner industries or businesses, exacerbating poor people's economic problems. Frequent violations of environmental standards and the failure of government regulators to adequately police the activities of industrial polluters convinced many African Americans that policy makers and business leaders still viewed them as second-class citizens to be exploited and abused.

Black homeowners in the Houston suburb of Northwood Manor were the first to use the antidiscrimination provisions of the Civil Rights Act to challenge the placement of a waste dump in their neighborhood. Environmental justice scholar and activist Robert Bullard noted that the middle-class character of the community made it "an unlikely location for a garbage dump – except that over 82 percent of residents were African American." Many families had moved there to escape landfills that undermined their quality of life in their previous neighborhoods. When they learned that city officials had issued a permit to a private company to construct a dump near their homes in Northwood Manor, residents formed Northeast Community Action Group and filed a class-action lawsuit in 1979 to halt the project. Although the case was unsuccessful, city leaders were sufficiently chastened by the protest to avoid locating any more waste facilities in black neighborhoods for the rest of the twentieth century.[12]

In 1982 protests by residents in Warren County, North Carolina, against the state's decision to store thousands of tons of contaminated soil in their community received support from national civil rights organizations and pushed environmental racism into public view. The SCLC, the CRJ, and members of the Congressional Black Caucus all joined with local activists in their effort to prevent the dumping. The CRJ's Charles Cobb linked the demonstrations to the earlier freedom movement, stating, "We must move in a swift and determined manner to stop yet another breach of civil rights. ... The depositing of toxic wastes within the black community is no less than attempted genocide." Public condemnation failed to convince state leaders to find an alternative, and trucks began hauling soil to the landfill in mid-September. Over the next two weeks police arrested more than 400 people who tried to block access to the site. The state remained undeterred and the protesters ultimately failed to prevent the dumping, but their efforts helped to raise awareness of discrimination and catalyzed studies by government agencies, civil rights groups, and academics that lent empirical support to activists' claims regarding the racially biased distribution of industrial waste. As in the Houston case, residents' actions signaled to political leaders that African Americans were no longer willing to accept the designation of their neighborhoods as waste sites. "Nobody thought people like us would make a fuss," Warren County minister Luther Brown observed.[13] In subsequent decades, black passivity could no longer be so easily assumed.

The 1990s saw several victories for the environmental justice movement. When authorities in California failed to adequately implement a federal mandate to test children for lead exposure under the Medicaid program, civil rights groups helped parents to sue the state and win a settlement that resulted in testing of 557,000 poor children. Activists in Louisiana organized demonstrations and signed on to a lawsuit that succeeded in blocking construction of a plastics manufacturing plant in St. John the Baptist Parish in 1992.[14] In St. James Parish, a community that was already ranked third in the state for toxin levels, poor black people formed St. James Citizens for Jobs and the Environment in September 1996 after learning of Shintech Corporation's plans to build a polyvinyl chloride manufacturing plant next door to their homes. The group found support among white environmentalists who were also concerned about the state's notoriously high pollution levels, creating an interracial coalition that used legal action and appeals to federal officials to delay construction of the factory. In June 1998 a three-member delegation traveled to Shintech's headquarters in Japan to explain their concerns to the company's top executives. In September, Shintech canceled its plans to build the plant.[15]

The movement gained momentum at the national level as well. Black community struggles forced white Americans to recognize that their NIMBY (Not In My Back Yard) politics often had PIBBY (Place In Black Back Yards) consequences. Organizations such as Greenpeace and the Sierra Club began to pay more attention to race and class inequality, helping to broaden the mainstream environmental movement into new areas and bringing useful allies into the fight against racism. Pressure from environmental justice groups led the EPA to create an Office of Environmental Equity in 1992, later renamed the Office of Environmental Justice during the Clinton administration. Clinton also created the National Environmental Justice Advisory Council, bringing representatives of community groups, environmental justice organizations, government, and industry together to help shape EPA policy. When state officials in North Carolina discovered problems at the Warren County landfill that threatened leakages of dangerous contaminants, the new provisions for citizen participation enabled activists to convince political leaders they could detoxify the chemicals at the site instead of moving them to some other unfortunate community. In February 1994 the president issued Executive Order 12898 requiring government agencies and entities that received federal funds to consider the environmental impact of planning decisions on poor and minority communities and avoid administering policy in a discriminatory manner.[16]

Activists in Louisiana cited Executive Order 12898 to protest the United States Nuclear Regulatory Commission's (NRC) approval of plans to locate a uranium enrichment plant in Claiborne Parish. Planners' nationwide search to choose a site for the project focused telescopically on regions, states, counties, and communities that grew progressively blacker at each stage of the decision-making process. Robert Bullard explained, "African Americans constitute about 13 percent of the U.S. population, 20 percent of the southern states' population, 31 percent of Louisiana's population, 35 percent of Louisiana's northern parishes ... and 46 percent of Claiborne Parish." Black people made up 65 percent of the population in the final six communities considered and 97 percent of those living within one mile of the eventual site choice at LeSage. Residents in the surrounding communities thought they had a good case for charging the NRC with environmental racism. In May 1997 three administrative judges on the NRC's Atomic Safety and Licensing Board agreed that the agency failed to adequately consider the likely impact of the uranium enrichment facility on citizens or the racial implications of the site choice, as required by Executive Order 12898. The private company that had applied for permission to build the plant abandoned the project. In addition, the organizing effort and eventual victory helped to propel several of the local activists involved into political office in the late 1990s.[17]

Environmental justice activists in the United States realized that people in other parts of the world faced similar battles to their own in an era of global economic policies that encouraged corporate exploiters to seek out the poorest nations and least powerful communities to avoid regulations that might interfere with their activities. In 1991 the first National People of Color Environmental Leadership Summit in Washington, DC, was an international affair involving 650 delegates from every state as well as Mexico, Chile, and Puerto Rico. Participants discussed a range of social justice issues that included health, housing, transportation, and the treatment of workers as well as problems related to toxic industries and waste. The conference resulted in the adoption of 17 principles of environmental justice that helped to guide activism inside and outside the United States in subsequent decades. Representatives from every continent and 18 nations attended a second summit in October 2002. They included members of civil rights organizations as well as religious, labor, and student groups who viewed environmental justice as an essential element in the global struggle for human rights. Activist Peggy Morrow Shepard outlined the inclusive view that motivated participants at the summits and in grassroots struggles waged in every nation: "[We] defined the environment holistically as being where we live, work, play, pray, and learn. Those of us in the movement see our concerns as interrelated: disinvestment, transportation, poverty, racism, pollution, deteriorating housing, land use and zoning, health disparities, environmental health, and sustainable development."[18]

A similar belief in the interconnectedness of social problems motivated civil rights lawyer and community organizer Van Jones to establish the Ella Baker Center for Human Rights in Oakland, California, in 1996. The center's initial focus on helping young black people avoid the racist traps laid for them by the criminal justice system expanded to include efforts to simultaneously improve environmental conditions, increase job opportunities, and keep African Americans out of jail through the Green Collar Jobs Campaign. "Quite simply, Oakland is under-employed and over-polluted," the Baker Center website noted. "We can solve both of these problems by making sure that the emerging 'clean and green' economy comes to Oakland, and that the jobs go to people coming out of prison or at risk for going in." Jones later founded Green For All, a national organization dedicated to the task of forging broad alliances of environmentalists, unions, social justice activists, and eco-friendly entrepreneurs to create a "green New Deal" with the same transformative power as the interracial coalitions of the 1930s. "We can take the unfinished business of America on questions of inclusion and equal opportunity and combine it with the new business of building a green economy, thereby healing the country on two fronts and redeeming the soul of the nation," he wrote in 2008. Barack Obama's election to the presidency in November that year offered the potential for these goals to be realized. Obama's policy proposals closely paralleled Jones' vision, promoting green energy and jobs as a way to revive Americans' economic fortunes. In March 2009 Obama chose Jones to be a special advisor to the White House Council on Environmental Quality.[19]

Battling Racism in the Criminal Justice System

Jones and other activists also succeeded in highlighting racial disparities in the legal system in the late twentieth century. Blatant discrimination often proved easier to challenge than less visible forms, and the criminal justice system provided some of the best cases for action. Police brutality, racial profiling, and the harsher sentences black Americans received compared with white people convicted of similar crimes concerned many civil rights groups in the late twentieth century. In 1978 the SCLC led 400 protesters on a march through Gadsen, Alabama, after police shot and killed a black man pulled over for drunk driving.[20] Similar incidents in other cities over the next few decades often drew African Americans into the streets in mass protests aimed at pressuring police departments to change their ways. In 1995 a black businessman with no criminal record died of suffocation while in police custody in Pittsburgh, Pennsylvania, raising suspicions of foul play by the five officers involved. Authorities' failure to adequately punish the officers sparked demonstrations by the NAACP and community organizations as well as a boycott by high school students. Activists viewed the killing as just the latest demonstration of disrespect for black life that had long characterized the actions of law enforcement officials.[21] A similar pattern of violence existed in New York. After police beat Liberian immigrant Ernest Sayon to death during a drug raid in 1994, protesters rallied and picketed law enforcement agencies to denounce this and other uses of excessive force. Three years later, Haitian immigrant Abner Louima was beaten and sodomized by officers after being arrested for double parking. Thousands of New Yorkers expressed their anger by marching on city hall and speaking out against Mayor Rudolph Giuliani, whose tough crime policies coincided with a 62 percent rise in complaints of police brutality in the city.[22]

Activists also organized to fight more subtle forms of discrimination in the criminal justice system. A lawsuit filed by Robert Wilkins after he was stopped and searched by a Maryland state trooper in 1992 led to a settlement requiring the state to begin collecting data to determine whether race played a role in officers' decisions to pull over drivers. Pressure from civil rights groups convinced several other states to study the practices adopted by their law enforcement agencies, producing strong evidence that racial profiling existed and that it fostered unjustified harassment of nonwhite citizens. In 1999 North Carolina, Connecticut, and Florida all passed legislation requiring state highway patrol officers to document racial patterns in their law enforcement activities and make them available to the public. At a conference held in Washington, DC, in June, civil rights leaders, government officials, and police chiefs from around the nation agreed that racial profiling must end. President Clinton ordered federal agencies to investigate the problem and work to ensure the fair treatment of all citizens by national law enforcement officers. Later that year the threat of a Justice Department lawsuit forced the New Jersey State Police Department to enter into a consent decree aimed at eliminating racial profiling by the agency, and in 2003 the state legislature passed a law banning the practice in all law enforcement. In June 2003 George W. Bush issued guidelines to federal law enforcement agencies that prohibited them from targeting individuals or neighborhoods because of their ethnic make up except in certain instances relating to antiterrorism investigations.[23]

No black person regardless of income or status was immune from racial profiling, and the issue mobilized African Americans across all social classes. It was harder to generate sympathy for convicted felons who were presumed guilty of the crimes that resulted in their incarceration. Nonetheless, a movement for prisoners' rights emerged alongside the civil rights movement in the 1960s and 1970s, led by activists who viewed racist law enforcement and punitive criminal justice polices as another link in the chain of black oppression stretching across the centuries. The Southern Center for Human Rights, founded in 1976, explained its mission as "ending capital punishment, mass incarceration, and other criminal justice practices that are used to control the lives of poor people, people of color, and other marginalized groups." In the prisons, inmates filed grievances and lawsuits, attacked guards who abused them, and occasionally engaged in large-scale uprisings to draw attention to the inhumane conditions that existed in the nation's jails. On the outside, family members and other supporters organized prisoners' rights groups and lobbied to reform crime prevention strategies, sentencing laws, and prison administration. Understanding that the black faces of a large proportion of the nation's incarcerated population facilitated the wider society's toleration of abusive practices, reformers worked to humanize inmates and link their fate with that of other Americans. Citizens United for the Rehabilitation of Errants adopted the slogan: "Today's prisoners are tomorrow's neighbors." Activist Ramona Africa noted, "These people are not separate from us; they are us and we are them. What we allow to happen to them, leaves the door open for it to happen to us."[24]

Declining crime rates, the costs of maintaining prisons, and the failure of drug policies that emphasized punishment over rehabilitation brought many Americans over to the reformers' side in the early twenty-first century. In 2000 voters in California approved a measure offering treatment instead of prison for people accused of minor drug offenses, and in subsequent years 13 other states made similar modifications aimed at keeping nonviolent offenders out of jail. Supreme Court justice Anthony Kennedy reinforced the arguments of prisoners' rights groups when he asserted that current crime prevention policies were counterproductive in a speech to the American Bar Association in 2003. In response to Kennedy's remarks, the lawyers' organization initiated a study that resulted in recommendations to abolish mandatory minimum sentences, provide alternatives to jail, and increase efforts to eliminate racial bias in the criminal justice system. Two years later, the Supreme Court struck down federal sentencing guidelines and restored judges' power to consider the totality of circumstances before meting out punishment. In 2008 the Pew Center reported that many states facing serious overcrowding in their prisons were seeking ways to avoid spending billions of dollars on building new facilities. In Texas, legislators from both political parties agreed to reverse some of the tough crime policies they had enacted in previous decades. Rather than keep building new prisons, they decided to alter parole practices and treat low-level offenders more leniently to reduce the number of inmates the state needed to accommodate in the coming years. State senator John Whitmire commented, "It's always been safer politically to build the next prison, rather than stop and see whether that's really the smartest thing to do. But we're at a point where I don't think we can afford to do that anymore."[25]

The Struggle for Equal Education

Political leaders' reevaluation of their decisions and the realization that the nation's resources might be better spent on educating and employing people rather than locking them up came too late to save many African Americans from the lost opportunities that resulted from the diversion of funds away from such social investments after the 1960s. The struggle for educational equality saw some small victories during this period but encountered powerful obstacles to the ultimate goal of ensuring quality instruction for all children. In many communities civil rights activists spent decades trying to overcome resistance to school integration only to find that inadequate funding of public education presented even greater problems than segregation in the late twentieth century.

Historian Cynthia Fleming's account of developments in Wilcox County, Alabama, illustrates the difficulties that activists continued to encounter after the passage of civil rights legislation. The county's political leaders and education officials were adamant segregationists who flatly refused to obey the law. A decade after *Brown v. Board of Education* black students who applied for admission to white schools were still being turned down. Black parents' complaints convinced the Justice Department to file a lawsuit in November 1965 to force the county to desegregate its schools. Local officials responded with a letter to parents warning of the dire consequences of integration and requesting voluntary cooperation in maintaining segregation. "[In] an effort to prevent the destruction of the school system of Wilcox County as we know it and realizing what is best, we are asking that you promote and encourage your children in the schools in which they are now attending," they wrote.

Twenty-one black students ignored the school board's suggestion and enrolled at white schools when the system desegregated under a court-ordered freedom of choice plan in August 1966. Some of these pioneers abandoned the effort after facing constant harassment and violent attacks from other students while teachers and principals stood by. Others, like high school student Larry Nettles, refused to be deterred. Nettles challenged the velvet racism of a white teacher who consistently used the term "Nigra" to refer to black people by raising his hand in class one day to ask, "Isn't that pronounced Nigger?" The teacher stopped using the word after that. Nettles' determination to stand up to racist abuse helped him to endure two more years at the school, and in 1969 he became the first African American to graduate from Wilcox County High School.

Nettles was one of only a very small number of black students who attended white schools under the freedom of choice plan. In 1970, noting that 97 percent of African American children remained in the black schools, federal officials ordered the county to adopt a comprehensive rezoning plan to achieve a more racially balanced student body in every school. That spring, a group of segregationists founded Wilcox Academy, a private, all-white facility that provided an alternative to the public school system. School superintendent Guy Kelly took no action to implement the new integration plan. Beginning in fall 1971 black students engaged in a mass boycott of the schools and daily protest marches to pressure Kelly to obey the law. The young activists persevered for months despite expulsions, arrests, and violent attacks by police against protesters. Since the county received education funding based on daily school attendance, the boycott provided the protesters' greatest leverage. One year after the protests began the school board finally agreed to adhere to the integration order and allow expelled students back into the schools.

Black people's travails were not over, however. Many white families refused to send their children to the public schools after 1972. The boycott and the loss of large numbers of white students to Wilcox Academy left the county's education funds severely depleted, and white residents showed little interest in trying to raise money for school improvements now that most of the students in the system were black. School officials met a requirement to integrate the teaching faculty as well as the student body by firing many black teachers and replacing them with inexperienced young white teachers from the Volunteers in Service to America program. The superintendent added to the disruptions by randomly reassigning teachers throughout the system without regard to their areas of expertise.

Black residents were convinced that county officials were intent on sabotaging the education system and decided that the solution was to elect African Americans to public office. White leaders tried to avert black political control through economic reprisals against voters, intimidation, and fraud, but in 1982 the county finally elected a black school board. The new board members inherited a bankrupt, unaccredited, deteriorating school system, however, and lacked the financial resources needed to save it. In the early twenty-first century Wilcox County schools remained as segregated and as unequal as they were in the 1950s, and racial separation seemed as natural and inevitable to young white people as it was to their parents. "It's basically just a tradition that there's no interaction between blacks and whites," one youth stated.[26]

Education reformers in Boston engaged in a similarly protracted struggle, with slightly better results. In the early 1960s city officials refused to acknowledge that the treatment of white and black students in the school system was in any way unequal, claiming that black children's underperformance resulted from their "culturally deprived" backgrounds. According to white political leaders, African Americans were just not as interested in education as other people. "We have no inferior education in our schools," claimed one official. "What we have been getting is an inferior type of student." A committee of black parents led by Ruth Batson carefully researched conditions in the schools and amassed enough evidence to demolish these arguments, documenting overcrowded classrooms and unsafe buildings, outdated and racist curricula, the exclusion of black students from college preparatory courses, and average per pupil spending of $340 for white children and $240 for black children.[27]

Like their counterparts in the South, Boston activists engaged in direct action protests and civil disobedience to draw attention to the problems, causing the governor of Massachusetts to commission a study that concluded discrimination did exist in the school system and that it interfered with black children's education. In 1965 state legislators passed a law that denied public funding to any school that was more than 50 percent black in an attempt to force a more equitable distribution of students and resources, leading to another decade-long struggle between school officials who stalled its implementation and black parents committed to securing better education for their children. Finally, in 1974, an NAACP lawsuit secured a federal court ruling that found the city guilty of deliberately maintaining segregated schools and ordered immediate integration through a combination of busing and redrawing district lines.[28]

As in Wilcox County and countless other communities, Boston activists' problems did not end with the legal victory. Administrators' failure to prevent white students from harassing African Americans who attended South Boston High School prompted local activists to request that the school be put into receivership. After hearing testimony from students describing the name-calling and physical attacks they endured every day, federal judge W. Arthur Garrity placed implementation of the city's desegregation plan under the direct control of the courts. Over the next decade Garrity issued more than 400 additional orders aimed at improving school facilities and equalizing educational opportunities for black children in Boston. According to NAACP lawyer Thomas Atkins, the Boston case helped to push other school districts around the nation into complying with desegregation orders and provided examples of effective measures that could be used to integrate schools.[29]

Along with problem schools like South Boston High there were numerous instances of peaceful and successful integration. Journalist Jon Hillson noted that only a handful of Boston's 162 schools were responsible for the troubles that attracted so much media attention in the 1970s. In most parts of the city desegregation occurred peacefully and the quality of education offered to black children improved greatly as a result. Garrity's orders did not aim simply for numerical racial balance in the schools regardless of the costs to children and their families, as critics of the judge often argued. The desegregation plan included new curricula, provisions for more parental involvement, and other measures that aimed to improve education for all students in the system. White parent Evelyn Morash appreciated the enhancements. "The school one of my children is going to was a mess before it opened," she said. "That is the way it probably was kept when it was segregated. ... But with the parents coming around, with busing opening it up, it has been all cleaned up. There is a teacher-pupil ratio there that has meant more time for individual attention."[30]

Interaction among white and black children attending integrated schools broke down individual prejudices on both sides of the racial divide. Black political scientist Jim Hill, a veteran of desegregation efforts in Louisville, explained that it was harder "to maintain the wall of racism when you're faced with the humanity of those other people. When you sit with them and talk with them they're no longer evil demons, they're friends who end up at your birthday parties and go with you to football and baseball games." Integration offered more important benefits than opportunities for interracial socializing, though. For black children a far more significant result was access to the same educational resources and economic opportunities that white children enjoyed. Attending integrated, middle-class schools offered the chance for inclusion in the institutions and processes that facilitated college attendance and successful careers for Hill and other young black people who benefited from forceful efforts to ensure desegregation in the early 1970s.[31]

Gaining entry to white schools did not end the struggle for equal education. The practice of "tracking" – placing students into separate classes according to academic ability – increased after the mid-1960s and in many cases seemed designed to maintain segregation within ostensibly integrated schools. In Washington Parish, Louisiana, white students predominated in the higher level classes and the lower tracks were virtually all black. A study of New York City public schools in the 1970s found similar racial correlations in around 200 cases and described the criteria used to place minority students in low-ability classrooms as "vague and subjective." Several researchers who analyzed the use of tracking in schools throughout the nation in the 1990s concluded that student placement was related more closely to race than to academic ability. Regardless of test scores or other measures of achievement, black and Latino students remained more likely to be placed in remedial classes. On the other hand, many white students of average ability were placed in honors or "gifted" classes thanks to the intervention of their parents. Administrators concerned with keeping wealthier families' support for public schools almost always accommodated these demands. "School districts have been willing to trade off black access to equal education opportunities for continued white enrollments in the school system," one study noted.[32]

Civil rights activists tried to challenge such practices without much success. Despite evidence that tracking led to unjustifiable disparities in education, the courts deferred to school administrators' claims that it enhanced instructional efficiency and helped to stem white flight. In-school segregation therefore remained a feature of American schools throughout the late twentieth century. A lawsuit filed against the board of education in Rockford, Illinois, in 1993 demonstrated that racism permeated that city's school system. In addition to tracking students by race into separate and unequal classrooms, Rockford's "integrated" schools maintained segregated entrances, bathrooms, and lunch times for white and black children. A lower court judge ordered a variety of remedies including the admission of qualified black students to higher level classes, but an appeals court later eviscerated the order. The new ruling even struck down a provision that allowed for reevaluation of students who were stuck in 12-year remedial tracks. Without legal remedies, individual families were left to fight the system alone. Clifford Williams' mother protested when Rockford officials placed him in a class for students with "behavioral disorders" despite his high grades and insisted that they test him for the gifted program. He scored in the 90th percentile and became one of only two black students admitted to the class. The time and persistence it took to force such changes could be exhausting. "I wonder how many people just gave up," Williams' mother mused.[33]

Ongoing frustrations caused some parents to abandon the entire cause. As conditions in poorer school districts deteriorated, middle-class black families joined their white counterparts in seeking alternatives to their local public schools. One black professional admitted that within his circle of friends and colleagues living in Washington, DC, "Very few of us sent our kids to our neighborhood public elementary schools." Most deployed the same methods as white Americans who had forsaken public education: private schools, moving to wealthier districts, or using their social and political connections to secure places for their children in better-funded magnet schools. All of these parents were progressives and included civil rights lawyers, the founders of non-profit agencies, and the boards and staff of community organizations. Legal scholar Mari Matsuda understood their choices, but in a 2004 article commemorating the fiftieth anniversary of *Brown v. Board of Education* she urged middle- and upper-class Americans to rejoin the struggle for quality education. If people looked inside the crumbling buildings where black and poor children received their education, Matsuda asserted, they would see "heroic teachers and real learning occurring alongside unconscionable neglect of human needs. ... Without witnesses, without the influence and entitlement that educated parents bring, it is hard to muster the political will to provide the simple things we need to fix our public schools."[34]

With or without such support, Americans who relied on the public education system continued to fight the misallocation of resources that interfered with their children's schooling. When integration efforts achieved only limited success and the federal courts indicated their willingness to allow resegregation in the late twentieth century, civil rights activists shifted their focus to demanding more funding for predominantly black schools to bring them up to the same standard as their white suburban counterparts. Many state constitutions contained clauses mandating that a certain level of education be provided to every resident. Reform-minded lawyers and judges seized on these provisions to pressure state legislatures into addressing educational disparities. Kentucky, for example, guaranteed its citizens an "efficient system of common schools," but fell short of providing that in many of its poorer school districts. In response to a lawsuit filed in 1989, the state Supreme Court developed a set of standards that defined an adequate education and ordered political leaders to make sure it was met, leading to sweeping reforms in school funding that elevated Kentucky to third in the nation in per pupil spending. Legal action in New Jersey forced that state to fund urban districts at the same level as the richest suburban districts and improve student learning through smaller class sizes and changes in curricula. By 2004 more than 10 states were under court orders to alter their funding mechanisms and distribute resources more equitably.[35]

Some analysts questioned whether spending more on black schools without addressing broader community problems could result in truly equal educational opportunities, however. More money was essential but in itself was not enough to overcome the obstacles to learning that poor children encountered in their daily lives: economic insecurity; unhealthy environments; distressed families; and constant threats to their emotional and physical wellbeing. "Even in those cases where per pupil spending in an inner-city district may approach the levels of surrounding suburbs, other forms of inequality remain entrenched," noted Jonathan Kozol. He urged activists not to be mollified by promises of "separate but equal" education and to push instead for solutions that integrated both the people and resources of wealthy and poor neighborhoods, which must include efforts to overcome residential segregation.[36]

Fair Housing Activism

Civil rights leaders well knew that housing segregation and its attendant concentrations of unemployment and poverty underlay inequalities in other areas of American life. "One of the most dangerous trends facing our nation is the constant growth of predominantly Negro central cities ringed by white suburbs," Martin Luther King Jr. observed in a speech delivered at Ohio Northern University shortly before his death. The SCLC led a series of protests in Chicago from May to July 1966 to highlight the exclusion of black people from the city's all-white suburbs and demand action from city hall. After meeting with Mayor Richard Daley, King concluded that the mayor was not racially prejudiced but did not understand "the depth and dimension of the problem." Many white residents were even less amenable to the idea of integrated neighborhoods than the mayor. The racist violence that met black activists' attempts to march in the white suburb of Cicero prompted King to comment that he had "never seen, even in Mississippi and Alabama, mobs as hostile and as hate-filled" as he saw in Chicago. Meetings with city officials, business leaders, and representatives of local community groups elicited promises to place families in public housing without regard to race, end discrimination in lending for home purchases, and improve relations between white and black people in the city through interracial dialogue. The Daley administration failed to enforce the agreements, however, and Chicago remained a segregated city.[37]

Activists also lobbied Congress to pass and enforce national laws aimed at ending housing discrimination. The National Committee Against Discrimination in Housing (NCDH) played a leading role in these efforts. Founded by a coalition of civil rights and community groups in 1950, the NCDH pushed for the adoption of fair housing practices in federal agencies and government-subsidized home construction projects over the next two decades. Its efforts were instrumental in securing presidential executive orders prohibiting discrimination in federally funded housing and in convincing Congress to pass the Fair Housing Act in 1968. Local chapters throughout the nation then worked to make sure the legislation was enforced. The NCDH developed educational materials to apprise minority renters and home buyers of their rights and pioneered the use of housing audits (systematic testing to compare the treatment of white and black home seekers) to monitor compliance with the law. These efforts were vital to uncovering persistent discrimination in the housing industry. In the 1970s the NCDH helped black plaintiffs file hundreds of lawsuits against property owners, realtors, and suburban governments that continued to circumvent the law. Its efforts secured court rulings that extended fair housing legislation to cover subtle forms of discrimination such as racial steering as well as more blatantly racist actions.[38] Fair housing advocates also convinced the Carter administration to enact the Community Reinvestment Act of 1977. The act required federally insured banking institutions to make loans in the same communities from which they took in deposits, including non-white neighborhoods they had previously redlined.

In the following decade activists worked to overcome challenges posed by President Reagan's lax approach to civil rights enforcement. The number of fair housing lawsuits filed by the government dropped from about 30 lawsuits per year in the 1970s to only two cases during the first two years of the Reagan administration. Fair housing groups and their supporters in Congress pushed Reagan to take more forceful measures to combat housing discrimination in later years. As a result of this pressure federal agencies increased their efforts to identify and punish violators and in 1988 the president signed the Fair Housing Amendments Act into law. The legislation empowered HUD to initiate legal proceedings when it had "reasonable cause" to believe discrimination had occurred and set hefty fines that grew progressively higher for repeat offenders.[39]

The passage of these amendments coincided with the formation of the National Fair Housing Alliance (NFHA), a coalition of local organizations that carried on the struggle for integrated housing after the NCDH closed down in 1990. The NFHA worked with HUD to secure funding and authority for non-profit organizations as well as state and local fair housing agencies to process complaints, conduct housing audits, negotiate settlements, and take legal action against discriminators. The program worked well until the late 1990s, when Congress cut funding and imposed new restrictions that impeded the work of fair housing groups. The loss of many experienced staff members at HUD led to a growing backlog of complaints and an increasingly antagonistic relationship between the federal agency and local fair housing organizations. The situation grew worse during George W. Bush's presidency. At hearings before House representatives held in June 2002, fair housing advocates expressed suspicion that the administration was deliberately trying to undermine civil rights enforcement. Eighteen months into his presidency, Bush had still not appointed a HUD secretary and the agency was staffed with people who had little expertise in the areas they were supposed to monitor. These officials had thousands of cases awaiting resolution and seemed intent on preventing new ones from being added to the pile. "When you call, the intake person, who is not trained in what is covered by the law, and what the courts have decided since 1968 about the law will oftentimes reject a complaint," stated NFHA president Shanna Smith. Fair housing groups also faced challenges from HUD investigators who questioned their right to bring cases although their standing to do so was clearly established under the law. Many groups declined to apply for funding from HUD and stopped filing complaints through the agency because of its staff's hostility and incompetence.[40]

Inconsistent enforcement of the law meant that direct action protests remained a feature of open housing activism in the post-civil rights era. In 1987 SCLC leaders in Virginia targeted the whitest city in the state, Colonial Heights, as the site for demonstrations aimed at drawing attention to persistent housing segregation. Less than one percent of the town's 16,500 residents were African American. A retired black military officer who supported the protest recalled that he had wanted to buy a home in Colonial Heights after returning from service in Vietnam in 1969, but a real estate agent told him he could not. Instead, he and other African Americans were redirected to nearby Petersburg, a mostly black city. Black students and faculty at Virginia State University (VSU) who patronized white-owned businesses in Colonial Heights often received less than friendly service. "[They] talk to you like you are the lowest of the low," one student stated. Civil rights leaders thought the undisguised antagonism was aimed at discouraging black people from settling there. "We have every reason to believe that there is effort and intent to keep Colonial Heights all-white," Curtis Harris told reporters.

Outside observers gained a sense of what Harris meant on April 4, when 600 marchers descended on the town to request that its leaders assist in widening the economic prospects of poor black people who lived in Petersburg and other surrounding areas. They asked city officials to grant jobs and construction contracts to African Americans and use black teacher trainees from VSU in the public schools instead of white students recruited from colleges farther away. In a scene that recalled white Chicagoans' response to open housing activism 20 years earlier, a crowd of local residents equal in size to the SCLC group greeted the marchers with Nazi salutes and shouts of "Niggers go home!" Local resident Robert Fuller wore a Confederate flag as a cape and told reporters that he was there "for white supremacy," adding that he did not want black people to "tear up Colonial Heights the way they have done with Petersburg." Sitting on her car next to a sign reading "We don't need murders, rapes, stabbings and robberies," Frances Vaden complained that she did not understand why black people were protesting. "Nobody is telling them they can't live here," she said. The Colonial Heights city council agreed. In a statement rejecting the SCLC's demands, council members asserted, "The charge that this city is a bastion of racism is as false as false can be. We have no feeling, covert or overt, of discrimination against anyone."[41]

Individual vs. Institutional Racism

The council's statement echoed similar assertions by federal officials who dismissed accusations of racism even as they implemented polices that clearly harmed large numbers of black Americans. In 1983 attendees at the SCLC's annual convention listened incredulously to a speech by William Bradford Reynolds that claimed Reagan's record on civil rights was better than previous presidents' and deserved "praise from all quarters." Audience

members challenged this assessment, citing Reagan's opposition to extension of the Voting Rights Act, weakening of affirmative action policies,
attempts to dismantle the Commission on Civil Rights, and general insensitivity toward black people. Perhaps most insulting was the administration's assumption that it had an image problem rather than a policy problem.
Reverend C. T. Vivian explained to Reynolds, "It's not simply a matter of
perception. The central thing to be understood about this administration is
you've attempted on every hand to destroy any real attention to enforcement of civil rights. This administration doesn't seem to want to deal with
the reality of racism in this country."[42]

Part of the problem was Reagan's understanding of racism as encompassing only intentional acts of discrimination by individuals. In contrast,
civil rights leaders were concerned not just with individual bigotry but the
systemic inequalities that disadvantaged black people. For these reasons
supporters of racial equality took on Reagan's broader social policies as
well as the administration's weak civil rights record. ACORN's response to
cuts in government housing programs for low-income people was one of
the most innovative and dramatic examples of such activism. In the 1980s
ACORN organized squatting campaigns that encouraged homeless families
to move into and repair abandoned buildings in poor neighborhoods (see
Figure 4.1). The families and local activists then pressured local governments to provide the additional resources needed to revitalize economically
depressed communities. ACORN members also established tent communities called "Reagan Ranches" in 35 cities to draw attention to the consequences of the president's housing policies. In a demonstration joined by
more than 200 civil rights and community groups, 40,000 homeless people
and their supporters marched on Washington in October 1989 to demand
a restoration of federal funding to pre-Reagan levels. Noting that the government had recently allocated $1 billion to people in South Carolina made
homeless by Hurricane Hugo, Ohio governor Richard Celeste proclaimed,
"We need billions for the poor souls made homeless by Hurricane Ronnie."
After meeting with the march's organizers, HUD secretary Jack Kemp
agreed to set aside some of the agency's low-income housing for homeless
families and to impose new conditions on community development grants
to local governments so that more of the money was directed toward
helping poor people.[43]

ACORN and other fair housing advocates also worked to make sure
banks complied with the Community Reinvestment Act. Initially reluctant
to lend to minority home buyers, banks found a profitable new market
providing home mortgage loans to qualified black and Latino borrowers.
Fair housing activism and stronger enforcement of civil rights legislation by
the Clinton administration in the 1990s increased lending in nonwhite communities and helped to expand home ownership among black families. In

Figure 4.1 ACORN members take over an abandoned building in New York to protest Reagan-era economic policies that exacerbated problems like poverty and homelessness, 1985
Source: Larry C. Morris/New York Times

these same decades, however, deregulation of the financial system brought new actors into the home mortgage business whose reckless lending practices almost brought down the entire global economic system in the early twenty-first century. Private mortgage companies, Wall Street investment firms, and unregulated subsidiaries of regular banks realized huge profits by expanding the credit market to include poor people and separating the act of lending from the risks that it traditionally entailed. Mortgage brokers encouraged borrowers to take out loans they could not afford, then sold the debts to investors, who bundled them into mortgage-backed securities that were traded to other investors around the world. Brokers earned fees for the mortgages they closed regardless of whether the loans were ever paid back, and the purchasers of the loans were not responsible for verifying borrowers' creditworthiness. People of very modest means who had trouble saving the required deposit or meeting the income threshold for traditional loans found they could purchase homes with interest-only or adjustable-rate mortgages and no down payment. The same was true of wealthier property investors seeking to profit from rising home prices. Easy credit and the assumption that property values could only increase fueled a speculative bubble that eventually burst when overextended homeowners began defaulting on their loans.[44]

Some analysts blamed the Clinton administration and community groups like ACORN for encouraging banks to loan money to people who could not pay it back, but fair housing advocates never supported the risky lending practices that led to the financial meltdown. In 2006 ACORN tried to warn industry leaders and government regulators that these loans were a ticking time bomb in a study titled *The Impending Rate Shock*. "In far too many cases, alternative mortgages are being sold to consumers who can only afford the initial lower-payments but will not be able to afford the higher payments that will come when either the interest-only period or the initial 'teaser' rate period ends," the report stated. Counselors working with low-income, first-time home buyers found that brokers often did not give borrowers a choice of loan products or explain how the complex mortgages they were selling really worked. Many people who qualified for lower-cost loans were not fully informed of their options and were steered into sub-prime products instead. Low-income and minority neighborhoods were disproportionately affected by such tactics. Even comparing lending among people of similar income, African Americans were more likely than white Americans to receive high-interest, subprime loans. ACORN urged government officials to impose stricter controls on the mortgage industry, including better enforcement of fair housing laws and requiring lenders to underwrite loans based on borrowers' capacity to make payments over the entire life of the loan and at the highest potential rates.[45]

Federal regulators ignored these recommendations, and the consequences of the "rate shock" rippled through the global financial system two years later. The mortgage crisis threatened to erase the advances in black home ownership that had occurred since the 1960s, along with the economic security and potential for providing better opportunities to the next generation that accompanied the acquisition of property. Many of the problematic loans were refinances of existing mortgages that families used to send children to college or make home improvements. Some loan firms actively sought out elderly or poorly educated homeowners and talked them into borrowing excessively high amounts. One retired couple in Atlanta ended up owing $176,000 on a house worth $100,000 after a broker manipulated them into a series of refinances. Another resident of the same neighborhood took out a $67,000 home improvement loan in 2005 that later ballooned to $102,000, with an adjustable interest rate that could reach up to 17 percent. Unscrupulous agents who filled out loan documents for pensioner George Mitchell falsely reported that he earned $4,725 per month and had

$8,000 in savings. When Mitchell's daughter came to witness the loan signing, she intended to convince her father not to finalize it. "I read through what I could understand," she recalled later. "It was really thick, and I don't know legalese, especially when it comes to loans. The only question that I had for [the loan officer] was, Could he cancel it, honestly?" The bank representative told her that canceling the loan was impossible. Within two months of the signing, Mitchell fell behind on his payments.[46]

By 2008 black neighborhoods in Atlanta and other cities were experiencing a tsunami of home foreclosures. Every estimate of the amount of lost wealth this represented placed it in the billions of dollars. Forty years after the passage of the Fair Housing Act, a national commission chaired by former HUD secretaries Jack Kemp and Henry Cisneros concluded that "insufficient fair lending enforcement and a resistance to more vigorous regulation of the subprime market" had created a crisis that could result in "neighborhoods with abandoned homes, eroding tax bases, increased crime rates, and a loss of wealth in minority communities which will represent the greatest loss of wealth to homeowners of color in modern U.S. history." As millions of middle-class white Americans learned when the effects of the economic crisis reached their own communities, the damage was not confined to black neighborhoods. "The 'ghetto lending' practices of the 1960s have metastasized, spreading across class, race and regional boundaries," observed legal scholar and *Nation* columnist Patricia Williams in July 2008. "If such practices began in neighborhoods where there was disrespect for the property rights of certain Americans, it's come round to bite us in the tail. We are all in the ghetto now."[47]

Amidst a financial crisis rooted in weak civil rights enforcement and the free market economic policies that prevailed in the late twentieth century, many white people finally realized that their experiences and those of African Americans were interconnected. Civil rights activists who worked to overcome racism in the post-civil rights era knew that the colorblind individualism adopted after the 1960s was an inadequate response both to ongoing injustices that limited black people's prospects and to social transformations that affected all Americans. Struggles for equality in the post-civil rights era frequently revealed tensions between citizens who viewed racism as a systemic problem that had broad implications for the whole society and those who defined it in terms of personal prejudices that were of relatively little importance. The outcomes of these debates shaped the fate of the nation along with that of African Americans.

To See or Not to See: Debates over Affirmative Action

Colorblindness is an absurd concept. The only way I can live in a color-blind society is if I have a bag over my head. (Eva Paterson, 2006)[1]

Soon after the Civil Rights Act banned racial discrimination in employment in 1964, the struggle to fulfill its goals revealed a need for stronger measures to overcome individual racists' reluctance to hire black workers as well as the structural disadvantages black people faced in the job market. In the late 1960s civil rights activists, government policy makers, and the federal courts promoted procedures that moved beyond nondiscrimination and required employers to take "affirmative action" aimed at ensuring equal opportunities for African Americans. Initially relying on outreach and training programs to recruit black workers into areas where they were underrepresented, these policies evolved into results-oriented approaches that set numerical hiring targets for employers to meet within specified time frames.

Although affirmative action was an effective way to move black people into areas of the economy that had previously excluded them, many Americans viewed it as a system of racial quotas that unfairly discriminated against white people. Debates over the morality and efficacy of "seeing race" in the context of hiring decisions occurred against a backdrop of economic restructuring that made it harder for all workers to find well-paid, secure employment in the late twentieth century. Opponents seeking to abolish affirmative action programs found a receptive audience among white Americans who sensed a threat to their competitive advantages just when they could least afford to lose them. Some African Americans also spoke out against group-based remedies for racism and argued that everyone must rely on their own individual efforts instead. Other analysts expressed ambivalence about supporting controversial measures that enhanced black people's chances of finding jobs but fell well short of the broad social reforms needed to ensure real equality. Civil rights activists recognized the limits of affirmative action but nonetheless mobilized to defend the practice against attempts to undermine it. Their efforts preserved an important means of overcoming institutional racism and ensured that the programs endured into the twenty-first century.

The Limits of Colorblindness

Ending employment discrimination was a paramount concern in black Americans' struggles for justice. Protests against segregation in the 1950s and 1960s often included requests that local governments and businesses hire black workers. Pressure from civil rights groups persuaded the city commission in Montgomery, Alabama, to add four black police officers to its all-white force in May 1954, 18 months before the same activists organized a boycott of segregated buses that made national headlines. Equal employment opportunities for African Americans were among the demands made by black leaders during civil rights protests in Birmingham in 1963. After CORE members successfully integrated two department stores in St. Louis, Missouri, in 1960, they followed up with requests that African Americans be employed as clerks, salespeople, and in other positions that were traditionally reserved for white workers. In 1962 CORE leader Gordon Carey outlined the organization's push for "'compensatory' hiring," explaining, "We are approaching employers with the proposition that they have effectively excluded Negroes from their work force for a long time and that they now have a responsibility and obligation to make up for their past sins."[2]

Whitney Young also believed that special efforts were needed to address black unemployment. Speaking at a meeting of the NUL in September 1962, Young suggested that overcoming the consequences of centuries of racism might require "a decade of discrimination in favor of Negro youth." The following year Young called for a "domestic Marshall Plan" to address black disadvantages in education, housing, and employment, modeled on the $17 billion in economic aid the United States sent to its European allies after World War II. Just as the nation stepped in to aid the victims of war, drought, hurricanes, and other disasters, he argued, so must it assist African Americans to overcome the historical consequences of slavery and segregation. Young urged businesses to actively recruit black workers and develop training programs to prepare more African Americans for jobs. "This does not mean the establishment of a quota system," he asserted. "But, because we are faced with the hypocrisy of 'tokenism,' where the presence of two or three Negro employees is passed off as integration, we are forced, during the transitional stages, to discuss numbers and categories."[3]

Not everyone agreed with this approach. White minister and *Christian Century* editor Kyle Haselden supported the immediate desegregation of all aspects of American life but viewed compensatory programs as "a subtle but pernicious form of racism" that destroyed black initiative and punished innocent white Americans for crimes their ancestors committed. Noting that many of the nation's poor people were undereducated white Americans who faced similar obstacles to black people in the job market, Haselden called instead for "a nationwide crash program for the education, training and employment of the underprivileged ... based not on race but on need." Black leaders A. Philip Randolph and Bayard Rustin also preferred broader programs aimed at ensuring full employment and a decent standard of living for all Americans. In 1963 Rustin warned against demanding differential treatment for African Americans. Poor black people's problems were inseparable from those of poor white people, he asserted, and the only real solution was "a political and social reform program that will not only help the Negroes but one that will help all Americans."[4]

Segregationists dismissed activists' claims regarding black people's employment problems entirely. Louisiana senator Allen Ellender denied that racism had anything to do with the low numbers of black people employed in skilled occupations, contending that African Americans were "attempting to use their color to camouflage their lack of capability." Others portrayed any means of ensuring equal employment opportunities as granting special privileges to African Americans. Opponents of President Kennedy's Civil Rights bill charged that the provisions outlawing job discrimination amounted to a system of racial quotas that unfairly advantaged black workers. In 1963 *U.S. News & World Report* printed a story summarizing the proposed legislation under the misleading headline, "Forced Hiring of Negroes," and suggested that under the new rules the government could order "hiring of Negroes instead of white applicants."[5]

Supporters of the legislation worked hard to allay such fears. Senator Hubert Humphrey noted that there was nothing in the bill that required employers to favor black people over white workers. Title VII of the act simply prohibited discrimination and was "designed to encourage hiring on the basis of ability and qualification, not race or religion." The final version of the Civil Rights Act made it illegal for most employers to discriminate against individuals because of their "race, color, religion, sex, or national origin" and contained a provision specifically stating that covered entities were *not* required to "grant preferential treatment to any individual or to any group ... on account of an imbalance which may exist" in the number employed. Initially, only companies employing 100 or more workers were required to adhere to the new rules, with provisions for gradually extending coverage to those with 25 or more employees. The legislation created the Equal Employment Opportunity Commission

(EEOC) and granted the new agency limited powers of enforcement. People who believed they had been unfairly denied employment filed complaints with the EEOC, which investigated the allegations and negotiated with employers to devise appropriate means of redress. Complainants could bring legal action if conciliation efforts failed to reach an acceptable settlement.[6]

Historian Timothy Minchin's research on labor practices in the southern textile industry shows that constant pressure by civil rights organizations and local activists was necessary to make equal employment opportunities a reality in the late twentieth century. Immediately after passage of the Civil Rights Act black people began testing the Title VII provisions. In Hillsborough, North Carolina, a group of black women met together and decided to apply for work at area textile mills and file complaints with the EEOC if they were turned down. Their experiences demonstrated that company officials had no intention of hiring black Americans regardless of the law. At one plant Annie Belle Tinnin and her sister learned from the office manager that "they didn't hire Negro ladies there." Desperate for earnings that could supplement the meager wages she earned as a seasonal laborer, Romona Pinnix tried repeatedly to get a job with the same company. "I went there – I let him know I went there wanting employment," she recalled later. "I didn't care if it was that day; I wanted it. And he let me know he didn't hire colored women." Josephine Jennings' experience demonstrated that employers who did not want to risk accusations of racism could easily circumvent the law in less obvious ways. In a complaint to the EEOC in 1969 Jennings wrote, "I was denied a position allegedly because of my weight. I believe that the real reason I was not hired was because of being too black rather than being too fat."[7]

A few African Americans were already employed in the textile industry but they were confined to the lowest paid jobs. The Civil Rights Act inspired many of these workers to push for opportunities to advance to higher positions. They too came up against the racial prejudices of employers who assumed black people were best suited for menial labor. At the Dan River Mills in Virginia, white supervisor Wyllie Smyka contended that black workers preferred unskilled labor because it gave them "less responsibility and more free time." In letters to their local NAACP branches and government officials, African Americans complained of unequal pay scales, abusive supervisors, and not being informed of opportunities for promotion. Black employee Paul Gene McLean explained in plain terms his insistence that job vacancies at J. P. Stevens and Company be publicized in accordance with the law: "I want a better job and when it comes open I want to know about it." Similarly, a group of black men who filed an EEOC complaint against a mill in North Carolina in 1971 asserted, "The Negroes in our department were not put in this world just to do the hard, common work. ... The Civil Rights Act gives us certain privileges and we would like to exercise these rights now."[8]

The thousands of complaints the EEOC received in its first few months of operation completely overwhelmed its tiny staff and budget. After just one year, the agency had a backlog of 3,000 cases waiting to be processed, and the stacks of paper kept growing. Two decades later, program analyst Everett Crosson reported: "We were initially programmed for something like about 2,500 charges. We received 6,000. We've been dying ever since."[9] The EEOC's weak enforcement powers also undermined its effectiveness. In May 1967 EEOC chairman Stephen Shulman told a senate subcommittee that about half the agency's efforts at conciliation failed to persuade employers to comply with the law. The long delays in processing cases and failure to force recalcitrant employers to stop discriminating disappointed many black workers. According to Whitney Young, the EEOC's ineffectiveness fostered "disillusionment and lack of confidence" among African Americans. As a result, he warned, black people were "rapidly losing faith in the democratic process."[10]

Origins of Affirmative Action

Like Young and other proponents of stronger measures to move black workers into jobs, President Johnson and his advisors ultimately concluded that racial equality could not be achieved through colorblind policies that ignored the continuing impact of past discrimination on African Americans. In April 1964 Assistant Secretary of Labor Daniel Patrick Moynihan suggested that although the idea of "unequal treatment for the Negro" sounded suspect, "it may be that without unequal treatment in the immediate future there is no way for them to achieve anything like equal status in the long run." Moynihan had read Whitney Young's proposal for a domestic Marshall Plan and concluded that the unique historical circumstances facing black people warranted "some form of special treatment." President Johnson expressed an identical view when he addressed the students and faculty of Howard University in June 1965. In a speech that is widely regarded as marking the administration's shift away from race-neutral to race-conscious approaches to civil rights, Johnson asserted: "You do not take a person who, for years, has been hobbled by chains and liberate him, bring him up to the starting line of a race and then say, 'you are free to compete with all the others,' and still justly believe that you have been completely fair. ... Equal opportunity is essential, but not enough."[11]

In September 1965 Johnson issued Executive Order 11246, stepping up efforts that had begun in previous administrations to eliminate discrimination by federal agencies and contractors. The order required government departments to develop equal employment opportunity programs and charged the Department of Labor with making sure that businesses receiving federal contracts took "affirmative action to ensure that applicants are employed, and that employees are treated during employment, without regard to their race, creed, color, or national origin." Contractors were required to submit reports outlining their employment practices and risked lawsuits, losing their contracts, and being declared ineligible for future consideration if they failed to demonstrate adherence to the law. The Office of Federal Contract Compliance (OFCC) was created within the Labor Department to monitor the activities of contractors. In subsequent decades the OFCC and the EEOC acted as the principal enforcers of equal employment opportunity legislation.[12]

Both agencies struggled to develop effective methods of ensuring employers' compliance. As the EEOC had discovered, reliance on investigation and conciliation of thousands of individual complaints was time consuming and failed to yield satisfactory results. Intentional discrimination was difficult to prove on a case-by-case basis because employers could always fabricate non-racial reasons for not hiring particular applicants. Other ways of circumventing the law, such as advertising jobs through word of mouth or placing notices in places where only white people were likely to see them, might never come to the EEOC's attention. Such problems convinced administrators that analyzing company records to identify patterns of discrimination was a more fruitful approach. In 1966 the EEOC began requiring businesses to file reports showing the racial composition of their workforces. Though the agency still lacked any real enforcement powers, the reports helped to identify industries and companies that might be persuaded to voluntarily hire more African Americans after being confronted with evidence that black workers were being "underutilized."[13]

The OFCC also gradually moved toward a model that relied on data collection and statistics to measure progress in combating discrimination. Administrators emphasized that they did not much care how contractors went about increasing employment opportunities for nonwhite workers as long as they achieved satisfactory outcomes. In 1967 OFCC director Edward Sylvester urged companies to "apply the same kind of imagination and ingenuity" they used to solve other business problems. "There is no fixed and firm definition of affirmative action," he stated. "Affirmative action is anything that you have to do to get results." At first, most contractors offered only vague promises to reach out to underrepresented groups and did not significantly increase the number of black workers they hired. An additional problem was that the unions that supplied much of the labor on federally funded construction projects generally excluded black workers. In St. Louis, Missouri, the combined membership of the building trades unions included only three African Americans out of more than 5,000 workers.

Similar imbalances existed in other cities, leading OFCC officials to demand that contractors and unions develop ways to increase black participation in all aspects of construction work, from apprenticeship and training programs to hiring for skilled positions on projects. These efforts culminated in the adoption of the Philadelphia Plan, a policy initiative that set out specific guidelines for affirmative action and served as a blueprint for employment practices that spread throughout the economy in the late twentieth century.[14]

Initially proposed in November 1967, the Philadelphia Plan required successful bidders for federal building jobs to submit employment plans designed to produce "minority group representation in all trades and in all phases of the construction project" before contracts were finalized. The original version of the Plan avoided imposing precise numerical requirements on employers and allowed for flexibility. Labor Department officials viewed this feature as a strength, but their colleagues in the GAO thought differently. Comptroller General Elmer Staats expressed concern that the Plan imposed additional requirements on employers after contracts were awarded and did not clearly define a minimum standard for approving affirmative action measures. In November 1968 Staats ruled the Plan illegal and it was shelved for the remainder of President Johnson's term. The Nixon administration revived the Plan and tried to overcome the GAO's objections by setting more specific criteria in its affirmative action guidelines. The new Plan set target ranges for the percentages of minority workers to be hired and required contractors to make "good faith efforts" to meet them. The GAO again declared the Plan unacceptable, this time arguing that it violated Title VII of the Civil Rights Act by forcing employers to make hiring decisions that were based on race. Attorney General John Mitchell overruled the GAO and asserted the legality of the Plan. After encountering some opposition in Congress the new rules were allowed to go forward in December 1969.[15]

Extending and Strengthening Affirmative Action in the Nixon Era

In February 1970 Secretary of Labor George Shultz issued a directive extending coverage of the Philadelphia Plan to all businesses that contracted with the federal government, bringing a quarter-million employers and one-third of the nation's labor force under its purview. The following year, the Labor Department added women to the list of underrepresented groups from which contractors were expected to actively recruit workers. In 1972 Congress made amendments to the Civil Rights Act that empowered the Department of Justice to bring lawsuits against city, county, and state governments that excluded black people from public employment. These cases along with private suits altered the employment practices of more than 50 public agencies across the nation between 1972 and 1980. Congress also strengthened the enforcement abilities of the EEOC with the Equal Employment Opportunity Act of 1972, authorizing the agency to take violators to court instead of merely negotiating with employers. The EEOC aggressively exercised its new powers, filing hundreds of lawsuits against labor unions and corporations whose employment records suggested a pattern of discrimination. Meanwhile, HEW pressured educational institutions that received federal funds into altering their hiring and admissions procedures by requiring them to submit affirmative action plans. Either by court order or voluntarily to avoid trouble, most businesses, government agencies, and universities that were covered by civil rights legislation adopted administrative practices that included goals and timetables for increasing minority participation.[16]

The Nixon administration's role in rescuing and expanding affirmative action puzzled contemporaries and historians. Why would a Republican president whose political base was almost entirely made up of white voters and who opposed rigorous enforcement of civil rights measures in most other areas promote a policy that many people viewed as offering preferential treatment to African Americans? One reason was that Nixon's appointees to the Labor Department were no less interested than their predecessors in getting results. After a few months of observing the practices that shut black workers out of the construction industry, Assistant Labor Secretary Arthur Fletcher concluded that the only way to open up these jobs was by setting clear targets for employers to meet. "Without such targets ... the interminable ineffectiveness of the government programs would go on," he explained. "I had not come to Washington to preside over a continuation of the ineffective programs of the past." Many unions seemed like little more than ethnic social clubs, restricting entry to the family and friends of existing members. "In essence, public taxes were being used to take care of a family clan called a union," Fletcher stated. "So I asked the question, Are we in the business of taking care of the Kawaski family?" Fletcher dismissed claims that no suitable African American workers were available, noting that "Italians with green cards who couldn't speak English ... were working on federal contracts [while] those same unions and contractors were saying they couldn't find qualified blacks." Similarly, Secretary Shultz found the elevated unemployment rate for black workers unacceptable and stated that conducting "business as usual" was an inadequate response.[17]

Nixon proved receptive to the arguments of his Labor Department officials. The president did not want to completely alienate black voters by appearing to be oblivious to their needs, and enhancing the employment prospects of African Americans was consistent with his belief that bringing them more fully into the capitalist system could solve the nation's racial problems. The political calculations of the president and his advisors were also evident at staff meetings where the possibility of driving a wedge between the civil rights and labor movements, two core Democratic constituencies, were discussed. Nixon highlighted the divisive potential of the Plan in a meeting with Republican leaders a few days before the congressional vote that determined its fate: "Make [civil rights] people take a stand – for labor or for [civil rights]." Policy advisor John Ehrlichman recalled that after the opposition in Congress was defeated, the president seemed very pleased at having created "a political dilemma for the labor union leaders and civil rights groups."[18]

Labor leaders responded angrily to the Philadelphia Plan, arguing that it threatened white workers' jobs and unfairly singled out the building trades unions when the percentages of African Americans employed in many other areas of the economy were just as minuscule. The Plan's narrow focus on the construction industry caused some civil rights leaders to conclude that Nixon's real aim was to divide working-class Americans along racial lines and weaken opposition to business-friendly policy initiatives. Black congressman Augustus Hawkins doubted that the initiative was the best way to ensure equal employment opportunities and wondered why the president ignored other ideas in favor of a relatively limited approach that was inadequate for solving rampant joblessness in African American communities. Though willing to support the proposal if it was extended to other industries on a national scale, Hawkins emphasized: "It must be understood that this plan is only one, and not necessarily the best of the tools for opening opportunities."[19]

Compared with other policy alternatives, affirmative action was a fundamentally conservative response to the problems at hand. This method of addressing black people's troubles contrasted greatly with proposals floated just a few years earlier that focused on generating enough jobs for all workers. In 1966, for example, President Johnson's Commission on Technology, Automation and Economic Progress released a report that urged the federal government to provide employment in the public sector for displaced workers to help ease the transition to a more technologically advanced economy. The following year Martin Luther King Jr. and the NAACP's Roy Wilkins called for a $30 billion economic aid package to solve the crisis in the nation's inner cities. Similarly, in 1968 the National Advisory Commission on Civil Disorders recommended creating 2 million new jobs in the private and public sectors. As Kevin Yuill observes, next to these proposals "a demand that a few African Americans be hired on building sites in specified cities ... appeared paltry indeed."[20]

Angry White Men

Whereas civil rights activists' ideas for more sweeping government action focused on expanding the number of job opportunities available, affirmative action simply tried to enhance black workers' competitiveness for a limited number of positions. This approach provoked strong reactions from white Americans accustomed to competing only among themselves, particularly in the context of the plant closings and layoffs that characterized the next few decades. The high pay, health and retirement benefits, and job security that many workers secured through unionized manufacturing employment in the 1950s and 1960s were not as widely available to their children and grandchildren. Later generations instead experienced declining living standards and increasing economic insecurity. Michael Goldfield analyzed the political choices open to white workers facing circumscribed employment prospects in the late twentieth century: "One can attempt to understand the broad economic trends and organize for more justice, greater union organization, and a larger safety net. This puts people in sharp conflict with the most powerful forces in the country. Or one can pick a scapegoat."[21]

Affirmative action made an easier target than the corporate and political elites whose decisions created the new economic order. Moreover, many Americans genuinely perceived the practice as an indefensible violation of national ideals. Opponents of color-conscious approaches to solving racial problems cited provisions in the Civil Rights Act to cast affirmative action efforts as illegal deviations from the colorblind practices mandated by the legislation. During discussions of the Philadelphia Plan, several senators argued that requiring employers to adopt goals and timetables for minority hiring amounted to imposing quotas, a practice that was banned under Title VII. Secretary Shultz maintained that this was an inaccurate interpretation of the policy. The Plan did not set rigid targets but flexible ranges for businesses and unions to aim for. Contractors who failed to meet these targets were not punished as long as they could show they had made some effort to achieve them. Making sure that all workers had an equal chance to compete for positions did not mean making race the sole criterion for employment, Shultz asserted. "You take [race] into consideration in that you must provide yourself with a reasonable range of choice in the hiring process," he explained. "However, that is not the same thing as saying that when it comes to hiring people, you have to decide between A and B on the basis of race."[22] Shultz's reasoning failed to convince many critics of the Plan, and the equation of "goals and timetables" with "quotas" remained a common practice in debates over affirmative action in later decades.

Nor could the reassurances offered by government bureaucrats erase the sense of loss that many white men felt when they were forced to concede

places in apprenticeship programs, construction jobs, police and fire departments, higher education, and skilled professions that they had long monopolized to nonwhite workers and women. Building trades union members
saw nothing wrong with the nepotism that excluded outsiders from their
organizations and viewed their ability to pass the benefits of membership
on to future generations as a sacred right. One Philadelphia construction
worker stated, "Some men leave their sons money, some large investments,
some business connections and some a profession. ... I have only one
worthwhile thing to give: my trade." Many white people saw themselves
as innocent victims of policies that advanced black interests at their own
expense. In challenging the promotion of a black co-worker over himself,
Birmingham fire fighter James Henson acknowledged that something needed
to be done to address the inequities created by the city's long history of
racism. "But they want me to pay for it," he stated, "and I didn't have
anything to do with it. I was a kid when all this [discrimination] went on."[23]

From the point of view of many African Americans, however, no white
person was completely innocent, and opposition to affirmative action was
just another attempt to preserve a racist system that accorded unearned
privileges to all white Americans whether they realized it or not. Black fire
fighter Carl Cook likened the benefits that white people accumulated
through centuries of racial exclusion to stolen property. Cook argued that
the current generation of white Americans lived off wealth that had been
wrongly appropriated from black people, and protestations that "we didn't
rob the bank" held little weight on the scales of justice.[24] Cook and other
supporters of affirmative action saw it as a way to dismantle structures
and practices that unfairly advantaged white people. The policies did not
target racist individuals but the systemic forms of racism that all the nation's
citizens had a collective responsibility to address. Using Julian Bond's football game analogy, it was like adding 142 points to the black team's score
in order to truly "play fair."

Breaking Down Institutional Barriers

Early decisions by the courts in employment discrimination cases upheld
the view that racism was not reducible to individual prejudices but encompassed institutional procedures that perpetuated injustice, whether or not
the procedures were developed with that intent. In *Quarles v. Philip Morris*
(1968) a district court in Virginia ruled that companies could not maintain
seniority systems that, because of past discrimination, effectively blocked
opportunities for advancement by black employees even after overtly
racist practices were eliminated.[25] In determining whether an employment
practice was legitimate, the court decided, discriminatory effects outweighed

innocent intent. In 1971 the Supreme Court reached the same conclusion in a case brought by black workers against Duke Power Company in North Carolina. Before passage of the Civil Rights Act the company hired African Americans only for menial custodial positions. After 1964 Duke allowed black workers to apply for higher paying jobs, but it also imposed new qualifications and testing requirements for those jobs. In a state where only 12 percent of black men had graduated from high school, few African Americans met the new employment standard. The Court accepted the contention of civil rights lawyers that policies resulting in "disparate impact" (such as the rejection of nine times as many black workers as white, as was the case with the Duke tests) were illegal. "Practices, procedures, or tests neutral on their face, and even neutral in terms of intent, cannot be maintained if they operate to 'freeze' the status quo of prior discriminatory employment practices," explained Chief Justice Warren Burger. The consequences of employers' actions rather than the motivations were the real test of what was allowed under the law.[26]

Having established that racism could be systemic and evident in disparate consequences as well as individual and motivated by malignant intent, the courts initially upheld color-conscious remedies for addressing the nation's racial problems. In 1969 several white teachers sued the superintendent of schools in Newark, New Jersey, after the school board altered promotion procedures to allow more African Americans to move into administrative positions. The decision was aimed at fostering better relations with the black community during a time of extreme racial tension in the city. The school system needed people who were sensitive to the problems of black children and parents, a quality that previous methods of promotion had not measured. The judges who decided the case rejected the plaintiffs' discrimination claim, stating that although the new policy aimed to facilitate the appointment of more black administrators, "the ultimate objective of the Board was to promote those persons most qualified to suit the needs of the Newark school system." The Third Circuit Court of Appeals cited the New Jersey case when it upheld the racially targeted approach of the Philadelphia Plan in *Contractors Association of Eastern Pennsylvania v. Secretary of Labor* in 1971. Arguing that Congress did not intend to "freeze the status quo and to foreclose remedial action" when it passed the Civil Rights Act, the Court stated: "Clearly the Philadelphia Plan is color-conscious. Indeed the only meaning which can be attributed to the 'affirmative action' language ... is that Government contractors must be color-conscious. ... In other contexts color-consciousness has been deemed to be an appropriate remedial posture."[27]

The Supreme Court reached a more ambivalent conclusion in *Regents of the University of California v. Bakke* (1978), a case that signaled a shift away from unqualified support for affirmative action. Allen Bakke, a white man who was rejected twice for admission to the medical school at the university's Davis campus, charged racial discrimination after discovering that the program reserved 16 out of the 100 available places each year for nonwhite students. Bakke argued that the admissions process amounted to a system of racial preferences and denied him the right to equal treatment. The university countered that ensuring a diverse student body was important to its institutional needs as well as broader social goals such as creating role models for minority youth and enhancing medical services to nonwhite communities. The Court ruled that the medical school's practice of setting aside a specific number of places for nonwhite students was unconstitutional and ordered Bakke admitted to the program. However, the justices upheld the general principle underlying affirmative action by accepting diversity as a legitimate state interest and allowing race to be considered as one factor, though not the only factor, in college admissions.[28]

With legal backing from the courts and strong enforcement by federal agencies, affirmative action enabled millions of nonwhite Americans to find places in skilled occupations, professions, and educational institutions that had previously excluded them (see Figure 5.1). Black enrollment at the

Figure 5.1 Engineer Delores Brown testing circuits for a government communications satellite, 1973
Source: Unknown/National Archives and Records Administration 306-N-2594

nation's major universities increased from 27 percent to 34 percent between 1972 and 1976. Businesses and unions that had contracts with federal agencies recorded strong increases in the number of African Americans they employed, and the proportion of apprenticeships held by black trainees doubled between 1970 and 1980. In the same decade, the number of African Americans holding middle-class jobs as managers or professionals grew by 70 percent. Black employment increases in the public sector were even greater, reaching 1.6 million workers by 1982. The consensus among government officials, business leaders, and civil rights lawyers involved in monitoring employment practices was that affirmative action worked. As Nancy MacLean notes in her study of the struggle for equal employment opportunities, "The expansion of the ranks of the better-off black working class and middle class and the tiny but growing black elite since the peak of the civil rights movement is one of the great success stories of recent history."[29]

Attacks on Affirmative Action

Critics of affirmative action were not impressed by evidence that it helped to break down the barriers to black economic advancement. Many people viewed the programs as illegal quota systems that benefited unqualified black Americans and harmed more deserving white citizens. In 1969 Robert Earl Holmes wrote to Mississippi congressional representative William Colmer to complain that the Farmers Home Administration was granting too many loans to African Americans and leaving white farmers without assistance. "Many Negroes in this area are receiving loans on smaller tracts of land than my land, and many of these people are poor credit risks, and it appears to me that they are being given special consideration at the expense of White people," he stated. Similarly, Alabama businessman George Thomas maintained that in the federal government's "unwarranted zeal to appeal to minority races, discrimination in reverse has been created." The *Citizen* promoted the same narrative of white victimhood in an article explaining the issues at stake in the *Bakke* case. According to this account, Allen Bakke's lawsuit challenged college admissions policies that "established racial quotas to determine the numbers of whites to whom they must deny admission." In 1978 the magazine hailed the Supreme Court's ruling in the case as a victory for "whites' rights."[30]

Political leaders who recognized the power of racially divisive issues reinforced such interpretations in their attacks on affirmative action. Richard Nixon reversed his initial support for race-conscious policies after concluding that he did not need black voters and focusing his attention on drawing more white working-class Americans away from the Democrats.

In 1972 the president told the Republican nominating convention that the nation was facing the prospect of a "quota democracy" that undermined traditions of meritocracy. Ronald Reagan's campaign speeches asserted that federal agencies' insistence on goals and timetables was "in effect a quota system both in hiring and in education." In the 1980 elections the Democratic Party's endorsement of affirmative action met with a Republican Party platform that attacked "bureaucratic regulations and decisions which rely on quotas, ratios, and numerical requirements to exclude some individuals in favor of others."[31] Civil rights groups rightly feared an assault on color-conscious policies when President Reagan took office the following year.

Reagan believed that requiring employers to work toward targets for minority hiring encouraged them to place racial considerations above everything else and violated the nation's colorblind ideals. "We must not allow the noble concept of equal opportunity to be distorted into federal guidelines or quotas which require race, ethnicity, or sex – rather than ability and qualifications – to be the principal factor in hiring or education," he told supporters after receiving his party's nomination to the presidency. In a radio speech delivered in 1985, Reagan warned, "There are some today who, in the name of equality, would have us practice discrimination. ... These people tell us that the government should enforce discrimination in favor of some groups through hiring quotas, under which people get or lose particular jobs or promotions solely because of their race or sex." The president then appropriated the language of the civil rights movement itself to rationalize his position, noting: "Twenty-two years ago Martin Luther King proclaimed his dream of a society rid of discrimination and prejudice, a society where people would be judged on the content of their character, not the color of their skin. That's the vision our entire administration is committed to."[32]

Unlike his predecessors and the federal judges who determined that affirmative action was a justifiable response to the intractability of racism in the United States, Reagan recognized none of the complexities or the limits to colorblindness that were exposed in the years following passage of the Civil Rights Act. His criticisms ignored the wealth and privileges that generations of white Americans had accrued at black expense, thus reducing a policy designed to address the massive disparities that resulted from the different historical experiences of black and white Americans to one that accorded benefits to people "solely" on the basis of skin color. He defined racism as individual prejudice, never mentioning the systemic forms of discrimination that continued to operate after the end of legalized segregation. Reagan failed to consider whether affirmative action might be moving the nation toward the realization of King's dream by increasing the number of African Americans employed in professional positions and undermining stereotypes that defined black people as unfit for anything except menial labor. Instead, he adopted a simplistic formula that equated efforts to secure a more just social order with the morally reprehensible practices that maintained white supremacy in an earlier era. In this analysis, noticing race for any reason was racist. Differential treatment based on group membership rather than individual characteristics was wrong. Affirmative action equaled Jim Crow.

Americans who shared Reagan's views expected the new administration to abolish affirmative action. At first, the situation seemed promising. Within days of the president's inauguration Senator Orrin Hatch announced plans to investigate "the ridiculous quota system" of federal equal employment opportunity programs. However, subsequent debates and resistance to policy initiatives revealed divisions among Republicans, their supporters in the business community, and within the Reagan administration itself that ultimately stymied efforts to end affirmative action. Against Hatch's assertions that the programs were burdensome and unnecessary, black Republican William Coleman noted that 50 percent of the nation's black youth were unemployed and that the overall jobless rate for African Americans was double that of white workers. Coleman challenged Hatch to explain how he would address the problem if race-conscious policies were abandoned. When the Justice Department asked the Republican mayor of Indianapolis to cease implementing an affirmative action plan that had increased the proportion of African Americans in the city's police force from 6 percent to 14 percent, he refused, citing the program's positive impact and widespread acceptance among residents as reasons for allowing it to continue. Forty-nine other cities across the nation also rejected pressure from administration officials to alter their employment policies.[33]

Though some business leaders and organizations supported plans to eliminate or amend equal employment opportunity regulations, others viewed the programs as beneficial to their own enterprises and the nation as a whole. After the White House floated a proposal to revoke all executive orders mandating goals and timetables, outlaw the use of statistical evidence to determine discrimination, and forbid employers from granting preference to members of minority groups, the president of the National Association of Manufacturers wrote to President Reagan to defend the existing system. He noted, "Since [Executive Order 11246] was signed into law, dramatic progress has been achieved in incorporating talented minorities and women into our workforce. ... Executive Order 11246 has benefited our country and should be continued to ensure the continued participation of all segments of our society in the nation's economy." Large corporations doing business with the federal government were accustomed to measuring their activities quantitatively and did not see the imposition of goals and timetables for minority hiring as an undue burden. Some companies that had no federal contracts and were not under any obligation to develop affirmative action plans did so anyway, believing equal employment opportunity practices to be good for business.[34]

The leaders of the three federal agencies responsible for enforcing the regulations also held divergent views. William Bradford Reynolds in the Justice Department emerged as one of the administration's most outspoken critics of affirmative action, denouncing goals and timetables and promising to support "*individual* opportunity" over "*group* entitlements." Similarly, Attorney General William French Smith asserted: "Our goal must always be genuinely color-blind state action." In response, EEOC acting chairman J. Clay Smith Jr. argued that colorblindness meant the continuation of racism and that "to treat discrimination as merely an individual problem insures the perpetuation of employment practices our nation has resolved to eradicate." Along with the EEOC, officials in the Labor Department defended the use of statistics to determine underutilization of minority workers against Reynolds' attacks on the practice.[35]

Facing opposition from civil rights groups, business leaders, state and local governments, and members of their own party, Reagan and his advisors eventually abandoned legislative efforts to end affirmative action. Instead, their antagonism toward the policy was expressed through administrative measures that weakened the enforcement of equal employment opportunity laws. Staff and budget cuts at the EEOC and the (now renamed) Office of Federal Contract Compliance Programs (OFCCP) left those agencies unable to pursue the aggressive approaches they had used to prevent employment discrimination in the 1970s. During Reagan's two terms in office, the OFCCP suspended only two contracts compared with 13 suspensions during President Carter's one term. In 1982 Reagan chose Clarence Thomas, an African American lawyer who opposed affirmative action, to take over as chairman of the EEOC. Under Thomas' leadership the agency reverted to investigating and prosecuting discrimination cases on an individual basis rather than identifying patterns of discrimination or filing class action lawsuits. This approach was even less effective in the 1980s than it had been in the 1960s. Thomas reported in 1983 that many people believed the Reagan administration was not interested in enforcing civil rights legislation and thought the laws no longer applied. Consequently, some employers were "surprised" when the EEOC initiated conciliation proceedings and proved more reluctant to settle cases than previously.[36]

Opponents of affirmative action could also take heart from some significant backtracking on the issue by the federal courts. Two Supreme Court rulings in 1989 revealed a new skepticism regarding the validity of color-conscious approaches. In *City of Richmond v. J. A. Croson* the Court struck down a program that reserved 30 percent of city construction funds for minority contractors. Justice Sandra Day O'Conner stated in the majority opinion that race-conscious policies were presumptively suspect and could only be deployed after being subjected to "strict scrutiny" to determine that they served a "compelling state interest" and addressed specific incidents of past discrimination. A few months later the Court's ruling in *Wards Cove Packing Co. v. Antonio* rejected the idea that disparate impact alone was evidence of discrimination, reversing its earlier determination in *Griggs*. The decision made it more difficult for plaintiffs to demonstrate that they had been denied equal opportunities and shifted the burden of proof from employers to employees. In response, supporters of affirmative action in Congress moved to clarify and strengthen the nation's equal employment opportunity laws by proposing legislation that restricted challenges to court-approved affirmative action plans, allowed the use of statistics to prove discrimination, shifted the onus back to employers to demonstrate that they had not discriminated, and increased financial penalties for law-breakers. President George H. W. Bush and some legislators initially resisted the changes but after some slight modifications to the original bill the Civil Rights Act of 1991 was signed into law.[37]

Direct Action to Open Employment Opportunities

Activists did not rely solely on the legal system to open up job opportunities for African Americans. Filing cases was costly and time-consuming, and the results did not always adequately address black workers' problems. As Nixon- and Reagan-era judicial appointees replaced judges who had sympathized with the freedom struggle in the 1960s, lawsuits became increasingly less effective in addressing employment discrimination. By the late 1990s civil rights lawyers preferred to try to settle cases through negotiation rather then risk the consequences of hostile rulings by the courts.[38] Boycotts, picketing, rallies, and demonstrations therefore remained important tools in the fight against racism. Direct action protests proved to be a valuable tactic for pressuring employers in the post-civil rights era. The black middle class was expanding and businesses seeking to maximize their markets feared upsetting African American consumers. Overt racism no longer had any legitimacy in the minds of most Americans, making it easier to shame violators of the new social norms into altering their behavior. Civil rights groups often found that threatening to draw public attention to discriminatory practices could quickly persuade corporations or government entities to consider black people's concerns.

The SCLC used the power of black dollars to good effect in its Operation Breadbasket program in the late 1960s. Groups of ministers visited business owners and managers to assess the extent of black employment within companies and suggest hiring goals based on the number of African Americans available in the local workforce. If negotiations were not successful activists organized boycotts and picketing to bring employers into line. According to Martin Luther King Jr., it was rarely necessary to take this step because most business owners were "keenly aware of the Negro's buying power and the consequent effect of its withdrawal." During eight months of operations in Chicago, the SCLC successfully pressured 11 companies to provide a total of 800 new positions or promotions to African American workers that represented over $7 million in increased income for the black community.[39]

Jesse Jackson headed Operation Breadbasket in Chicago and played a large role in its achievements. Under his leadership the program expanded to include training programs for aspiring black entrepreneurs and efforts to encourage consumers to patronize African American businesses. Jackson chafed under the constraints of working under the direction of others at the SCLC, however, and the resulting tension ended with his resignation in December 1971. A few days later Operation PUSH opened its headquarters in the South Side of Chicago. Although Jackson was often criticized for making brash statements to the media and failing to cooperate effectively with other civil rights organizations, Operation PUSH emerged as a powerful tool for mobilizing black Chicagoans' political and economic resources. Weekly rallies that combined church services, singing, and political speeches kept supporters enthused and engaged in the fight against racism. Meanwhile, PUSH's continued efforts to pressure corporate America to channel a fairer share of the nation's wealth to African Americans secured undeniable economic benefits. In 1981 PUSH assessed the business practices of the Coca Cola Company and found no African Americans on its board of directors, no black franchises or distributorships out of thousands spread across the nation, and a negligible percentage of advertising dollars spent with black-owned firms. The group then launched a nationwide campaign to publicize these failings and force changes in the way the company operated. Subsequent negotiations secured an agreement from Coca Cola to provide $1.5 million in loans to encourage black entry into the business and to name an African American to its board of directors.[40] Similar campaigns against dozens of other corporations over the next few decades also succeeded in breaking down some of the barriers to the full inclusion of black people in the nation's economy.

Other civil rights groups also recognized the power of economic pressure. The NUL responded to California governor Pete Wilson's attacks on affirmative action programs by canceling plans to hold its annual convention in the state in 1996. The decision cost California an estimated $10 million that the gathering would have generated for the economy. The following year several organizations including PUSH, the NUL, and the NAACP threatened to boycott and picket Texaco gas stations after the company's top executives were caught on tape making racist remarks about black people and plotting to destroy evidence related to an employment discrimination suit. Five weeks later, Texaco agreed to implement programs to hire and promote more minority workers, provide incentives to supervisors who met diversity goals, develop partnerships with minority-owned businesses, and create internship and scholarship programs to facilitate the recruitment of nonwhite youth into the oil industry. Civil rights leaders hailed the plans as setting a new standard for other corporations to follow. Emanuel Cleaver, president of the National Black Conference of Mayors, noted the implications of Texaco's past conduct for debates over affirmative action programs and other policies to address persistent racism. "This incident has made a very eloquent statement that African-Americans are not paranoid, particularly when it comes to employment issues," he stated.[41]

Diverse Criticism and Defenses in the 1990s and Beyond

Such evidence notwithstanding, opposition to affirmative action continued into the twenty-first century. Criticisms came from an increasingly diverse range of Americans offering perspectives from both ends of the political spectrum. Some attacks were plainly racist, as in the anonymous fliers mailed to 15 black students at the University of California at Berkeley in February 1995: "Rejoice you crybaby niggers. It's affirmative action month. When I see you in class it bugs the hell out of me because you're taking the seat of someone qualified." Other objections emphasized colorblind ideals or contended that the policies harmed more than they helped African Americans. Black scholar Shelby Steele, for instance, viewed the evolution of 1960s antidiscrimination measures into a system of "set-asides and other forms of preferential treatment" as a betrayal of the civil rights movement's original goals. "By making black the color of preference, these mandates have reburdened society with the very marriage of color and preference (in reverse) that we set out to eradicate," he argued. Steele thought affirmative action elevated unprepared African Americans to positions that they were ill-equipped to handle, leading to the perpetuation of stereotypes regarding the inferior abilities of black people. White Americans' racist beliefs were thus confirmed, while African Americans who secured advancement through affirmative action suffered debilitating self-doubt. African American sociologist William Julius Wilson questioned the benefits of affirmative action from a different perspective, arguing that it had driven white working-class voters out of the Democratic Party while doing little to address the problems of poor black people. Several other analysts also highlighted the limits of affirmative action and called for replacing color-conscious policies with class-based programs that addressed broader social problems. According to political scientist Jim Sleeper, rebuilding interracial coalitions through more broadly based assistance to disadvantaged Americans offered a way for progressive reformers to "find their way out of the thicket of race and move towards economic justice."[42]

Defenders of affirmative action countered opponents' arguments by pointing out that the use of other criteria apart from individual merit to distribute resources was hardly a break from tradition, asserting that African Americans were fully qualified for the positions they held, and questioning the effectiveness of class-based approaches. Studies of college admissions policies found no universities that admitted students solely on the basis of their academic qualifications. Non-academic factors such as age, athletic ability, or other talents all influenced admissions decisions, and a significant portion of places were reserved for the children of alumni, donors to institutions, and political leaders. In response to suggestions that affirmative action stigmatized black people, one University of California admissions officer noted that other "undeserving" students, such as those with low test scores but wealthy parents, did not appear to suffer from this problem.[43] For most African Americans, what counted most was that they were in college, earning the degrees that were their keys to a better future than past generations had enjoyed.

The hiring decisions of employers also typically considered attributes other than applicants' academic and professional résumés, including vague criteria such as temperament or collegiality – in other words, the ability to "fit in" and get along with other employees. In the days before affirmative action this meant that white male-dominated businesses and universities tended to hire only more white men. Such cultural affinities, along with the social networks that remained a key means through which many white Americans secured jobs even after the 1960s, undoubtedly promoted some people of mediocre abilities to positions they would not have secured without these connections. In a study conducted in the mid-1990s, legal scholars David Wilkins and Mitu Gulati found that black applicants hoping to find positions at the nation's largest law firms had to be "superstars" to be hired whereas many white job seekers with average records found employment with relative ease.[44] If anything, African Americans often had to be smarter and work harder than their white competitors to even be considered for the positions they sought.

Evidence of continued job discrimination against African Americans of all social classes in the 1990s caused some observers to conclude that replacing race-conscious policies with class-based remedies was premature. According to Stephen Steinberg, the persistence of racist practices by employers more than the lag in education and skills that left black workers unprepared for the postindustrial economy was responsible for high unemployment rates in African American communities. Many businesses remained reluctant to hire black people even for low-wage service jobs that required little education, citing "cultural" factors that supposedly made them poor employees. Steinberg argued that reducing racial inequality to a subset of class inequality was an inadequate response to the problem and ignored "the ways in which the black experience was fundamentally different from the experience of other ethnic groups." Indeed, the nation had been down that road before, in the 1930s and 1940s when New Deal reformers assumed that the job creation programs and social welfare policies they initiated would automatically raise black people's living standards along with those of white Americans. Instead, both individual and institutional racism ensured an uneven distribution of benefits, and the consequences remained evident decades later. Taking on the Supreme Court's insistence that race-based policies must be designed to correct specific historical injustices, Ira Katznelson argued a case for affirmative action grounded in evidence of deliberate discrimination against African Americans in the New Deal and post-World War II initiatives that were most responsible for creating the white middle class. Racially targeted policies were necessary to create the black middle class that would have emerged if African Americans had received their share of the benefits accorded by the federal government's home loan policies, subsidization of suburbia, Social Security, and the GI Bill.[45]

The argument over race-conscious policies continued in the courts as well. In 1996 the Fifth Circuit Court of Appeals cast doubt on the future of affirmative action in college admissions by ruling in *Hopwood v. University of Texas Law School* that the goal of maintaining a diverse student body was not a good enough reason to justify using racial criteria. The University of Texas appealed the decision with support from the Clinton administration, but the Supreme Court declined to hear the case. In 2003, however, the Supreme Court invalidated *Hopwood* with its decision in *Grutter v. Bollinger*, which upheld race-conscious admissions policies at the University of Michigan. The Court received more than 60 briefs from supporters of the university, including civil rights groups, government agencies, corporations, and retired military leaders, collectively promoting a new rationale for affirmative action that emerged at the turn of the century: that in the age of globalization and the threat of international terrorism, diversity was a legitimate state interest and an appropriate goal for the nation's educational institutions and businesses to pursue. The majority opinion maintained that evidence cited in numerous academic studies as well as the briefs received by the Court proved the benefits of diversity were "not theoretical but real."[46]

Recasting affirmative action policies as diversity initiatives that served the public interest helped supporters to reclaim the debate from those who stressed their impact on individuals. One group of constitutional scholars argued that the programs involved "not a simple trade-off among individuals in different racial groups, but rather a patriotic effort by all Americans to hasten the day when we can truly say that we have become a color-blind nation." Most people appeared willing to accept the need for affirmative action when they understood the policy in this way. Public opinion polls showed that the majority of Americans opposed initiatives that were described as "quotas" and "racial preferences" but supported efforts to increase employment and educational opportunities for members of groups that had historically been treated unequally. In 1997 a ballot initiative aimed at ending minority contract set-asides in Houston, Texas, failed to pass after the city council reworded the proposition to ask voters if they wanted to end "affirmative action for minorities and women" instead of whether they wanted to ban "preferential treatment." Supporters of set-asides also ran a series of television advertisements during the campaign that highlighted the racial progress of the past few decades. One spot featured Mayor Bob Lanier explaining that white men secured 95–99 percent of city contracts before affirmative action and they currently still received 80 percent. "Let's not turn back the clock to the days when guys like me got all the business," he urged voters.[47] In Houston and other American communities, citizens responded favorably to affirmative action when it was placed in historical context and its purpose clearly explained.

People on both sides of the debate believed the election of the nation's first African American president in 2008 vindicated their position. Proponents of affirmative action programs saw evidence of their effectiveness in the new willingness of millions of white Americans to cast their votes for a black man. The young voters and grassroots organizers who propelled the Obama campaign came of age in an era when it was normal to encounter African Americans as college students, professors, doctors, lawyers, journalists, government officials, and in other skilled professions, so they were more open than previous generations had been to the idea of a black president. Meanwhile, opponents of affirmative action interpreted Obama's success as proof that the programs were no longer necessary. Ward Connerly argued that white voters' support for Obama showed that the United States was not a racist nation and affirmative action was "an idea whose time has passed." Connerly considered the election results a potent new weapon in ballot initiatives planned for 2010 that aimed to ban the practice in Arizona and Missouri. "We will say, 'How do you account for the election of Barack Obama?'" he stated.[48]

Obama's victory had significance far beyond its meaning for African Americans or the implications for race-conscious employment practices. Affirmative action was a valuable tool for overcoming systemic racism but remained an inadequate solution to the unemployment and poverty that afflicted millions of white Americans as well as poor black people. Many participants in the interracial progressive movement that formed the basis for Obama's election campaign believed it was time to return to the broader visions for social justice that characterized the 1960s. The new president's call for Americans to recognize their "individual responsibility *and* mutual responsibility" for solving the nation's problems expressed the aspirations of activists who struggled to ensure economic inclusion and democratic participation for all citizens in the late twentieth century.

★ **6** ★

IS THIS AMERICA? ELECTORAL POLITICS
AFTER THE VOTING RIGHTS ACT

You don't have to be crazy to be a mayor. But it helps. And to be a Black mayor, you really have to almost be a masochist. (Maynard Jackson, 1976)[1]

In August 1964 civil rights activist Fannie Lou Hamer testified before the Credentials Committee at the Democratic national convention in an attempt to persuade party leaders to seat delegates of the interracial Mississippi Freedom Democratic Party instead of those chosen by the white supremacists who controlled the regular state party. After describing the beatings, murders, and other violence that met black people's attempts to participate in the political process in Mississippi, Hamer stated, "If the Freedom Democratic Party is not seated now, I question America. Is this America, the land of the free and the home of the brave, where we have to sleep with our telephones off of the hooks because our lives be threatened daily because we want to live as decent human beings, in America?"[2]

The efforts of Hamer and other black southerners who risked their lives in the voter registration campaigns of the early 1960s bore fruit a year later when President Lyndon Johnson signed the Voting Rights Act into law. This achievement did not automatically assure full citizenship for African Americans, however. The road to meaningful participation in the nation's political life lay strewn with obstacles, necessitating new battles to ensure that African Americans gained representation in government. Opponents of the freedom movement circumvented voting rights legislation with new measures designed to limit black political influence. Characteristics of the American electoral system that hindered participation by poor people also interfered with African Americans' ability to make their voices heard at election time. When black people were elected to public office they found their ability to enact reforms hamstrung by structural limits on their power as well as concerted attempts to undermine and intimidate black political leaders. Even as the landmark voting rights legislation empowered African Americans, the struggle to fulfill its promise revealed weaknesses in the nation's democracy that raised the question again: Is this America?

Black Political Empowerment and White Resistance

The Voting Rights Act outlawed the literacy tests and other practices southern states had used to prevent African Americans from voting and allowed for federal registrars to be sent to counties where few black people had been able to register in the past. To prevent racist lawmakers from devising new ways of disfranchising black voters, Section 5 of the act required states and political subdivisions that had a history of discrimination to submit any proposed new election procedures for approval by the Justice Department. The legislation's impact on voter registration rates for black southerners was immediate and dramatic. In Mississippi, the proportion of eligible black voters who were registered increased from 5 percent in 1960 to 61 percent in 1976. Over the same period the number of African Americans registered to vote in all 11 southern states grew from 1.5 million to 4 million.[3]

Civil rights activists knew that massive black voter registration alone could not topple the segregationist social order in the South. Black southerners needed to learn the mechanics of the electoral system to secure political power and gain a voice in the decisions that affected their lives. In 1966 SEDFRE initiated a leadership development program designed to teach African Americans how to use the democratic tools made available by the Voting Rights Act to maximum effect. Local activists attended SEDFRE workshops to learn how to build political organizations, run candidates for office, and win elections. Prospective candidates received instruction on every aspect of the process, from printing campaign leaflets to getting out the vote and monitoring polling places on election day. SEDFRE also worked to develop "citizen leaders" among those who were not interested in running for office but stood ready to pressure local officials to respond to their concerns. This approach was in keeping with the philosophy of grassroots organizing that influenced SNCC and CORE's work among black southerners in the early 1960s. As veterans of those earlier efforts, SEDFRE activists knew that real social change came from the bottom up rather than through the actions of a few charismatic leaders or elected officials. Leadership development workshops empowered ordinary people to influence political decisions by showing them how government worked and encouraging regular communication (through protests, if necessary) with their representatives.

In the late 1960s and early 1970s SEDFRE trained thousands of local activists in hundreds of communities across the nation. As African Americans

were elected to public office SEDFRE followed up its leadership development initiatives with programs to assist newly elected black officials.
Executive director Marvin Rich explained, "We helped to get some of these
people elected simply by showing them methods of campaigning. Now they
want help in functioning more effectively in their new responsibilities."
SEDFRE offered training and technical assistance to dozens of first-time
mayors, school board members, aldermen, and state legislators to make
sure they understood their public duties. The organization also researched
and disseminated information to black elected officials regarding resources
that were available from federal agencies to support infrastructure improvements, public services, and other economic development projects in their
communities. This help proved invaluable to black office holders, whose
white predecessors frequently refused to orient them to their new positions
and who often contended with undisguised hostility from colleagues and
administrators.[4]

The thought of African Americans voting and holding office frightened
many white Americans. Their views regarding black people's political skills
were shaped by horror stories of Reconstruction that falsely depicted the
nineteenth-century experiment in interracial democracy as an exercise in
general incompetence and misrule. More importantly, wealthy citizens who
enjoyed cozy relationships with elected officials and frequently shaped
policy according to their own economic interests worried about disruptions
to the system if new actors entered the field. As Victor Ullman noted in the
Nation, the election of black southerners to political office could force white
people to relinquish their monopoly over the region's resources and share
its bounty more evenly with their African American neighbors. Mississippi
senator and plantation owner James Eastland, for example, owned thousands of acres of rich Delta land that had a market value of $400 or $500
an acre but was appraised by the county tax assessor at only $3.14 an acre.
"Suppose the current Sunflower County tax assessor ... were to be defeated
for re-election and a Negro tax assessor elected by Sunflower County's
8,000 registered Negro voters," Ullman speculated. "Would there be a tax
reappraisal of those 5,000 Eastland acres?" Scenarios such as this prompted
one white Mississippian to advocate "lawful resistance from now on, organized on every level, in order to prevent Negro political domination."[5]

Resistance to black political empowerment took both lawful and unlawful forms. Threats, intimidation, and violence against African Americans
who tried to participate in the electoral process continued well beyond the
1960s. *Newsweek* reported in August 1971 that three black people had
been murdered in Mississippi in what seemed like a warning against political activity during preparations for state and local elections later that year.
A black candidate in the town of Moss Point who announced plans to
request a recount after losing a primary election in 1973 received a phone

call from a man suggesting that he reconsider. "He knew where my little girl went to school ... who picked her up and what time she got out of school ... and I had best not cause any trouble," the candidate stated. Residents of Port Gibson noted that registering to vote was a simple and fast process for white people in the town but for African Americans it could take hours to complete. Questions asked of black applicants resembled an "interrogation" and included unrelated inquiries such as "Do you own the house you're staying in?" and "Does your employer know you're registering to vote?" Such tactics raised the specter of evictions or job losses and aimed to dissuade black people from registering. A study undertaken by the Commission on Civil Rights in 1981 found that "economic and physical reprisals for voting or for assisting others to vote" continued to pose problems for African Americans in many communities.[6]

White officials also acted to limit black political influence through "second generation" disfranchising measures designed to annul black votes. In the late 1960s legislators in many states enacted new election laws that, given most white people's refusal to vote for any black candidate, made it impossible for African Americans to be elected to public office. Counties that were subdivided into smaller political units for the purposes of electing county supervisors and school boards switched to at-large elections to avoid the possibility of African Americans being elected from majority-black districts. Elected positions such as school superintendent were changed to appointed positions in many communities. Many states gerrymandered political districts to break up concentrations of African American voters and weaken black political power. Mississippi, for example, adopted a congressional redistricting plan in 1966 that sliced up the state's Second District and dissolved its mostly black population into districts where African Americans were outnumbered by white voters. Representatives of the previously much whiter First District who opposed the measure knew their colleagues were deliberately seeking to dilute black voting strength and warned of legal challenges the state could face if it adopted the plan. "We all know the Negro situation was the main factor," Representative Odie Trenor asserted. According to the *Jackson Clarion-Ledger*, "Backers of the plan did not deny that the Delta area was split up to divide the heavy Negro vote."[7]

Battles in the Courts

States did not submit these changes to the Justice Department for approval because they did not directly affect the right to vote. In the context of racial bloc voting, however, the new laws meant black people's votes were much less likely to lead to the election of their chosen representatives than white people's votes were. Civil rights activists argued that vote dilution was prohibited under the Voting Rights Act and engaged in legal action to force adherence to the law. Black voters in several states filed lawsuits challenging discriminatory election rules, and in *Allen v. State Board of Elections* (1969) the Supreme Court considered whether new regulations adopted by Mississippi and Virginia were covered by voting rights legislation. Attorneys from the Lawyers' Committee argued convincingly that the Voting Rights Act was intended to protect African Americans against exactly the kinds of subterfuges the state governments had undertaken, leading the Court to decide that the Section 5 preclearance provision applied to "any state enactment which altered the election law of a covered State in even a minor way." In *White v. Regester* (1973) the Supreme Court extended the reach of voting rights law further by ruling that at-large elections violated the equal protection clause of the Fourteenth Amendment if their effects were to deny black or Latino voters the chance to elect "legislators of their choice." These rulings blocked the advance of second generation disfranchising measures and cracked open the closed election systems that had deprived African Americans of opportunities to serve in public office. Nationwide, the number of black elected officials at all levels of government increased from 1,469 to 4,890 between 1970 and 1980.[8]

The 1980s and 1990s saw the Supreme Court reverse course on the issue of voting rights. *City of Mobile v. Bolden* (1980) overturned a district judge's finding that at-large elections for the city commission and school board implemented before 1965 were discriminatory because they effectively ensured no black candidates were ever elected. The higher court ruled that unequal effects were an inadequate standard for demonstrating a violation of the law and that plaintiffs must also show discriminatory intent. Although lawyers in the *Mobile* case eventually did prove the system purposely denied African Americans representation in government, demonstrating racist intent was difficult and expensive. Civil rights groups successfully lobbied Congress to restore the effects standard that the courts had assumed in earlier interpretations of the Voting Rights Act. In 1982 legislators extended Section 5 for 25 years and reworded Section 2 to make clear that the effects of an election change could be used to determine whether discrimination had occurred.[9]

These amendments, subsequent court rulings, and the partisan interests of legislators encouraged some states to actively create electoral districts in which members of racial minorities were the majority. Minority-majority districts greatly enhanced black candidates' chances of being elected and generated significant increases in the number of black office holders in the 1990s. In the first half of the decade the number of African American congressional representatives jumped from 26 to 41. Another 563 black people served in state legislatures, and 7,781 held local office. At the same time, however, minority-majority districts came under attack from analysts who viewed them as unconstitutional and immoral. Abigail Thernstrom, for example, argued that the Voting Rights Act only protected the right to vote and was not meant to guarantee the election of black people to political office. In *Shaw v. Reno* (1993) the Supreme Court sided with white plaintiffs in North Carolina who thought the creation of two minority-majority districts in the state's congressional redistricting plan violated voters' right to a colorblind election process. In a decision that was widely criticized by legal scholars for its disingenuous and contradictory reasoning, the Court denounced minority-majority districts as a form of "political apartheid" that attempted "to segregate the races for the purposes of voting." As J. Morgan Kousser noted in *Colorblind Injustice* (1999), the ruling ignored a long history of "racial and partisan gerrymandering" for the purpose of limiting black political power that most white Americans had never seen fit to challenge. The only thing different about the redistricting plans of the early 1990s was that, for the first time, they empowered nonwhite voters.[10]

    Shaw and subsequent court rulings essentially halted the creation of new minority-majority districts and allowed the redrawing of existing districts to restore white majorities. Despite some observers' assertions that racism no longer affected voting patterns and that black candidates' problems stemmed from their politics not their skin color, civil rights activists were justifiably concerned by the loss of districting mechanisms that had played a crucial role in increasing black representation in government. Most white Americans in the late twentieth century were not ready to cast their ballots for African Americans who ran for public office regardless of party affiliations or policy positions. Throughout the 1970s and 1980s black mayors of major cities typically won with more than 90 percent of the African American vote and less than 20 percent of white residents' support. David Lublin's study of congressional elections between 1972 and 1994 found that, controlling for a range of other variables, racial demographics almost always predicted electoral outcomes. Out of 5,079 elections Lublin examined, African Americans won in districts with white majorities only 72 times. As late as 2008, racial prejudices influenced the preferences of many voters in the presidential election. During the close contest for the Democratic nomination between Hillary Clinton and Barack Obama, journalist JoAnn Wypijewski reported on a conversation she had with some Clinton supporters in Springfield, Ohio. One man vowed to campaign for Republican John McCain if Obama became the Democratic nominee. Asked why, the man stated that Obama was "too inexperienced." Pressed by his friends for further explanation, the man finally admitted the real reason he could not support Obama: "Because he's black."[11]

Challenges Facing Black Elected Officials

Convincing nervous constituents that the world would not fall apart if they were governed by a black city council, a black mayor, or a black president was an uphill battle that continued even after African Americans were elected to office. Attempts to address the long-neglected needs of poor people or open access to government jobs and contracts to African Americans were construed by some residents as "antibusiness" or "antiwhite" actions. In Cleveland, Ohio, white law enforcement officers accused Mayor Carl Stokes of "political pandering" when he tried to introduce reforms to cut down on police brutality. Black leaders who rejected the advice of white officials and instead implemented their own initiatives invited charges that they were "arrogant." Most African American officials took care to emphasize that they did not seek to replace white dominance with black dominance and only wanted to share power and resources more evenly. For white leaders accustomed to monopolizing political decision making, though, power sharing represented a loss of control. Political scientist Adolph Reed Jr. observed that in cities like Atlanta, Georgia, where the white business leadership chose government officials from among their peers and set policy within the plush confines of their private clubs before the 1960s, "the election of any black mayor ... would have increased the degree of inconvenience suffered by elites, if only by forcing them to venture into City Hall to conduct those of their affairs that involved the public sector."[12]

Many white people were convinced that the election of black people to public office spelled certain doom for their communities. During a mayoral race in Detroit that pitted African American Richard Austin against a "law and order" candidate who manipulated white racial fears to win a narrow victory in 1969, one resident wrote to Austin stating, "All you BLACKS know how to do is have illegitimate children, drink, tear up schools, rob, rape, and constantly expect to get handouts from tax-paying whites! If by any fluke you become mayor of Detroit, you will be mayor of a dung heap because any WHITE who is able to do so will move out." After Coleman Young was elected mayor of the city in 1973, thousands of white residents fled to the suburbs, depriving the new black administration of badly needed tax dollars, businesses, and jobs. White flight also accelerated in Gary, Indiana, after Richard Hatcher assumed the mayor's office in 1968. The white suburb of Merrillville incorporated as a separate entity after state legislators granted an exemption from a law that prohibited suburban areas from incorporating, and residents of Glen Park also lobbied for de-annexation from the city. The local newspaper stopped using the name of the city on its masthead and often printed stories that were critical of the mayor's initiatives. Hatcher faced additional opposition from Gary's Chamber of Commerce and its main industrial employer, U.S. Steel, both of which fought the mayor's efforts to raise tax revenues to pay for economic development projects and social services.[13]

White hostility added to the already daunting tasks that faced black elected officials of the post-civil rights era. The transformation of the nation's largest cities from booming manufacturing centers to postindustrial basket cases was well under way by the late 1960s. Many urban black mayors assumed leadership of their communities under circumstances that resembled clean-up crews after a wild party where guests had trashed the premises and made off with every bit of furniture in the house. Deindustrialization and job losses, suburban secession, declining tax bases, growing populations of poor people, and cuts in federal assistance challenged the abilities of the most talented administrators. In Gary, the number of downtown businesses dropped from 500 in 1960 to 40 in 1979. Between 1967 and 1982 Chicago, Detroit, and Philadelphia each lost roughly half of their manufacturing jobs. By the time black mayor David Dinkins took office in New York in 1990 the city had a one billion dollar deficit, 75,000 homeless people, and a need for 250,000 more housing units. Schools, hospitals, and other social services were inadequately funded, and deteriorating roads, bridges, and water mains looked ready to crumble. Hamstrung by financial constraints and powerless to solve problems that lay largely beyond their control, black mayors were often attacked for mismanagement, even though white mayors of declining cities fared no better.[14]

Black elected officials in the rural South also faced significant challenges. In Uniontown, Alabama, a community of just over 2,000 people where two-thirds of the residents were black and poor, African Americans were excluded from the political process and from the provision of government services until black mayor Andrew Hayden and three black city council members were elected in 1972. The new administration was eager to address the inadequacies in housing, employment, education, health services, and infrastructure that plagued the town. Sixty percent of homes were classed as substandard and many people lived in houses without running water or indoor toilets. Sewage systems were primitive, streets were unpaved, and garbage collection was non-existent in black neighborhoods. Many residents suffered from malnutrition. The schools were starved of funds and offered a less than basic education devoid of laboratory science, music, art, or vocational programs. In one school the principal paid for paper himself and rationed it to students.

Uniontown's black voters hoped to end the racism and neglect that created these conditions when they elected the newly integrated city council, but Hayden and his colleagues were frustrated in their efforts to implement reforms because of debts they inherited from the previous administration. Tiny Uniontown owed $1.5 million dollars to creditors located as far away as Boston and California. According to one account, some of these people "operated with unprecedented zeal" to demand repayment immediately after Hayden took office. Even after the council spent half of its federal revenue sharing funds on debt reduction, a substantial amount of money remained outstanding. "Because of the inherited fiscal problems, natural priorities arising from the election mandate have necessarily been submerged in unnatural priorities arising from creditor pressures," noted a report prepared by SEDFRE in April 1973. "Whereas an expansive program is needed by the community, a fiscally conservative program has been dictated by financial realities."[15] Like their big city counterparts, black political leaders in small southern communities struggled to secure even modest improvements for their constituents within the bounds dictated by economic circumstances.

White voters who feared that political empowerment of African Americans would lead to significant policy shifts or a redistribution of resources need not have worried. Black people might control the government but white Americans controlled the wealth, and it did not take long for most black elected officials to realize that they remained junior partners to the nation's business leaders when it came to making decisions about the direction of their communities. The case of Atlanta illustrates this dynamic. White political dominance over the city was broken in 1973 with the election of Maynard Jackson to the mayor's office. Jackson received 95 percent of the black vote and the support of a few white moderates, including some key corporate backers such as the chairmen of the Coca Cola Company and the city's two largest banks. One banker explained, "I'd always been persuaded that Maynard was going to be elected. So I thought somebody in the business community better get behind this guy so that we'd have a line of communication."[16]

Jackson attempted to balance the needs of African American constituents against the priorities of the city's business elite within the context of what he called "exaggerated black expectations" combined with "exaggerated white anxiety." Initiatives aimed at increasing grassroots participation in decision making and improving social services to poor people met with hostile reactions from business owners and developers who believed city funds were better spent on the construction of shopping malls, convention centers, and other projects to revitalize downtown Atlanta. Aware that he could not afford to alienate corporate supporters and persuaded that business-friendly policies were necessary to create jobs and attract outside investment to the city, Jackson soon began diverting resources away from black neighborhoods to focus on rebuilding the central business district. Rather than generating jobs for African Americans, however, the construction projects more often tore up communities and displaced black residents while skilled workers imported from outside Atlanta reaped the benefits of the employment opportunities that were generated.[17]

Despite the demonstrated limits of policies that provided government subsidies to corporate elites in hopes of improving conditions for poor people, Jackson's successor Andrew Young continued the business-oriented approach. Immediately after his election in 1981 Young sought the cooperation of the city's business leaders, telling them, "I didn't get elected with your help, but I can't govern without you." Young informed constituents who were concerned about the city's growing poverty and inequality that government intervention was not the solution to social problems. "Politics doesn't control the world," he stated. "Money does. ... If you want to bring about what we preachers preach about – feeding the hungry, clothing the naked, healing the sick – it's going to be done in the free market system."[18]

Elected officials who demonstrated too much ideological independence from the prevailing economic assumptions risked sharp truncations of their political careers. In 1971 black Republican Charles Freeman Joseph was elected mayor of Benton Harbor, Michigan, a community with a population that was 80 percent African American located in a county that was 80 percent white. According to Joseph, the county was the northern equivalent of a southern plantation and completely controlled by "the Chamber of Commerce, Whirlpool Corporation, and an all-white industrial and business organization called the Area Resources Improvement Council." Whirlpool's executives chose or served as the political leadership and appointed their associates to the boards and commissions that determined who profited from economic development efforts. Schools and neighborhoods in Benton Harbor were segregated, and local taxes as well as federal funds were spent mostly in white communities. By the late 1960s the city was in a state of advanced decay. One-fourth of its population was unemployed and 38 percent of its housing was substandard. Nearly half of the town's residents depended on public assistance. Those African Americans who were lucky enough to have jobs were largely confined to low-paid work in white households and factories. When black people began to demand action from their local officials, white leaders turned to Joseph. "The white power structure ... thought I was the kind of person who would play the role of a 'spook by the door,' " he stated. "They felt that if anybody could control people in the community ... maybe I was that person." When Joseph instead began speaking out against the system and calling attention to the plight of poor black people, the county's real rulers responded with a concerted and ultimately successful effort to remove him from office.

During the four years he served as mayor, Joseph was "under constant daily attack and pressure." The local newspaper offered only negative accounts of his reform programs, and the Chamber of Commerce sabotaged efforts to secure federal funding for antipoverty projects by writing to government agencies to ask them not to approve grants to Benton Harbor. Banks encouraged many businesses to relocate to the suburbs by refusing to make loans in the city. Council members who opposed Joseph's plans disrupted meetings and the police placed the mayor under surveillance in an attempt to find evidence of illegal activity. Citizens who supported him were threatened with evictions, the loss of jobs or welfare benefits, denial of credit, and home foreclosures. Anonymous callers harassed Joseph and his family with threats of physical violence. Finally, after Joseph and his allies on the council voted not to renew the city manager's contract in December 1975, disaffected factions charged the mayor with official mal-feasance and organized a recall referendum. The effort succeeded amidst a vicious media campaign, efforts to bribe voters, and intimidation of Joseph's supporters at the polls. "I no longer believe the American system is what I thought it was," Joseph wrote in an account of his ordeal. "Democracy will never be in this country until we have a generation of people disassociated from money and power. ... It is time for us to stand up and tell big business to stop running our governments."[19]

Mayor Joseph's experience was not unusual. A study by Mary Warner of the National Association of Human Rights Workers uncovered similar treatment of black elected officials across the nation in the mid-1970s. Dozens of African American office holders ranging from commissioners of small southern towns to United States congressional representatives encoun-tered one or more of the techniques deployed by Joseph's enemies in Benton Harbor: media bias; obstruction of legislative agendas; false charges of corruption; surveillance by law enforcement agencies; bribes; threats; and other forms of intimidation. Cleveland mayor Carl Stokes reported: "I was investigated by everyone from Cleveland's lowliest Polish housewife to the highest agencies of the United States government: my own Police Department, all the Cleveland area newspapers, the strike force set up to fight organized crime, the Justice Department, the Internal Revenue Service, were all in Cleveland and anywhere I'd ever been, investigating me because of rumors, allegations and accusations."[20]

Black politicians were not immune to the temptations of power, and investigations into their activities sometimes uncovered genuine abuses. In most cases, though, investigators found no evidence of illegal activity or uncovered only minor infractions that were the result of innocent over-sights. Maryland state senator Clarence Mitchell suffered through several years of scrutiny by the Internal Revenue Service (IRS) and the Justice Department before it was determined that he had not engaged in any tax evasion and that the federal government instead owed him $234. Congressional representatives Shirley Chisholm and Ralph Metcalfe were similarly vindicated after being accused of official misconduct. Between 1969 and 1975 the nation's taxpayers funded more than one hundred IRS audits and other probes into the activities of black elected officials that ended with the charges being dropped for lack of evidence. The eventual exonerations, often not reported by the media after months of coverage that essentially declared black officials guilty, could not undo the damage done to elected leaders' reputations and their relationships with constituents. Many survivors either lost their positions to challengers or chose not to run for office in subsequent elections.[21]

The racial and political motivations that lay behind some of these investigations of black elected officials were hard to miss. When Georgia state representative Henrietta Canty visited her local IRS office to challenge the $14 the agency said she owed, a staff member greeted her saying, "Mrs. Canty, you too? They're auditing all our black politicians." Tax audits of Fayette mayor Charles Evers and more than two dozen other black leaders in Mississippi prompted an editorial in the *Winston County Journal* that stated, "This does smack of harassment and makes one wonder just how the IRS is motivated." Evers viewed the investigations as representing "the same kind of obstacle Blacks have always had to fight ... First they came at us with guns and crosses, then they tried to steal our elections, and now it's the IRS." The extent and the recurring patterns that were evident in reports of abuse led Congressman William Clay to charge that an organized conspiracy existed to "undermine, humiliate, jail, and destroy black leaders who dared challenge a repressive and unresponsive racist society."[22]

Historian Derek Musgrove's analysis of such claims found that although black leaders may have exaggerated the sinister implications of their experiences, the perception that they were being unfairly singled out for attention had some basis in reality. Many African Americans were elected to office at a time when the public's confidence in politicians was shaken by the Watergate scandal and this partially accounts for the overly suspicious treatment they received from the media and law enforcement agencies. At the same time, some Republicans sought to undermine their political opposition by accusing black Democrats and other detractors of corruption. In the Nixon era black elected officials were caught up in the president's broad abuses of power and his attempts to destroy his critics on the left. The Reagan and George H. W. Bush administrations also used federal law enforcement agencies to target their enemies. In the 1980s and early 1990s black elected officials were five times more likely than white political leaders to come under investigation by government authorities. Musgrove concluded that efforts to paint black elected officials as unfit for office were a continuation of powerful white southerners' resistance to the civil rights movement and aimed to prevent a reemergence of the progressive political coalitions of the 1960s.[23]

Despite these challenges, the number of African Americans serving in public office increased steadily in the late twentieth century, reaching 9,430 in 2002. Within the fiscal and ideological limits of the times, the black leaders of small southern towns and declining industrial cities faced challenges that often proved insurmountable. Nonetheless, modest improvements in housing, education, and employment made a real difference in some black people's lives. Richard Hatcher was unable to stem white flight and business disinvestment in Gary, but the policies he implemented benefited constituents like the senior citizens who moved into newly built low-cost housing, the young people who participated in job training programs, and the welfare mother who was included in urban planning under the Model Cities program and went on to become a state legislator. The employment of more African Americans in government positions, awarding of city contracts to minority businesses, and improvements in law enforcement in many communities also represented significant advances. The greater accessibility of black elected officials compared to white political leaders in previous administrations made it easier for constituents to air grievances and pressure governments to act. As Adolph Reed Jr. noted, "Objectives that not very long ago required storming city council meetings – for example, getting streets paved, street lights or stop signs emplaced – can now be met through routine processes."[24]

Institutional Obstacles to Political Participation

At the state and national levels, black legislators' ability to move policy in a progressive direction was constricted by their minority status within governing bodies and the Democratic Party's rightward drift after the 1960s. With help from supportive white representatives, African Americans could sometimes secure enough votes to pass measures that benefited poor people, such as the extension of federal minimum wage legislation to cover domestic workers in 1974. In Mississippi, black representatives found allies among some of the younger, moderate white political leaders and managed to implement educational reforms and improve access to health care for low-income families in the 1980s. Such coalitions became harder to forge as New Democrats who viewed association with "black" issues as a political liability gained influence within the party. Republicans' hostility toward the freedom struggle meant they were unlikely to attract many black votes, so Democrats took African Americans' support for granted and worked to break down their own image among white Americans as the party of "special interests." Jesse Jackson expressed the frustration many black people felt regarding the lack of political options when he stated, "It doesn't matter to us whether we're riding on a donkey or an elephant if both of them are walking slowly and going the wrong direction."[25]

Jackson set out to convince the Democratic Party to change its ways by running for president in 1984 and again in 1988. Although he knew victory in the party primaries was unlikely, he thought his candidacy might boost

African American political participation and force party leaders to pay more attention to black people's concerns. Jackson aimed to build a "Rainbow Coalition" of the dispossessed that included ethnic minorities, women, and working-class white people who were suffering along with African Americans in the Reagan era. "Just as we displaced racial violence, we must replace economic violence with economic justice," he explained. Jackson cited plant closings, corporate greed, unemployment, homelessness, and cuts in social services as examples of economic violence and urged people to join together to challenge policies that privileged the wealthiest Americans over most other citizens (see Figure 6.1).[26]

Jackson's message resonated with many black Democrats and they turned out in large numbers to vote for him in the primary elections. To most white voters, however, Jackson was "the black candidate" representing ideas they had repudiated when they elected Reagan in 1980. White southern support for the Republican Party solidified in the 1984 elections, the promise of an interracial grassroots movement was not realized, and the campaign degenerated into what many perceived as a personal quest for power by Jesse Jackson. Democratic Party leaders were not persuaded

Figure 6.1 Jesse Jackson with members of United Rubber Workers Local 310 in Des Moines, Iowa, 1988
Source: Jim Wilson/*New York Times*

to renew their commitment to racial equality and economic justice, responding instead with token concessions to Jackson and an even more cautious policy agenda shaped by the DLC. In 1988, Jackson's victories over Massachusetts governor Michael Dukakis in several early primaries alarmed some powerful Democrats and sparked what one analyst called a "de facto 'Stop Jesse Movement.'" After securing the nomination Dukakis ran as a centrist, distancing himself from African Americans and refraining from actively seeking their support until the last few weeks of the election. The party's treatment of Jackson and Dukakis' lukewarm outreach efforts dampened black voter turnout in the general election and resulted in four more years of Republican rule under George H. W. Bush.[27]

Other factors in addition to the sense that neither major political party was really interested in advancing the freedom struggle had the effect of suppressing black participation in elections in the post-civil rights era. Paradoxically for a nation that saw itself as a model of democracy for the rest of the world, voting in the United States was not a simple endeavor. Apart from age and citizenship requirements, no consistent, nationwide election rules existed. State and local governments developed their own procedures and required a certain amount of effort on the part of voters. In many other nations people were automatically registered by their governments when they reached voting age, but Americans enjoyed no such coddling. Citizens had to learn about eligibility requirements, registration procedures and deadlines, and locations for registering largely on their own. Voters in many communities were further inconvenienced when they found that registrars' offices were closed outside of regular working hours. Changing residencies sometimes necessitated learning a new set of rules and going through the whole procedure all over again. On election day voters had to make sure they went to the correct polling place and provide proof of their identity if it was required. Depending on staffing levels and the availability of voting booths, they might then wait in line for hours before being able to cast their ballots. The primary elections and run-off elections that often preceded general elections meant multiple trips to the polls for citizens who wanted to have their preferences recorded in every phase of the process.[28]

None of this presented major obstacles to educated, middle-class Americans who owned cars and could afford to take time off work to register or vote. For many poor, elderly, and disabled citizens, however, the system posed significant barriers to participation. Economic disparities between white and black Americans meant that there were racial disparities in voting as well. In *Tyranny of the Majority* (1994) Lani Guinier outlined how these inequalities affected elections in Phillips County, Arkansas. Forty-two percent of African Americans in this rural community did not own cars compared with 9 percent of white residents. Thirty percent of black residents did not have phones compared with 11 percent of white people. There was no public transportation system in the county and paying for a taxi or a ride from neighbors or friends was expensive. Black residents' poverty posed difficulties to participation in all aspects of the electoral process both for voters and the candidates seeking to represent them. Without easy means of communicating with residents and getting them to the registrar's office or the polls, tasks like organizing volunteers, fundraising, canvassing, registering people, and getting out the vote on election day were formidable challenges. On the other side, these same factors made it easy for election officials seeking to discourage black voting to manipulate the process to their own advantage. In the 1980s polling places in Phillips County were moved "ten times in as many elections, often without prior notice and sometimes to locations up to twelve to fifteen miles away, over dirt and gravel roads." The county's run-off election requirement, necessitating two efforts to turn out voters in two weeks, added to black candidates' problems.[29]

The correlations between blackness and economic disadvantage meant that election rules that seemed neutral, practical, and fair often had the effect of suppressing black political participation. The run-offs mandated in many southern communities if no candidate received a majority of the vote in the first primary election were supposed to ensure that the eventual winner was elected with support from a majority of voters. Yet this rule was a major obstacle to black electoral victories and did not always realize its ostensibly democratic goal. Turnout often dropped between the first and second elections, and the victor in the second primary could win with fewer votes than were cast for the winner of a plurality in the earlier election. African Americans in Phillips County viewed the mechanism as simply a way for white people to "steal" elections, and the feeling that the system was rigged against them dampened many black people's enthusiasm for exercising their political rights. Local activist Julious McGruder contended that African Americans' sense of permanent exclusion smothered "all of the hope, all of the faith, the belief in the system."[30]

Felony disfranchisement laws were another means through which black political influence was weakened in the post-civil rights era. Most states restricted voting rights in some way for people convicted of serious crimes, and in many cases the punishment was extended beyond the years offenders spent in prison. In 48 states prisoners could not vote. Thirty-six states restricted the voting rights of people who were on probation or parole, and 13 states revoked felons' voting rights for life. These laws, combined with mass incarceration policies and racism in the criminal justice system, resulted in the disfranchisement of hundreds of thousands of black Americans. By the early twenty-first century one in 12 black adults was not allowed to vote. For black men living in states that permanently disfranchised felons the figure was one in four. Their physical presence, however, still counted for the purpose of determining the number of representatives accorded to political districts after each decennial census. In a situation that paralleled the effects of the three-fifths clause during slavery, the rural white communities where many prisons were located benefited from overrepresentation in government while the inner-city neighborhoods that were the main targets of the war on crime were further disadvantaged politically. In New York state, for example, 38 new prisons were built in the 1980s and 1990s, all located in sparsely populated, heavily white and Republican districts.[31] The federal funds and political strength that came with these facilities, along with the removal of a large and mostly Democratic-leaning segment of the electorate, provided incentives for some politicians to continue with the tough crime policies that sent large numbers of black Americans to jail in the post-civil rights era.

Political motivations were also apparent in debates over initiatives to make voting easier in the decades after 1965. High voter turnout, especially by low-income and minority groups, favored Democratic candidates. In contrast, Republican interests were served by discouraging poorer people from voting. Paul Weyrich, a leader in the movement to mobilize social conservatives in support of Ronald Reagan and other candidates who shared their values, explained: "I don't want everybody to vote. ... As a matter of fact, our leverage in the elections, quite candidly, goes up as the voting populace goes down." When President Jimmy Carter proposed legislation allowing election-day registration for federal elections, Republicans in Congress killed the plan, arguing that pre-registration was necessary to prevent voter fraud.[32] In 1992 George H. W. Bush also cited concerns about fraud when he vetoed a bill requiring states to encourage people to register to vote when they applied for drivers' licenses or government benefits. According to the *New York Times*, however, the 29 states that already had such registration procedures had seen "no recorded increase in cheating." Congress tried again the following year, and after supporters defeated efforts to filibuster the legislation President Bill Clinton signed the National Voter Registration ("Motor Voter") Act into law.[33]

The concerns about fraud expressed by opponents of electoral reform were not entirely unfounded. In two separate surveys of the history of elections in the United States from the colonial era to the early twenty-first century, historian Tracy Campbell and journalist Andrew Gumbel both concluded that unlawful or unethical manipulation of the democratic process was an American tradition.[34] Republican fears that Democrats might take advantage of relaxed voting rules to register non-citizens, criminals, dead people, and pets were understandable because it had all happened before. Neither party was innocent of past misconduct, however, and attempts to steal elections in the post-civil rights era more often involved suppressing turnout by legitimately registered voters rather than encouraging participation by people who were ineligible. Under the guise of preventing voter fraud, Republican operatives engaged in thinly veiled efforts to discourage African Americans and other nonwhite citizens from voting. Though adamant that these measures aimed only to protect the democratic process and not to suppress black votes, the Republican National Committee agreed to suspend its "ballot integrity" program in 1986 in response to a lawsuit and the public disclosure of an internal memo that cast doubt on its intentions. In the congressional races that year, a party leader in the Midwest urged southern associates to initiate a ballot integrity drive before the primary elections in Louisiana. "I would guess that this program will eliminate at least 60–80,000 folks from the rolls," she wrote. "If it's a close race ... this could keep the black vote down considerably."[35]

Both the institutional disadvantages African Americans faced in the electoral system and deliberate vote suppression deprived Democratic politicians of a significant source of support. Throughout the late twentieth century African Americans reliably supported the party's candidates nine to one over their Republican opponents. In a close election, preventing even a small number of black people from casting ballots could significantly influence the outcome. In the 1980 presidential election Ronald Reagan won several southern states only because hundreds of thousands of African Americans in the region did not vote. Reagan's margin of victory in South Carolina, for example, was 11,456. The number of unregistered black voters in South Carolina was 292,000. Depressed levels of black political participation enabled Reagan to secure similarly narrow victories in Arkansas, Tennessee, Alabama, and Mississippi.[36] Republican political dominance in the late twentieth century arguably relied on fake electoral majorities resulting from systemic obstacles and partisan political tactics that limited democratic participation by large numbers of citizens.

Voting Rights Activism and Electoral Reform

Civil rights activists responded to these problems with efforts to overcome institutional barriers to voting and increase black political engagement. In the months before the general election in 1984 dozens of civil rights and social justice organizations including the NAACP, ACORN, labor unions, and student groups worked to massively increase voter registration among minorities and poor people in hopes of turning Reagan out of office. Canvassers deployed innovative techniques such as registering people at welfare offices and on public transportation as well as going door to door in low-income neighborhoods to sign up new voters. Some activists engaged in direct action techniques that were reminiscent of the 1960s. The NAACP organized a march from Richmond, Virginia, to New York City that registered 35,000 people along the route. The United States Student Association recruited hundreds of volunteers for its Freedom Summer '84 voter registration drive, reprising the efforts undertaken by college-aged activists in Mississippi 20 years earlier. ACORN members staged sit-ins at registrars' offices in Bridgeport, Connecticut, to protest local officials' refusal to deputize volunteers to register people. A lawsuit joined by ACORN and several other groups eventually forced the officials to capitulate, and legal action in seven other states upheld volunteers' right to canvass in the waiting rooms of government agencies. Nationwide, the campaign succeeded in adding 12 million more people to the electoral rolls.[37]

Activists also tried to level the political playing field for candidates who could not afford to spend thousands of dollars on election campaigns. In 1997 the Georgia State Conference of NAACP Branches requested a court order mandating publicly financed elections after a black candidate in a state senate race lost to a white opponent who outspent him $270,000 to $16,000. Plaintiffs argued that the electoral system disadvantaged poor people and violated the equal protection and free speech provisions of the Constitution. Recognizing that the problem extended beyond black and white to encompass broader issues of democracy and class inequality, veteran civil rights activist Charles Sherrod stated, "Fact is, it's no longer just a race thing. The vote knows nothing but green. That's the color that we've got to concentrate on." The federal district court in Atlanta denied the plaintiffs the right to bring the case. Even after Congress passed new national campaign finance regulations with the McCain-Feingold Act in 2002, money continued to play a major role in the outcome of American elections.[38]

In the absence of more fundamental electoral reforms, activists' best hope lay with massive grassroots mobilization efforts to register new voters and ensure that they got to the polls on election day. In the 2000 elections the NAACP created the National Voter Fund and initiated a major campaign that recruited 5,000 volunteers to work on voter registration and Get Out the Vote efforts in 17 states. That year more than 1 million more black Americans voted than had cast ballots in 1996, and 90 percent of them supported Democratic candidate Albert Gore. The increase in black participation was one of the factors behind an extremely close contest and high voter turnout in Florida that overwhelmed the state's election system on November 7. Had the resulting confusion not interfered with many citizens' attempts to vote, Gore might well have won the presidency.[39] Instead, a combination of inadequate resources, bureaucratic incompetence, socioeconomic disparities, and partisan maneuvering conspired to send George W. Bush to the White House.

The events in Florida in 2000 exposed the multitude of problems that existed in the nation's electoral system and their particular effects on black voters. The state had 25 electoral college votes, a Republican governor who was Bush's brother, a secretary of state who had campaigned for Bush and co-chaired his election campaign, and a long history of racism. In the months before the election a badly mismanaged purge of the voter rolls focusing mostly on removing convicted felons deleted the names of thousands of eligible citizens from county voter lists. At the same time, aggressive voter registration drives by both political parties added an unusually large number of people to the rolls. Already underfunded and understaffed, county election offices were unable to cope with the burdens of verifying voter lists, processing new registrations, and informing new voters about election procedures. Many people arrived at the polls to find that election officials had no record of their eligibility to vote. Citizens whose names were not on the voter lists were legally entitled to cast ballots by affidavit if permission was granted by the county election supervisor, and some were able to do so. More often, however, phone lines to supervisors' offices were jammed for hours, authorization was never received, and voters either left in frustration or were sent home after the polls closed without being allowed to cast ballots. Compounding the chaos surrounding the voter lists were problems caused by some counties' use of antiquated voting machines and confusing ballot designs. A total of 180,000 ballots cast in Florida were thrown out because of undervotes (no clear marking of the ballot) or overvotes (ballots recording votes for more than one candidate) that made voters' preferences difficult to determine.[40]

In the weeks following the election the Florida attorney general's office received 3,600 complaints from citizens who were wrongly denied the opportunity to vote or who observed other irregularities at the polls. Many others reported their experiences to civil rights groups, leading the NAACP to file a class-action lawsuit against the state's election officials. The Commission on Civil Rights also investigated allegations of vote suppression. In June 2001 the commission released a report that concluded, "Many eligible Florida voters were, in fact, denied their right to vote, with the disenfranchisement disproportionately affecting African Americans." Every problematic aspect of the election had a greater impact on black Floridians than on white citizens. African Americans were more likely than white citizens to be purged from voter rolls based on the inaccurate list of suspected felons and less likely to receive assistance from poll workers when their eligibility to vote was in question. A poll worker in Broward County reported seeing "mostly African American and Hispanic voters being turned away because their names did not appear on the rolls" and stated that the clerk at her station "did not communicate with the voters and did nothing to encourage them to vote." The state's black citizens were also concentrated in poor counties where funding inadequacies were most acute. This in turn affected the extent of voter education and outreach, the number of polling places and staffing levels on election day, and the quality of voting technology used to record and count ballots. Seventy percent of African Americans lived in counties that used the two least reliable types of voting machines (punch card machines and optical scan systems with centralized recording). On election day, these counties were responsible for 65 percent of votes cast but 90 percent of rejected ballots. In rural Gadsen County, the state's poorest and blackest county, one in eight votes was not counted because of the spoilage problem. In mostly white Leon County, the rate of rejection was one in 500. Analysts concluded that overall about 14 percent of African American votes were discarded compared with only 2 percent of white people's votes.[41]

Many of the problems outlined in the commission's report were not unique to Florida. As scholar Allen Lichtman pointed out in expert testimony prepared for the investigation, disparities in the resources available to manage elections in different communities were the "real scandal" in the nation's electoral system. "Poor counties, whether in Florida or elsewhere, have always had a disproportionate number of votes not counted," he noted. Another study estimated that nationwide between 4 and 6 million votes were not counted in the 2000 election. In the wake of such revelations Congress passed the Help America Vote Act (HAVA) in October 2002, hailed by its proponents as the most significant civil rights legislation since the 1960s. The act set minimum national standards for registering voters and promised $3.9 billion in federal assistance to the states for projects such as upgrading voting equipment, educating voters, training poll workers, and maintaining accurate voter lists. It also required states to allow people whose eligibility to vote was unclear to cast provisional ballots on election day and verify their status later.[42]

These reforms still proved inadequate for ensuring equal access to the democratic process, however. Secretaries of state retained broad powers to determine exactly how to implement HAVA and some provisions of the act provided new openings for electoral malfeasance. Greg Palast argued in the *Nation* that requiring all 50 states to maintain computerized voter rolls actually increased the likelihood of more Florida-style purges of "ineligible" voters orchestrated by partisan election officials. The stipulation that first-time voters who registered by mail must present identification at the polls created problems for some citizens who lacked any of the types of identification that qualified. Many people expressed concern about states' rush to invest in electronic voting machines that were prone to errors and security breaches. Stanford University computer scientist David Dill warned, "If I was a programmer at one of these companies and I wanted to steal an election, it would be very easy."[43]

Civil rights organizations took action of their own in the wake of the 2000 elections to combat informal and deliberate disfranchisement of voters. Dozens of groups cooperated on creating the Election Protection

Program, an effort to monitor election practices and solve problems that interfered with citizens' ability to register or vote. The program recruited lawyers and trained volunteers to provide legal assistance to people who encountered difficulty negotiating the system. In 2004 the coalition maintained a direct presence in 25 states and handled more than 150,000 calls through its national hotline in the two weeks leading up to election day. Once again the NAACP, ACORN, and other organizations joined together in a massive drive to bring millions of new voters into the political process, recruiting at homeless shelters, public housing projects, beauty salons, high schools, and colleges. These initiatives were not enough to offset extremely well organized Republican efforts to get their own supporters to the polls. Many people also encountered the same kinds of obstacles to participation that characterized earlier elections, including long lines at polling places, inconsistent availability of provisional ballots, unhelpful poll workers, and voter intimidation. As usual, residents of poorer communities encountered the most frustrations while those in wealthier precincts cast ballots with relative ease.[44]

Under pressure from reformers, many states acted to alleviate such problems by extending the voting period beyond the 12 to 15 hours that polls were open on election day. Allowing people to cast ballots over a period of a few days or weeks helped to overcome many of the barriers to participation that disadvantaged poor people and made partisan efforts to suppress turnout more difficult. By 2008 residents of 32 states could vote early by mail or in person, and millions did so. In North Carolina, an NAACP-led coalition of 95 social justice organizations embarked on an initiative to persuade 1 million people to vote early in the presidential election. Mazie Butler Ferguson, a former CORE worker and SEDFRE scholarship recipient, was one of the coordinators of the "Souls to the Polls" effort and later reported on the results: "Hundreds of thousands of new voters registered and voted prior to election day. ... [On election day] many network commentators called North Carolina for McCain early in the evening before the early votes had been counted. BUT when the early votes were counted, Obama had carried North Carolina overwhelmingly. The early voting and Souls to the Polls made the difference in the outcome of the election in North Carolina."[45]

The Long Obama Campaign

Obama's victory reflected the work of civil rights veterans like Ferguson as well as millions of new recruits who joined the struggle in the late twentieth century. Obama was just four years old when the Voting Rights Act was passed in 1965. Raised under relatively privileged circumstances by his white mother and grandparents in Indonesia and Hawaii, his story was not one that the majority of African Americans shared or recognized as part of their experience. Nonetheless, the new president connected strongly to the history and achievements of the black freedom movement and acknowledged them as being intricately entwined with his own. His success owed much to the example of black leaders like Martin Luther King Jr., whose inspiring appeals to the nation's highest ideals echoed through Obama's own speeches. His political career built on the efforts of an earlier generation of black candidates and elected officials. Most of all, Obama's election was a legacy of the grassroots organizing model crafted by black activists in the mid twentieth century and carried into later decades by SEDFRE, ACORN, and the many other social justice organizations spawned by the civil rights movement. Political analyst Christopher Hayes observed a crucial difference between the Obama campaign and previous election bids he had covered. "This campaign's field operation is guided by a principle which is posted in every office: 'Respect, Empower, and Include,'" he explained. "Volunteers are not just used as chess pieces – they're developed into leaders and given tools to organize themselves, so they turn into force multipliers."[46]

Millions of Americans donated money and time to the Obama campaign, providing the financial and human power needed to canvass communities multiple times to register voters, educate them about local election procedures, and get them to the polls. The massive volunteer base gave unprecedented depth to these efforts and enabled Obama to set up field offices in states that were initially considered beyond reach for the Democratic candidate – and that he eventually won. Obama realized that, to paraphrase Ella Baker's astute observation regarding Martin Luther King Jr., he did not make the movement, the movement made him. "This is your victory," he told supporters in his acceptance speech, and went on to remind them that his election did not represent the end of their efforts: "This victory alone is not the change we seek – it is only the chance for us to make that change. ... It cannot happen without you."[47]

Obama's admonition recalled the sentiments expressed 40 years earlier by civil rights activists who knew that years of struggle lay ahead to ensure genuine social change after the legislative victories of the 1960s. Throughout the late twentieth century the fight to include black Americans in the nation's democracy continued in the courts, in the legislatures, at registrars' offices, at the polls, and in the streets. Sustained efforts to overcome barriers to participation achieved some important victories and made possible the election of the nation's first African American president. As the experiences of black elected officials demonstrated, however, political representation alone was insufficient to ensure meaningful reform. In addition to enforcement of civil rights laws and a voice in government, African Americans pressed for broader social justice goals in the post-civil rights era.

$\star$ **7** $\star$

FIR$T CLA$$ CITIZEN$HIP: STRUGGLES FOR ECONOMIC JUSTICE

This civil rights revolution is not confined to the Negro nor is it confined to civil rights, for our white allies know that they cannot be free while we are not and we know that we have no future in a society in which six million black and white people are unemployed and millions more live in poverty. (A. Philip Randolph, 1963)[1]

On January 31, 1966 a group of about 100 displaced agricultural workers in Mississippi moved their families into an abandoned air force base near Greenville and called on the federal government to put the site to use as a low-income housing project and job training center. In a telegram to President Johnson they explained: "We are here because we are hungry. We are here because we have no jobs. Many of us have been thrown off the plantations where we worked for nothing all of our lives. We don't want charity. We demand our rights to jobs, so that we can do something with our lives and build us a future." The protest drew attention to political leaders' failure to address the social crisis generated by the modernization of southern agriculture and resulting unemployment that left large numbers of black people without income, food, or shelter. These activists did not believe the government's responsibility to ensure racial equality ended with the passage of civil rights legislation. Their message to Johnson showed that they considered economic rights to be just as important in the freedom struggle as the political and legal rights won in the mid-1960s. Johnson's response was an early indication of the wall of resistance that met such arguments in the later part of the decade and beyond. On February 1, 140 military police descended on the base and evicted the protesters.[2]

In the decades after passage of the Civil Rights and Voting Rights Acts social justice activists struggled to place the right to adequate income at the center of national policies aimed at addressing racial inequality and the broader problems facing the United States as it transitioned to a postindustrial economy. The nation's political leaders never embraced this approach, however. Proposals to establish basic economic rights for all Americans through full employment initiatives and a stronger social welfare system met with indifference or outright hostility in the late twentieth century. African Americans responded to the government's failure to act by engaging in cooperative and self-help efforts to fill the gaps left by the withdrawal of support for antipoverty programs.

The Poor People's Campaign and Proposals for Full Employment Policies

The civil rights movement had always included an economic component. Many grassroots participants and leaders were working-class black people who were more interested in improving their incomes and living standards than integrating restaurants or other facilities that they could not afford to patronize. In July 1963 CORE worker Miriam Feingold reported from Louisiana: "One lady told me yesterday that she didn't care if the lunch counters everywhere were opened – she couldn't buy anything with the money she had. All she wants is a good job for her husband, and the chance to bring up her kids like everyone else's kids." In the mid-1960s CORE and SNCC's work in the rural South shifted from a focus on desegregation and voter registration to mobilizing poor people to demand a fair share of the nation's wealth. The goal was neatly summarized in a flyer announcing one local group's purpose as securing "Fir$t Cla$$ Citizen$hip [and] Fir$t Cla$$ Job$."[3]

Martin Luther King Jr. also spoke out eloquently against other forms of oppression apart from racism. At a press conference in December 1967 King asked Americans to consider the moral implications of "children starving in Mississippi while prosperous farmers are rewarded for not producing food. ... Or a nation gorged on money while millions of its citizens are denied a good education, adequate health services, decent housing, meaningful employment, and even respect, and are then told to be responsible."[4] He envisioned the mobilization of a multiethnic coalition made up of other poor and dispossessed groups in addition to African Americans. "As we work to get rid of the economic strangulation that we face as a result of poverty, we must not overlook the fact that millions of Puerto Ricans, Mexican Americans, Indians and Appalachian whites are also poverty-stricken," he asserted.[5] King was in the process of organizing members of all of these groups to participate in a poor people's march on Washington before his assassination in April 1968. His lieutenants in the SCLC continued the Poor People's Campaign (PPC) amidst the shock and grief of his death. In mid-May a multiethnic gathering comprising thousands of low-income Americans converged on the nation's capital to engage in lobbying efforts and mass demonstrations. Activists spent the next several weeks visiting the offices of federal agencies during the day and camping out in a makeshift tent city near the Washington monument at night.

The PPC's demands centered on guarantees of adequate income for all citizens through job creation, social welfare payments, and increased funding for the war on poverty. Participants argued that there was no excuse for allowing hunger and homelessness to exist in the wealthiest nation on earth. The United States had the resources to eradicate the problem if only its political leaders were willing to reorder their priorities. A pamphlet outlining the goals of the PPC contrasted the billions of dollars in government subsidies that southern plantation owners, large corporations, and middle-class homeowners received every year with the meager amounts spent on helping poor people to meet their basic subsistence needs. "Let America treat its poor children at least as well as its rich farmers," organizers suggested. "Let America subsidize the families in the rotting tenements at least as well as those in the affluent suburbs." The PPC called on legislators to enact an Economic Bill of Rights to ensure jobs at living wages for all citizens who could work and an adequate income for those who could not. Representatives of the various government agencies targeted by the march listened politely to the civil rights leaders and poor people they met with but prevaricated on specific actions they could take. The Department of Labor's response, for example, drew criticism from activists for merely describing "past, inadequate and irrelevant accomplishments while ignoring this, our most important demand – immediate jobs for the poor." Although protesters vowed to remain in Washington for as long as was necessary to force more serious efforts to address their concerns, police forcibly removed people and shut down the PPC's camp site on June 24 after the permit for the demonstration expired.[6]

National leaders' reluctance to accept responsibility for ensuring a more equitable distribution of resources only grew stronger in subsequent decades. In the 1970s opposition to government guarantees of economic security blocked efforts to enact full employment legislation proposed by Congressman Augustus Hawkins and strongly supported by civil rights, labor, and religious groups. The prevailing view among economists and policy makers assumed that maintaining some level of unemployment was necessary to control inflation. Business leaders also supported this arrangement because it ensured a ready supply of labor and curbed workers' ability to demand higher wages. Hawkins argued that the system aimed to protect "property rights instead of human rights [and] led to ... defining full employment in terms not of the number and kind of paid jobs but rather some politically tolerable level of unemployment." Between the 1940s and 1970s that level crept up from 2 percent to 7 percent, a figure that translated into millions of people unable to find work and one that was entirely intolerable to Hawkins and his supporters. Initially introduced in 1974, Hawkins' bill established the right to a job for all able-bodied adults and required the government to provide employment for surplus workers when the private sector failed to generate enough positions.[7]

Opponents of full employment policies countered that the legislation would interfere with the free enterprise system, result in inefficient and costly public works projects, and cause runaway inflation. Lower taxes and reliance on market forces were a better way to reduce unemployment than government intervention, they asserted. Hawkins' bill went through multiple revisions and was combined with another bill proposed by Hubert Humphrey before coming to a vote as the Full Employment and Balanced Growth Act in 1978. The language asserting that employment was a right was dropped along with the mechanisms for ensuring that everyone who wanted a job could find one. Congress passed the legislation in its weakened form and President Carter signed the act into law in October. Carter and his successors in the White House continued to place a higher priority on keeping inflation down than reducing unemployment. In the next three decades the nation's official jobless rate never fell below 4 percent (more than 5 million workers). The actual unemployment rate, including part-time workers who preferred full-time jobs, people who were ineligible for unemployment benefits, and those who had become too discouraged to look for work, was even higher.[8]

Debates over full employment legislation occurred against a backdrop of rampant inflation in the 1970s. By the middle of the decade inflation was increasing by 5–10 percent each year, leading some economists to advocate tightening rather than expanding job opportunities to bring wages and prices under control. Proponents of such policies became more influential as the decade progressed, arguing first for acceptance of a higher rate of unemployment and eventually calling for a deliberately engineered recession. In September 1977 economist Herbert Stein theorized in the *Wall Street Journal* that the nation's 7 percent unemployment rate was in fact full employment. Acknowledging that nonwhite workers' jobless rate was double that figure and that this was not acceptable, Stein maintained that full employment policies would not solve the problem because unemployed people did not really want jobs. "The heightened sense of national obligation to provide jobs – or, at least, a paycheck – had as its corollary a lowered sense of private responsibility to work," he claimed. The following year William Fellner of the American Enterprise Institute asserted that contracting the economy was the only way to bring inflation back to within reasonable limits. "No one wants the recession, but it's unavoidable," he stated. Such a policy might mean high unemployment for several more years, but there was "no other way." Arthur Okun, a former advisor to President

Johnson, concurred. "The [Federal Reserve Board] is not going to accommodate what is happening in prices. The Fed is going to give us a recession," he predicted.[9]

Sure enough, Federal Reserve chairman Paul Volcker began raising interest rates in 1979 to tighten the credit supply and force Americans into greater austerity. The *New York Times* reported in October that the Carter administration was determined not to allow recent price increases in housing and energy to spark another upward revision in wages. Volcker was aware of the likely effects of the rate hikes on workers' employment prospects and incomes, but he argued that there were no easy paths to economic recovery. "The standard of living of the average American has to decline," he stated bluntly. "I don't think you can escape that." By 1982 the unemployment rate was at 10 percent and labor unions' power to negotiate better pay and conditions for members was severely weakened. Inflation was tamed, but the costs were not evenly shared. Wealthy Americans who could afford to buy stocks or United States Treasury bonds benefited from the healthy returns on their investments while those with more modest incomes bore the brunt of the pain.[10]

The Welfare Rights Movement

Political leaders' refusal to enact measures guaranteeing jobs for all Americans spurred efforts to strengthen the social welfare system that unemployed people and their families relied on for survival. A nationwide welfare rights movement emerged in the late 1960s as activists looked for ways to address the southern agricultural crisis and its overflow effects on urban black communities. Many displaced black workers were not eligible for unemployment insurance and therefore relied heavily on the state public assistance programs that provided for those left out of other Social Security initiatives in the 1930s. Most states did not provide assistance to two-parent families on the assumption that able-bodied men could always find jobs. If the fathers left, however, their wives and children became eligible for Aid to Families with Dependent Children (AFDC). At hearings held by the state advisory committees of the Commission on Civil Rights in 1967, black women testified to the difficulty of keeping families intact in communities where few employment opportunities existed. "A man doesn't want to feel that he is going to take bread out of his child's mouth if he is really a man," explained an AFDC recipient in Cleveland, Ohio. "This means that he leaves. If he is not able to support his family adequately, he usually leaves." A minister from the same community stated that he found it difficult to counsel such men to stay with their families "because it is life and death that we are talking about."[11] In the late 1960s increasing numbers of black women and children turned to AFDC as a last desperate resort after jobs and men disappeared.

Civil rights workers in the South recognized early on that racist officials' control over public assistance programs allowed for forms of discrimination against African Americans that were as serious as segregation laws and the denial of voting rights. Maximum benefits paid under the AFDC program sat well below poverty level in every state, and strict eligibility requirements kept many needy families from receiving assistance. Stipulations that recipients must maintain a "suitable home" for children, for instance, empowered administrators to refuse or cut off welfare payments for any reason, including family members' participation in the civil rights movement. Economic reprisals by private employers combined with restricted access to the welfare system caused one CORE worker to conclude that "poverty purposely tightened" was a deliberate ploy on the part of white supremacists to discourage black organizing and force African Americans out of the region. An OEO official sent to monitor food distribution programs in Mississippi in 1966 offered a similar assessment. "Many of the very needy are disqualified from receiving food by arbitrary certification regulations," he reported. "There is ample evidence that the welfare program in Mississippi is discriminatory, punitive, dishonest and endowed with a feudalistic authority over human life and dignity."[12]

Racism lay behind many of these abuses but similar mistreatment was accorded to white people who relied on public assistance as well. In 1965 legal scholar Charles Reich outlined multiple violations of welfare recipients' basic rights that resulted from administrative rules meant to guard against the misuse of taxpayer funds. The residency requirements imposed by many states limited poor people's mobility and made it hard to relocate in search of work. Social workers' close supervision of recipients' private lives threatened their individual liberties. Unannounced inspections of people's homes were inconsistent with Fourth Amendment protections against unreasonable searches. No other segment of the population was subjected to this level of scrutiny, Reich noted. The system essentially made poor people into second-class citizens. "Today the nation's poor stand as far from the enjoyment of basic rights as did the Negro at the beginning of the Civil Rights movement," he concluded. Welfare mother Johnnie Tillmon noted that gender ideologies as well as race and class biases played a role in the rules governing the AFDC program. "The truth is that A.F.D.C. is like a super-sexist marriage," she stated. "You trade in *a* man for *the* man. ... *The* man, the welfare system, controls your money. He tells you what to buy, what not to buy, where to buy it, and how much things cost. If things – rent, for instance – really cost more than he says they do, it's just too bad for you."[13]

State governments' miscalculations of how much money people needed to meet basic needs was perhaps the biggest problem facing those who depended on the welfare system. In 1965 HEW reported that in 32 states "public assistance payments to families with children were only a portion of the amount the State itself had figured as the minimum on which a family could live decently." Alabama provided $15.00 per month per child, about half the level of need. Mississippi's payment of $34.00 per month for a family of four was the lowest in the nation and only one-third of what people needed to survive. Welfare recipients scrambled to make up the shortfall by borrowing money from relatives or friends, skipping meals, doing odd jobs, keeping children out of school when they could not afford to buy shoes or books, and recycling furniture and household items that wealthier neighbors left out with the trash. Stories circulating in the wider society about "welfare queens" who drove luxury cars and stocked their freezers with the most expensive cuts of meat bore no resemblance to the reality of recipients' lives. On the contrary, an inter-agency study undertaken by the federal government found, "Most persons receiving assistance do not receive enough money to make it possible for them to live at even a minimum level of decency and dignity."[14]

Many former sharecroppers and domestic workers who relied on public assistance viewed the subpoverty-level benefits and abusive practices of welfare officials as little better than the plantation system of the Jim Crow era. With encouragement from civil rights activists and community organizers, poor people formed local welfare rights associations to push for more generous payments and better treatment. Mothers for Adequate Welfare in Boston, the Welfare Recipients' League in New York, the Hinds County Welfare Rights Movement in Mississippi, the Clark County Welfare Rights Organization in Nevada, and dozens of other groups used mass rallies and sit-ins to highlight problems and pressure administrators to act. Some of the first demonstrations aimed simply to secure benefits that welfare recipients were entitled to under the law. In New York, for example, case workers were legally required to make sure all of their client families had items that were considered necessary to meet "minimum standards" for maintaining households, such as clothing, beds, linens, tables and chairs, cooking utensils, refrigerators, and stoves. Most recipients were unaware of the requirement and learned of it only after sympathetic welfare office staff supplied activists with copies of the minimum standards. Sydelle Moore recalled that when she and her neighbors saw the documents, they "couldn't believe the things that were in them. Coats and sweaters. ... There was a law in the books that said you were entitled to these things and we were going to try to get them." Welfare rights activists also helped to arrange fair hearings for people whose benefits were denied or cut off, forcing officials to defend their decisions and discouraging politically motivated reprisals.[15]

The welfare rights movement drew support from many of the same organizations and professionals who supported the civil rights struggle, including lawyers, social workers, religious leaders, academics, and students. In May 1966 George Wiley and two other former CORE activists founded the Poverty/Rights Action Center to help channel poor people's growing militancy into a movement that could carry the freedom struggle into new areas and force policy makers to address economic injustice. Five thousand welfare rights activists in 16 cities across the nation participated in mass demonstrations on June 30, and the following month representatives from 75 local groups met in Chicago to form the National Coordinating Committee of Welfare Rights Groups. Headed by Johnnie Tillmon, the committee spent the next year working with local groups to lay the groundwork for a national organization. In August 1967 300 delegates attended the first meeting of the National Welfare Rights Organization (NWRO) in Washington, DC. Although black women made up the largest proportion of the membership, the interracial composition of the movement was evident in the presence of poor white people and Latino activists as well as African Americans at the meeting. When George Wiley referred to the audience as "black folks" in a speech to the convention, Tillmon recalled, she passed him a note requesting, "Will you please quit saying black and say poor. ... 'Cause we [were] not talking in terms of black folks now."[16]

Welfare rights activists worked to convince recipients and the society at large that poor people were entitled to the same rights as other Americans, including the power to decide for themselves how to organize their lives and run their households. Much as black southerners had startled segregationists with demands for equal treatment in the civil rights era, the claim that public assistance benefits were *rights* challenged entrenched assumptions and policies that stigmatized the poor. Welfare recipient Joyce Burson remembered the feelings of relief and empowerment she felt when she attended her first welfare rights meeting: "I felt good, because number 1 I was finding out that I was entitled to some things that I needed ... I was hearing people say that you can do something ... you don't have to be ashamed because you're on welfare, you know, you are okay, you're a person, and it's not your fault." Scholar and activist Joseph Paull described the new mood in evidence at welfare offices across the nation in an article that appeared in the journal *Social Work* in 1967. "The idea has caught hold that poor people count for something and have rights; they do not have to put up with things as they are; conditions can be changed and there is a point in speaking up; there is somewhere to go and someone who will listen," he wrote.[17]

The concrete benefits that poor people could secure through educating themselves about the welfare system and demanding their full entitlements were as significant as the psychological impact. In the first week of one organizing campaign in Brooklyn, participants received payments totaling $150,000 after demanding that welfare officials adhere to state laws regarding the provision of basic needs and procedures for challenging decisions through fair hearings. Welfare rights activism thus offered immediate and tangible results that encouraged more people to join the struggle. The rewards were material goods such as furniture, clothing, and appliances that fulfilled real needs and signified inclusion in the nation's consumer society. As Felicia Kornbluh notes in her study of the movement in New York, welfare rights activists viewed participation in the economic market-place, along with access to the political and legal systems, as essential to achieving full citizenship.[18]

With help from civil rights lawyers, some welfare recipients took their grievances to court in an effort to ensure stronger legal protections for poor people. The Supreme Court heard its first welfare rights case in 1968, ruling in *King v. Smith* that an Alabama law denying benefits to women who engaged in sexual relationships with men was unconstitutional. The rationale for the law was that a woman who had a man in her life had someone who could support her family, an assumption that the testimony of Mrs. Sylvester Smith suggested was unfounded:

Q: Has Mr. Williams ever supported your children?
A: No.
Q: How do you know he's not able to support your children?
A: He can't support his own.[19]

In 1969 the Supreme Court ruled in *Thompson v. Shapiro* that state residency requirements violated the equal protection clause of the Fourteenth Amendment. As Justice William Brennan noted, the effect of the waiting period imposed by some states before poor families qualified for aid was to create two classes of citizens and deny one class "welfare aid upon which may depend the ability of the families to obtain the very means to subsist – food, shelter, and other necessities of life." The following year the Court heard testimony from welfare recipients, social workers, and lawyers regarding practices in the New York City Department of Social Services that created severe hardships for poor people seeking reinstatement after being dropped from the welfare rolls under suspicion of violating regulations. Alma Coldburn stated that during months of waiting for a hearing after her AFDC payment was suspended she was "constantly without money for food and other necessities." Attorney David Gilman told the Court that the average wait for an initial hearing was four to five months, and referees often adjourned hearings "arbitrarily without regard to the client's need for a speedy decision." Clients then had to wait at least another six weeks to have their cases heard, all the while trying to survive on no income. The Court ruled in *Goldberg v. Kelly* (1970) that welfare recipients must receive a fair hearing before rather than after their aid was revoked.[20]

The legal fight was part of a broader strategy to change the way Americans thought about public assistance programs and the people who depended on them. Government aid was not a privilege reserved only for those considered worthy, activists argued, but something that all poor people were entitled to by virtue of their need. Charles Reich explained, "The idea ... is simply that when individuals have insufficient resources to live under conditions of health and decency, society has obligations to provide support, and the individual is entitled to that support as of right." Participants in the welfare rights movement believed that poverty was caused by structural shifts in the economy that were beyond poor people's control. If the government was not willing to guarantee all workers jobs that paid adequate wages, then it must take responsibility for providing a minimum standard of living to those who were unemployed or underemployed through no fault of their own. In response to suggestions that the welfare rolls were packed with lazy people who ought to be forced to find jobs, activists cited studies showing that the vast majority of welfare recipients were children, parents with childcare responsibilities, and elderly, sick, or disabled Americans – people who could not work even if employment were available. A report produced by HEW in 1971 noted that the largest group of able-bodied adults on welfare was single mothers. Many of these women would have liked to hold jobs but faced significant barriers to employment, such as lack of transportation and childcare. Others preferred to stay home with their children and thought they had as much right as married middle-class women to decide whether to work as full-time mothers or in occupations outside the home. Welfare rights activists detested the double standard that heaped praise on white women who devoted all of their time to their families but cast black women as loafing, immoral parasites when they tried to do the same. When Senator Abraham Ribicoff suggested putting welfare mothers to work cleaning streets in New York City, NWRO organizer Beulah Sanders responded, "Senator Ribicoff, I would be the first welfare recipient to volunteer to clean up New York's streets if your mother and your wife were beside me."[21]

Activists' demands for increased benefits, relaxed eligibility criteria, and freedom from intrusive regulation of welfare recipients' private lives elicited sympathy from some Americans and outrage from others. A few politicians and administrators agreed that the modernizing economy and structural unemployment created a moral imperative to strengthen the social safety net. In New York, welfare commissioner Mitchell Ginsberg met with welfare recipients in June 1966 and conceded to their request to make supplementary grants available for families needing to buy school clothes for their children. Welfare officials in Massachusetts were also receptive to the movement and often discussed policy with activists. Staff at HEW consulted with leaders of the NWRO and acknowledged the importance of incorporating the views of welfare recipients into proposals for reform. "In the past, we used to consider what the reaction of Congress might be, how the states would respond," stated one HEW administrator. "Now we've begun to consider the recipients too: what would they think about what we're doing."[22]

In many other quarters, however, welfare recipients' demands met with incredulity and derision. Middle-class Americans whose economic security was enhanced by less visible government supports, such as tax breaks for homeowners and for parents with dependent children, could not see why public funds must be used to support less well off members of society. The widespread (and erroneous) belief that most people on welfare were African American meant that abuses of recipients' rights were not of great concern to the majority of citizens. Moreover, tighter economic circumstances pushed many married women with families into the workforce after the 1960s, making welfare mothers' assertion of their right to choose childcare over paid employment in the private sector seem like a request for unfair privileges rather than equal treatment. One woman expressed the frustration many Americans felt after reading about the NWRO's lobbying efforts in Washington, DC: "I am a working woman and can't afford a trip to Washington, but taxes are withheld from my salary – much of it going for this and other welfare handouts to many loafers, demanding undesirables, and just plain trash."[23]

Proposals for amending the Social Security Act introduced by Democrats in Congress in 1967 reflected Americans' divided opinions over welfare as well as state governments' concerns about swelling public assistance rolls and the increasing costs of providing for their poor residents. A requirement that states raise their minimum standards of need to more realistic levels and adjust them to keep up with inflation promised to alleviate the financial hardships many welfare recipients faced, but the amendments simultaneously set a limit on how many people could receive assistance. The legislation also included a work requirement for all able-bodied participants, including mothers, and cut benefits for those who refused placement in employment or job training programs.[24] The NWRO opposed the measure, arguing that it empowered officials to force people to labor for sub-minimum wages. "Training" for welfare recipients often seemed designed to turn them into "polite domestics" so that they might trade a life of poverty on welfare for a life of poverty scrubbing other people's floors. One African American woman who took a "homemaker aid course" in Gary, Indiana, observed that it was "rather unnecessary for a Negro to go to school to get a certificate to clean up someone else's house."[25] Activists argued that if state and federal officials truly wanted welfare recipients to achieve economic independence, they should train people for real jobs at real wages.

Despite the NWRO's criticisms, the Social Security amendments cleared Congress in December 1967 and President Johnson signed them into law the following month. Subsequent reforms of the welfare system over the next few decades grew progressively more draconian, influenced by assumptions that the root causes of poverty lay in the behavior of individuals not deficiencies in the economic system. In 1969 the Nixon administration proposed to replace the AFDC program with a Family Assistance Plan (FAP) that would have extended assistance to working people whose jobs did not pay enough to keep them out of poverty and provided a guaranteed income for every American family. Although welfare rights activists supported the idea in principle, the plan ensured a minimum annual income of just $1,600 for a family of four, well below the $5,500 that the federal government's Bureau of Labor Statistics determined necessary to meet basic subsistence needs. It also included the same kinds of work requirements that the NWRO had opposed in 1967. With support from the NAACP and the NUL, the NWRO advocated raising the income floor to $5,500 and making participation in training and job programs voluntary. Neither condition was met in revised versions of the bill, and it eventually died for lack of support from Democrats as well as Republicans in Congress.[26]

Rising unemployment in the 1970s added more people to the welfare rolls while reducing the tax revenues needed to pay for increased caseloads. Political leaders responded by cutting benefits and scapegoating welfare recipients. Opponents of public assistance programs portrayed them as threats to American values and the people who depended on them as frauds and cheats who were undeserving of aid. In this climate the NWRO was unable to maintain momentum or secure the tangible benefits for members that facilitated its growth in the late 1960s. Internal divisions among the leadership further weakened the organization and it disbanded in 1974. Without a national coordinating entity or allies in Congress activists were unable to prevent the erosion of welfare rights in the 1980s and 1990s. One of Ronald Reagan's first acts as president was to push through legislation that limited eligibility for public assistance to the truly destitute, pushing millions of poor people off the rolls. The president also urged states to place a greater emphasis on moving welfare recipients into the labor force through mandatory work requirements. The bipartisan Family Support Act of 1988 gave added impetus to this approach by requiring states to implement "job opportunities and basic skills training" programs to help AFDC families "avoid long-term welfare dependence." A critique of the legislation by social policy researcher Mimi Abramovitz noted that it might move some families off public assistance but was unlikely to do anything to reduce poverty. "Most state welfare-for-work programs place AFDC mothers in low-paying jobs," she wrote. Rather than meeting the real needs of poor families, the legislation seemed designed simply to cut costs and increase the pool of cheap labor available to employers. Echoing the reform agenda of earlier decades, Abramovitz called for "assuring economic security through income support programs for all families, with benefits at or above the poverty line and indexed to inflation" along with "full employment policies that provide jobs for all those ready and able to work."[27]

Even after the election of Democrat Bill Clinton to the presidency in 1992 there was little hope of reviving progressive approaches to ending poverty. Clinton did implement modest improvements such as raising benefits and expanding eligibility for food stamps, but he was no fan of the welfare system. He did not believe the federal government alone could solve social problems and preferred policies that encouraged involvement of the private sector, such as offering tax incentives to businesses willing to locate in economically depressed areas. After Republicans gained majorities in the House and Senate in the mid-1990s Clinton acquiesced to their plans to radically overhaul the welfare system. The Personal Responsibility and Work Opportunity Reconciliation Act of 1996 abolished the AFDC program and replaced it with Temporary Assistance for Needy Families (TANF). States received block grants from the federal government to operate programs within guidelines set by the legislation aimed at reducing welfare rolls. The act set a five-year lifetime limit on eligibility for public assistance and required states to place half of their welfare recipients in work or job training programs by 2002.[28]

Although the legislation did indeed result in fewer people on welfare, its success as an antipoverty measure was questionable. Some former recipients found stable, well-paid employment that offered a comfortable standard of living. Many more people were forced to take minimum wage jobs that left them worse off after the loss of medical benefits and added costs for transportation and childcare were taken into account. The number of Americans living below poverty level declined by roughly 5 million people between 1996 and 2000, a period that coincided with strong economic growth and greater employment opportunities. Poverty rose again during George W. Bush's presidency, however, and by 2006 the number of poor people stood at more than 36 million (12 percent of the population), the same as it had been in 1996.[29] In the first three years of the twenty-first century the number of children receiving welfare declined by 10 percent, but the number living in poverty increased by 11 percent. State and local governments' control over the program also allowed the reemergence of capricious practices that blocked aid to many needy people, particularly African Americans and Latinos. A study published by the Applied Research Center in 2002 reported many instances where TANF administrators had made racist statements, unfairly denied assistance, or misinformed nonwhite recipients. Researchers also uncovered racial disparities in the allocation of many states' block grant funds. In Georgia, for example, one county with a 98 percent white caseload spent $2,090 annually per child on welfare compared with $694 in a neighboring county where the clients were 96 percent black.[30]

Welfare rights activists continued to push for measures to ensure economic security for all Americans throughout the late twentieth century. Local groups such as the Massachusetts Welfare Rights Organization, Westside Mothers in Detroit, and Welfare Warriors in Milwaukee protested cuts in welfare services and pressured political leaders to address problems of poverty, homelessness, and hunger. Former NWRO staffer Wade Rathke founded ACORN in 1970 and over the next few decades built it into the largest organization of poor people in the nation. Similarly, Beulah Sanders and other activists established the National Welfare Rights Union (NWRU) to assist local groups in their efforts. Under the leadership of Marian Kramer, the NWRU worked to empower a new generation of welfare recipients in the 1980s and 1990s to assert their rights to adequate incomes and respectful treatment. Cheri Honkala, a welfare mother who headed the Kensington Welfare Rights Union (KWRU) in Philadelphia, recalled the inspiration she derived from Kramer: "Marian was a feisty woman who could walk into a welfare office and not kiss everybody's ass and not feel obliged to explain herself or apologize for being there. It seemed so sane to me. I had always wanted to do that but never had the courage."[31]

Welfare rights groups used mass protests, conferences, civil disobedience, lawsuits, and education efforts to fight negative stereotyping of poor people and draw attention to injustices. In 1981 activists in Maryland filed a class action suit against the state after it abruptly terminated benefits for thousands of people, resulting in a court order to place 35,000 families back on the rolls. In New York, 3,000 people marched on the state capitol and convinced legislators to raise public assistance payments to keep up with cost of living increases. The KWRU staged a series of well-publicized protests in Philadelphia in the 1990s that dramatized the links between inadequate incomes and the city's growing homeless problem. Many welfare recipients who were not lucky enough to secure subsidized housing lived in the streets because they could not afford the rents charged in the private market. Cheri Honkala and other KWRU members helped homeless families to set up tent cities at various locations in the city – a vacant lot, the newly constructed downtown convention center, the park that tourists passed through as they walked between Independence Hall and the Liberty Bell – to embarrass city officials and draw attention to the low priority accorded to meeting the needs of poor people. Journalist David Zucchino observed, "Cheri loved to make people uncomfortable. ... She was convinced that America sought desperately to keep its poor out of sight so as not to be reminded of the social policies she believed exacerbated poverty. If the country was going to turn its back on the poor, she was not going to let anyone feel ambivalent about it."[32] The KWRU's activities confronted policy makers with the consequences of their actions and prevented them from keeping poor people hidden from view.

In 1995 and 1996 welfare rights activists expressed their opposition to Republicans' proposed changes to public assistance programs through petitions, teach-ins, rallies, and sit-ins. The NWRU joined with the Women's International League for Peace and Freedom to produce publicity materials that challenged the prevailing assumptions about the welfare system. One series of posters featured photographs of prominent business leaders such as Michael Eisner of Disney Corporation and Daniel Tellep of Lockheed Martin under the heading "Who Gets Welfare?" Text below these images explained that AFDC payments made up less than 1 percent of the federal budget and contrasted the $14 billion spent on all social welfare programs in 1994 with the $104 billion doled out in subsidies to giant corporations. The posters also noted how millions of other Americans, not just those on welfare, relied on taxpayer-funded government services: "Everyone who drives on a toll-free highway, attends a public school or university, deducts mortgage interest payments from their income tax, or enjoys a national park is getting the equivalent of welfare from the federal government. In one way or another, we are all welfare recipients."[33]

As states implemented new programs focusing on moving people from welfare to work, activists fought to ensure that "workfare" did not exploit people or push them into positions resembling slave labor. In May 1996 the Welfare Warriors protested a bill passed by the state legislature in Wisconsin that required heads of families to work 40 hours a week for their welfare checks. "W2 is every large corporation's dream: *unpaid* temporary workers!" the group stated. The following year ACORN brought 1,000 people to Washington, DC, to protest similar programs around the nation that forced people to work for public assistance allowances that were far below the minimum wage. In New York welfare recipients assigned to cleaning city parks and streets engaged in sit-ins, slow downs, and demonstrations to demand better pay and working conditions. Some of these workers had been unionized city employees earning good wages and benefits before their jobs were cut during a recent budget crisis. Workfare in this instance was not a path out of poverty but a way for the city to extract people's labor more cheaply. Administrators made no pretense that the programs aimed to provide training or job placement. State senator George Pataki explained that workfare was essentially "community service. ... You are requiring them, week in and week out, to show up for public service work." According to Richard Schwartz, who headed New York's welfare reform program, workfare aimed simply to instill good work habits so that participants would be more competitive in the job market. "These are not real jobs, and it is a mistake for anyone on welfare to think they ever will be," he stated.[34]

Workfare participants demanded better. The problem was not welfare recipients' lack of a work ethic, they argued, but the shortage of jobs that paid decent wages and a lack of support services for single parents. Hundreds of people rallied at a welfare office in Manhattan in April 1997 chanting, "A day's work for a day's pay." Other demands included access to affordable health insurance and day care. With help from ACORN, workfare participants in New York organized into a union and called on city officials to recognize them as government employees entitled to the same rights as other workers. When Mayor Rudolph Giuliani proposed bringing nonprofit groups into the pool of workfare employers, 68 local churches and social justice organizations responded with a statement that denounced workfare programs and informed the mayor: "Rudy, We Will Not Be Your Slave Drivers."[35] If the government wanted people to "earn" their benefits, it must acknowledge workers' right to a living wage and fair treatment.

Welfare reform exposed recipients to greater exploitation in workfare programs but simultaneously brought new allies to the struggle. Most Americans considered it a matter of basic fairness that people who worked should earn enough to live on. At the turn of the century progressive coalitions of welfare rights activists, labor unions, civil rights organizations, churches, and student groups pushed for reforms that addressed the needs of low-wage workers as well as the unemployed. These efforts sometimes succeeded in transforming TANF policies from punitive efforts to push "lazy" welfare recipients off the rolls into programs that provided the supports necessary to lift families out of poverty. In some states income supplements, education and job training programs, health insurance, childcare, and transportation services were extended to low-income families whether they were on welfare or not. Activists also organized campaigns to pass legislation mandating that businesses pay workers enough to keep them out of poverty. Living wage ordinances passed in many cities across the nation in the late 1990s, including Minneapolis, Oakland, and Chicago.[36]

When TANF came up for reauthorization in 2002 welfare rights activists reiterated the goals that had motivated the movement since the 1960s: jobs for people who could work and adequate government support for those who could not. In a letter to the Department of Health and Human Services, the National Campaign for Jobs and Income Support suggested moving the focus of welfare reform away from reducing caseloads to reducing poverty. The coalition of social justice organizations proposed higher welfare payments, the expansion of eligibility, government job creation initiatives, and an increase in the minimum wage to move the nation toward that goal. "Only when we have a comprehensive and cohesive public policy to address the needs of low-income families and their barriers to employment will we be able to say that welfare reform has been a 'success,'" the letter concluded. Congressional debates over reauthorization offered no new policy initiatives, however, focusing instead on the number of hours recipients should be required to work each week and how much money to allocate to child care assistance. The TANF program remained largely unchanged for the remainder of George W. Bush's presidency.[37]

The Rural Southern Cooperative Movement

Activists seeking to create a more just economic order did not look solely to the government to solve social problems. In Louisiana black Catholic priest Albert J. McKnight urged African Americans to take control of their own destinies by pooling their resources in cooperative stores, farming enterprises, businesses, and credit unions. Starting with a small buying club that enabled members of his rural poor congregation to purchase groceries at lower prices than were charged in local stores, McKnight helped to establish more than 2,000 cooperatives throughout the southwestern part of the state by 1962. Civil rights workers who came South to work on voter registration projects in Louisiana and neighboring states in the 1960s adopted the cooperative model as a solution to the poverty and dependence that African Americans suffered within the white-dominated economic system. Activists joined together in the late 1960s to form the Federation of Southern Cooperatives (FSC) and secured funding from several foundations and the OEO to engage in cooperative organizing throughout the region.[38]

The FSC's staff and member organizations were comprised of veterans of the civil rights struggle who saw the cooperative movement as a continuation of their earlier efforts. Executive director Charles Prejean had worked closely with Father McKnight in Louisiana and supervised outreach projects in the state. John Zippert, who filled a variety of key positions in the FSC over several decades, was a former CORE volunteer who came to the South to work on voter registration and stayed to help organize the cooperative movement. The FSC's field staff consisted mostly of local activists who had been active in the civil rights struggle and in establishing cooperatives in their communities. Organizers viewed the cooperative movement as "poor people's economic response to the Civil Rights Movement," working to supplement the rights African Americans had won in the mid-1960s by encouraging projects designed to secure economic as well as political independence.[39]

The FSC established a strong record of achievement in improving conditions for rural poor black people that enabled it to secure modest levels of government support throughout the 1970s. The cooperative movement's emphasis on helping people to help themselves fit with political leaders' calls for greater self-reliance on the part of the black community. As FSC project director William H. Peace III noted, "The cooperative as viewed by our people is not welfare, a hand-out, or somebody else doing it for you. ... It is self determination, decision making, and participatory democracy in action. And it is the way to a better life for many of the people in our region." Officials in the Carter administration agreed that cooperatives were an effective means of fostering economic development in rural communities. Between 1976 and 1978 federal agencies granted more than $2 million to the FSC for a broad range of programs that included helping small farmers to switch from expensive fossil fuels to renewable energy sources and training displaced workers to rehabilitate substandard housing or build new homes for poor people.[40]

Southern elites were somewhat less appreciative of the FSC's efforts. Cooperative organizing empowered African Americans economically and fostered greater political activity among local black people in the region. Both of these developments challenged the dominance of powerful white residents. In 1979 a group of business and political leaders in Sumter County, Alabama, accused the FSC of misusing federal funds and demanded an official probe into its activities. Alabama district attorney J. R. Brooks launched an 18-month long investigation that ultimately found no cause for prosecuting anyone. The proceedings nonetheless cost the FSC millions of dollars in legal fees and lost grants, undermined member support, and damaged its reputation. Staff of the organization and their allies in the foundation community viewed the investigation as a politically motivated attempt to destroy the cooperative movement. "Since the formal legal abolition of 'Jim Crowism' one finds its 'de facto' re-emergence in more subtle and perhaps more dangerous forms," Charles Prejean observed. "In the case of FSC, it seems as if a more institutional approach is being used to frustrate and to nullify our rural Black socio-economic initiatives."[41]

The FSC entered the Reagan era severely weakened by its ordeal, only to face more financial problems after the new administration cut most of its government funding. After scaling back its programs in the early 1980s, the FSC merged with the Emergency Land Fund to become the Federation of Southern Cooperatives-Land Assistance Fund (FSC-LAF) in 1985. The FSC-LAF continued to work with rural poor people into the twenty-first century, providing training and support to cooperatives, lobbying for government policies to ensure the survival of family farms, promoting sustainable agriculture and fair trade, and engaging in community organizing and leadership development efforts. The FSC-LAF's response to the destruction wrought by Hurricane Katrina in 2005 contrasted starkly with the Bush administration's incompetence. In addition to providing food, clothing, shelter, and financial aid to more than 5,000 displaced people, the FSC-LAF offered training in how to navigate federal relief programs and workshops for those who were interested in using cooperatives and credit unions to help rebuild Gulf Coast communities.[42]

Black Self-help Efforts

Throughout the post-civil rights era black community organizations stepped in with assistance for poor families whose needs were neglected by political leaders. The government's failure to provide the public investments necessary to provide high quality education, affordable housing, economic security, and a healthy environment for all citizens convinced many African Americans that they could not rely on anyone but themselves to improve conditions in their neighborhoods. In the late 1960s the black power movement emphasized self-reliance rather than depending on white people for help and promoted the creation of black-controlled organizations, businesses, schools, and social institutions. Black nationalist groups such as the Black Panther Party, the Republic of New Afrika, and the Black Liberation Front combined revolutionary rhetoric urging people to assert their rights with concrete neighborhood improvement projects such as providing free meals, health care, and other social services in poor black communities. Black Panther Party members explained that such programs were "meant to meet the needs of the community until we can all move to change the social conditions that make it impossible for the people to afford the things they need and desire."[43] Police and government repression destroyed most of these organizations by the mid-1970s, but self-help projects remained a staple feature of black activism throughout the next several decades.

Sometimes these efforts reflected the views of social conservatives who argued that the abandonment of traditional values and growing numbers of single-parent families explained rampant poverty, drug use, and violence in black communities. In the 1980s and 1990s several new black organizations emerged that promoted Reaganite philosophies of individualism and self-reliance as alternatives to traditional civil rights approaches. Spokespeople for these ideas rejected the notion that racism remained a significant barrier to advancement and urged African Americans to rededicate themselves to the "family-centered traditions of earlier black Americans," including hard work, thrift, and religious faith. In February 1987 Robert Woodson of the Council for a Black Economic Agenda criticized black leaders who organized a mass demonstration to protest a Klan attack on African Americans in Georgia. "All it does is misdirect the limited resources and moral capital that we need urgently for other issues," Woodson complained. "More people died on the streets of Detroit last year than the Klan has killed in 10 years."[44] An example of what Woodson and others might see as a more fruitful approach could be found in Boston, where former gang member Eugene Rivers founded the Azusa Christian Community in one of the poorest, most crime-afflicted parts of the city and worked to draw black youth away from the streets and into the church. Rivers viewed religion as black people's "last best hope" and did not believe that racism alone was responsible for the deteriorating quality of life in the nation's inner cities. "The major problems confronting black people have nothing to do significantly with white people," he asserted. "White people are not black people's problem. Ultimately, black people are black people's problem."[45]

Many activists who believed the real solution lay with the creation of a more just economic order nonetheless recognized that individual accountability must also play a role in addressing social problems. When Whitney Young called for a domestic Marshall Plan in the 1960s, he emphasized that this did not mean exempting African Americans from "the independence and initiative demanded by our free, competitive society." Young advised African Americans to "exert themselves energetically in constructive efforts to carry their full share of responsibilities" by utilizing opportunities for education and civic participation. Programs initiated by the NUL in the post-civil rights era included efforts to combat drug abuse and teenage pregnancy. In 1984 the NUL joined with the NAACP in organizing a Black Family Summit that included discussions of how to help black youth avoid behavior that was harmful to themselves, their families, and communities. Similarly, the local SCLC chapter in St. Petersburg, Florida, created a Delinquency Prevention Task Force and organized mass demonstrations at public housing complexes aimed at driving out drug dealers. National SCLC leaders launched major campaigns against drugs and gang violence in the late 1980s and early 1990s that involved training black ministers in prevention strategies and offering support to poor families to help them resist the temptations of the drug trade. Countless smaller groups engaged in identical projects in their own neighborhoods, including programs for disadvantaged youth, drug rehabilitation centers, and organizations to help the families of incarcerated people.[46]

Black women were often at the center of these and other self-help initiatives. In 1980 Billye Avery founded the National Black Women's Health Project to increase awareness of common health problems among African Americans and empower people to take control over their physical wellbeing. Participants established local discussion groups, developed educational materials, and worked with health educators and providers to improve services for black women. Outreach activities drew on the social resources of black communities and used institutions such as churches and beauty salons to disseminate information. The project also identified "natural helpers" – women who had established reputations in their neighborhoods as trusted advice givers and problem solvers – and trained them as lay health providers. These efforts offered valuable assistance to African Americans who could not afford private health insurance and were poorly served by underfunded public health facilities.[47]

The National Council of Negro Women (NCNW) also developed creative solutions to address the shortfall in public resources available to black communities. In the decades after the 1960s the group sponsored dozens of programs that provided assistance to poor families and helped people to enhance their economic prospects through education and job training. In Mississippi the NCNW designed a program that enabled more than 6,000 families to become homeowners by donating "sweat equity" (labor) instead of making down payments for homes in cooperatively managed communities. Another project involved donating pigs to rural people who raised and bred them, then passed on two piglets from every litter to help other needy families.[48] In 1986 the NCNW took action to counteract the distorted image of African Americans presented in a television documentary titled *The Vanishing Black Family*. Dorothy Height explained, "We didn't think [the] piece was about the black family at all. It was about teenage pregnancy. And it showed only black teenagers – overlooking completely the fact that the majority of pregnant teens are white." The NCNW responded by organizing the Black Family Reunion, a national event that brought African Americans together from all over the country to reconnect with relatives and enjoy music, food, art, and games. Supplementing the festivities were exhibits offering information about job training programs and how to earn a high school equivalency degree as well as free medical screenings. One woman who attended the first reunion in Washington, DC, in 1987 praised the event for helping to expose her grandchildren to a world of alternatives. "You can get into gangs or you can get into good things," she stated. "This day has shown them that they have a lot more choices than they think." Annual Black Family Reunions were held in Washington and other cities throughout the late 1980s and 1990s. Height stated that these events helped to "awaken people to their rights, responsibilities, and opportunities" and generate "community energy to tackle our problems."[49]

Some analysts criticized self-help programs for reinforcing individualistic arguments that located the causes of social problems within black communities and absolved the rest of society from responsibility. In 1999 Adolph Reed Jr. warned: "Each attempt by a neighborhood or church group to scrounge around the philanthropic world and the interstices of the federal system for funds to build low-income housing or day care or neighborhood centers, to organize programs that compensate for inadequate school funding, public safety, or trash pickup, simultaneously concedes the point that black citizens cannot legitimately pursue those benefits through government." Though not necessarily disagreeing with Reed's argument, others viewed such projects as a vital lifeline for poor black communities that had few other options given the prevailing political climate. An NCNW member believed this work was "important in today's society for keeping a support structure" that kept people afloat after government resources were withdrawn.[50] Most activists recognized the need to exert continued pressure on business and political leaders to reinforce their efforts even as they struggled to do what they could with black people's own limited resources.

Despite increasing hostility from political leaders and many other citizens, participants in the freedom movement continued to press for recognition of poor people's economic rights after the 1960s. Their efforts kept ongoing injustices in public view and highlighted the effects of policies that enriched some Americans at the expense of others in the era of free market globalization. As many activists were aware, these problems were not unique to the United States. Social justice advocacy looked beyond the national context to global developments that tied black Americans' struggles to the cause of similarly oppressed people around the world in the late twentieth century.

★ 8 ★

ALL AROUND THE WORLD: THE FREEDOM
STRUGGLE IN A GLOBAL CONTEXT

*There is a section of the population that is just as present in the US,
and in England – the homeless, unemployed people, on the streets of
London – which is also there in the indigenous communities, villages,
and farmers of India, Indonesia, the Philippines, Mexico, Brazil. All
those who face the backlash of this kind of economics are coming
together to create a newer, people-centred world order. (Medha
Patkar, 2001)*[1]

African Americans' struggles for justice took place within the context of a
restructuring of the global economic system in the late twentieth century
that significantly altered other societies around the world along with the
United States. Advances in communication and transportation technologies
allowed for the rapid movement of information, money, products, and
people across national borders, facilitating international trade and cross-
cultural interaction on an unprecedented scale. At the same time, economic
theorists and policy makers in the world's wealthiest nations worked to
dismantle barriers to trade and investment that interfered with capitalist
activity. Proponents of such measures promised that they would spread
prosperity and democracy, but for many people they led instead to increasing economic insecurity and loss of control over the decisions that affected
their lives.

African Americans were among the first victims of policies that encouraged the privatization of resources, left the distribution of wealth to free
markets, and privileged the interests of banks and corporations over those
of poorer people. Some black activists cooperated with their counterparts
in developing nations in solidarity movements to challenge various forms
of racist exploitation that continued under this newest incarnation of capitalism. Toward the turn of the century many white people in the United
States and Europe also expressed concern about the economic, political,

and environmental effects of the system, joining other activists in a movement for global justice aimed at creating alternatives. Drawing inspiration
from the black freedom struggle and other social movements, participants
worked for the adoption of new rules that placed human needs above corporate profits and distributed the benefits of globalization more widely.

Constructing the Global Economic Order

Supporters of global capitalism portrayed it as the inevitable consequence
of technological developments and laws of economics that operated independently of government intervention. "Globalization, quite simply, is part
of the natural evolutionary process," asserted Canadian trade minister
Pierre Pettigrew. "It goes hand and hand with the progress of humanity,
something which history tells us no one can stand in the way of." As global
justice activist Naomi Klein countered, however, "Mother Nature doesn't
write international trade agreements, politicians and bureaucrats do."
Although basic features such as the exchange of goods and ideas had characterized human relations for centuries, the particular forms these activities
took in the late twentieth century resulted from actions taken by the heads
of state, treasury officials, central bankers, legislative bodies, and corporate
leaders of developed nations. Almost all of these actors were wealthy white
men whose decisions promoted their own interests on the assumption that
what was good for them was good for the rest of the world.[2]

The origins of the international economic order lay in an agreement
adopted by 44 nations at a conference in Bretton Woods, New Hampshire,
in 1944. At that time the dominant intellectual influences were the theories
of British economist John Maynard Keynes, who attributed the worldwide
depression of the 1930s to a collapse in demand for goods and services.
Keynes advocated free trade policies to foster prosperity for all nations by
providing access to international markets. At the same time, he believed
that markets were imperfect and government action was sometimes necessary to ensure full employment and sustain sufficient demand. During times
of recession, Keynes argued, governments should stimulate the economy
through measures such as tax cuts, deficit spending, and job creation programs to make up the shortfall in private sector employment.

Delegates at the Bretton Woods conference drew on Keynes' ideas in an
effort to stabilize the global economy and avoid another catastrophe like
the Great Depression. They established a system of fixed currency exchange
rates that made the United States dollar the standard currency for international trade. The value of other nations' currencies were set relative to the
dollar, which was itself redeemable for gold at a rate of $35.00 per ounce.
The agreement was mutually beneficial to the United States and its allies,

serving to solidify American economic power and facilitate other nations' recovery from the devastation caused by the war. The International Bank for Reconstruction and Development (World Bank), the International Monetary Fund (IMF), and the General Agreement on Tariffs and Trade (GATT) were also established in the 1940s to ensure that global demand was maintained at a healthy level. The IMF and World Bank provided loans that helped nations to rebuild, assisted with economic development efforts in poorer countries, and injected money into ailing economies threatened by recession. Meanwhile, multiple rounds of GATT negotiations gradually lowered the tariffs on imports that most nations used to insulate domestic industries from foreign competitors.[3]

Increasing international competition reduced the United States' share of global trade from 20 percent to 11 percent between 1950 and 1970, eating into corporate profits and undermining national prosperity. President Nixon attempted to enhance American manufacturers' ability to sell their products by abandoning the system of fixed currency exchange rates adopted under the Bretton Woods agreement. Now that other countries were competitive with the United States, Nixon argued, it was time to allow market forces to determine currency values in accordance with the relative health of each nation's economy. Nixon's announcement in August 1971 that the United States would no longer pay out gold in return for dollars aimed to devalue the dollar, thus lowering prices for domestic goods relative to their international competitors. This action failed to revive the American economy, however, because the OPEC embargo kept production costs and prices high and consumers continued to prefer foreign-made imports. At the same time, allowing currency rates to fluctuate destabilized the global financial system. In later decades speculative trading by investors seeking quick profits led to wild fluctuations in the value of some currencies that bore little relationship to the actual strength of national economies.[4]

American policy makers' actions and the growing influence of free market ideologies among administrators of the Bretton Woods institutions after the 1960s significantly shaped the fate of newly formed nations in Africa and Asia as they emerged from colonialism in the decades after World War II. These regions' position in the global economy resembled that of African Americans in the United States: a source of cheap, exploitable raw materials and labor that powered the economic growth of nations in Europe and North America, enriching white people but leaving the majority of the world's darker-skinned populations in poverty. Like the black elected officials who rose to power in the post-civil rights era, the leaders of decolonized countries found that political independence did not translate into economic independence. Moreover, many of the people who made up the post-colonial leadership in developing countries were educated in the United States or Europe and believed that following western models of modernization was the best way to ensure progress. These leaders relied on foreign investment and expertise to develop manufacturing industries, commodities for export, banking systems, and infrastructure as well as education and other social services for their people. Initially the IMF, World Bank, and foreign governments provided most of the necessary financial aid, but in the 1970s private banks and investors began to play a larger role. Western European and North American financial institutions were flush with deposits generated by the profits made from international trade, including significant amounts of money earned by oil producing nations after the OPEC embargo sent energy prices soaring. Investing in developing nations was deemed both lucrative and safe because commodity prices were rising, entire countries did not usually go bankrupt, and the IMF could always step in with rescue funds if governments were unable to repay the loans.[5]

Only the last of these assumptions proved to be correct. As the export industries of developing nations grew, increasing competition led to declines in the prices they received for their products. The Federal Reserve's decision to raise interest rates in the United States in the late 1970s caused private banks to raise rates on the money they had loaned to national governments around the world, precipitating a global financial crisis in the early 1980s when dozens of borrower countries proved unable to repay their debts. Allowing these nations to default on the loans risked the collapse of major international banks and worldwide depression. The IMF therefore provided the money governments needed to continue their payments to creditors. This measure saved the banks but did nothing to relieve borrower nations of their debt burdens. Many countries became trapped in a form of ongoing debt peonage, forever borrowing money to make interest payments on earlier amounts they had borrowed. In addition, the IMF imposed conditions that dictated the reorganization of economic priorities according to the free market ideologies that prevailed at the agency during the Reagan era. Convinced that too much government spending and political corruption were the main cause of the debt crisis, IMF advisors demanded that borrower nations implement American-style structural adjustment programs to restore fiscal responsibility, shrink the public sector, and free businesses from burdensome regulations. As in the United States, poor people in developing nations suffered most from the rising unemployment, cuts in social programs, and elimination of government services that resulted.[6]

Efforts by American policy makers to liberalize international trade also contributed to the hardships faced by many people around the world in the 1980s and 1990s. In 1986 the United States requested a new round of GATT negotiations aimed at further reducing tariffs and loosening regulations that hindered the international exchange of goods and services.

Resistance from farmers and small business owners in the United States and Europe who feared competition from large, multinational corporations stalled progress in these areas for almost decade, but a new agreement was finally reached in 1993 that achieved many of the goals pushed by free trade advocates. In 1995 the World Trade Organization (WTO) was formed as a successor to GATT to enforce compliance and serve as a venue for resolving trade disputes among the 109 nations that signed on to the agreement. The United States also worked to facilitate trade with its continental neighbors, finalizing the North American Free Trade Agreement (NAFTA) with Canada and Mexico in 1993. Proponents of the agreements argued that they would enhance global economic prosperity and improve living conditions for people in poor countries as well as wealthy ones by opening access to new sources of raw materials, technology, ideas, markets, and employment. According to GATT director Peter Sutherland, free trade produced "only winners, no losers."[7]

Economic Dislocation and Ethnic Conflict

In reality, laissez-faire economic policies extended around the world had the same impact globally that they had in the United States: large accumulations of wealth by some people and the relegation of millions of others to lives of poverty and insecurity. Labor activist Jeff Faux argued that the architecture of the global economy was not designed to benefit everyone but instead was "established to protect the interest of those who invest for a living, at the expense of those who must work." International agreements and the policies of the World Bank, IMF, and WTO reflected the views of corporate and financial elites who thought the most important element of any economy was the ability of capital to generate wealth. Their decisions placed maximizing profits ahead of everything else and neglected other concerns such as ensuring decent wages and conditions for workers, protecting consumers, or preserving the environment. In the new climate of deregulation corporations and banks sought out the lowest production costs and most lucrative investments with little thought to the social consequences of their decisions, and national governments competed with each other to offer the most business-friendly environment in an effort to attract capital. Many unionized factory workers in the United States and Europe lost their jobs when employers moved operations overseas to take advantage of cheaper labor. In the clothing manufacturing industry, for example, roughly 850,000 positions were redistributed from developed nations to poorer countries between 1980 and 1992. Average hourly wage rates in the developing nations ranged from 10¢ to $2.38 compared with $11.61 in the United States. Corporations' ability to leave if conditions were not to their liking undermined the power of labor unions and discouraged governments from implementing policies opposed by business leaders, such as higher taxes or more generous social services. Globalization thus simultaneously subjected many people to unemployment or lower incomes while limiting the ability of political leaders to respond with programs to alleviate workers' economic anxiety and help them adjust to the new order.[8]

The impact of economic liberalization was most severe in developing nations. Agricultural modernization displaced many small farmers and consolidated land ownership into the hands of a few native elites and foreign-owned agribusinesses. New manufacturing enterprises provided employment opportunities for only a fraction of those who lost their homes and livelihoods, and the jobs often paid subpoverty wages. In Indonesia, the parents of young women employed in factories producing goods for export had to subsidize their daughters' incomes to bring them up to subsistence level. Despite their willingness to labor for much less than their counterparts in other parts of the world, workers in developing countries could be no more certain that jobs would stay in their communities. American telephone company AT&T moved its assembly operations from Louisiana to Singapore in the late 1970s and exchanged its Singaporean employees for even cheaper labor in Thailand a decade later. In many countries fledgling local industries collapsed under the pressure of competition from international conglomerates that gained access to domestic markets through free trade agreements in the 1980s and 1990s, adding more unemployed workers to the hundreds of thousands who migrated to urban areas to find jobs. Cities were overwhelmed by the influx of poor people, and the structural adjustment programs imposed by the IMF left governments without the means to address problems of overcrowding, dilapidated housing, lack of sanitation, and crime. In some countries where states lost legitimacy and citizens were left to fend for themselves, violent conflicts broke out as people competed for access to scarce resources.[9]

Poverty and war drove many inhabitants of these regions to seek better opportunities outside of their home countries. In the early twenty-first century a World Bank study counted just over 190 million people in the global migrant stream. Western nations including the United States, the United Kingdom, France, and Germany, whose leaders had encouraged the adoption of measures that disrupted the lives of millions of people in the developing world, were among the top ten destinations.[10] Some native-born people in the racially and culturally homogenous societies of Western Europe expressed alarm over increasing numbers of immigrants from former colonies and from nations in Eastern Europe making the difficult transition from communism to capitalism after the end of the Cold War. The 1980s and 1990s saw the emergence of racist, neo-fascist movements in Europe that blamed immigrants for social ills such as rising unemployment, declining wages, and overburdened public services. In France the right-wing National Front campaigned openly as the party of white supremacy and called for the expulsion of Africans, Arabs, and other foreigners. Gangs of white youths in Germany, the United Kingdom, and the Netherlands violently attacked nonwhite people and burned down homes, businesses, and mosques in immigrant communities. Mainstream political leaders decried the violence but often legitimized xenophobic sentiments by enacting restrictive immigration policies and promising not to allow Europeans' traditional cultures to be "swamped" by new influences. Immigrants served as convenient scapegoats for governments seeking to deflect blame away from the economic policies that were the real source of the problems afflicting these societies.[11]

The same dynamics were evident in the United States. Although many Americans took pride in traditions of openness and the nation's past history of incorporating newcomers, some were disturbed by this latest infusion of diverse peoples. Eighty-four percent of the 36 million foreign-born residents of the United States in 2006 came from countries in Latin America, Asia, and Africa, a development made possible by civil rights era legislation banning racial discrimination in immigration. An estimated 11 million more immigrants from those regions lived in the country illegally. This shift in the ethnic composition of the nation concerned nativists like Pat Buchanan, whose book *Death of the West* (2002) warned that the United States faced the threat of extinction unless something was done to restrict the flow of people from alien and inferior cultures to its shores. Similar sentiments lay behind the successful movement to pass Proposition 187 in California in 1994, which denied access to public services such as education and medical care to illegal immigrants and their children. As scholar Evelyn Hu-DeHart observed, many Americans no longer saw immigrants as valuable additions whose presence enriched the nation economically and culturally. Instead, the new arrivals from developing nations were labeled as "terrorists, criminals, welfare cheats, and freeloaders, social burdens who exacerbate our urban crime problem and severely strain the public resources that our taxes support."[12] As in Europe, some political leaders seized on these issues to explain native-born Americans' economic woes, framing immigration as the natural outgrowth of the freedom and opportunity on offer in the United States rather than the consequence of global dislocations that accompanied the spread of capitalism.

In many communities immigrants competed directly with black workers for jobs in unskilled positions for which there was already a surplus of applicants. Some employers preferred to hire laborers from Latin America or the Caribbean over African Americans, claiming that black people did not want the jobs and performed poorly when they were hired. A more important reason underlying this discrimination was that immigrants, particularly those who were undocumented, were easier to exploit than native-born citizens. Workers whose visas were tied to their jobs or who were living in the country illegally could be persuaded to accept virtually any wages or conditions. In 2003 a report on abuses of agricultural migrant workers by labor contractors and growers in Florida stated plainly: "Slavery exists today." As in the nineteenth and early twentieth centuries, families worked for long hours under conditions resembling peonage, lived in squalid housing unfit for human habitation, and risked physical violence if they tried to leave. In Florida and elsewhere employers easily stifled attempts to resist the system with threats of deportation or a well-timed visit by immigration officials. Workers at a laundry service in New York discovered the risks of asserting their rights after demanding the company pay them $159,000 in back wages they were owed. Within a few days, the Immigration and Naturalization Service (INS) raided the work site and deported 10 undocumented employees. According to Christian Parenti, the INS frequently colluded with companies that employed immigrants to intimidate workers and ensure a cheap, docile labor supply.[13]

Abusive practices that were no longer tenable when applied to African Americans could still be used to control the immigrant labor force in the post-civil rights era, with consequences that negatively affected the prospects of both groups. Black workers were displaced from low-wage jobs as employers filled those positions with people who would work for even lower pay. One study in California found a significant drop in the number of African American janitors between 1977 and 1985 along with a decline in wages from $13.00 an hour to just above the minimum wage. The pattern of employing immigrants instead of native-born workers affected positions higher up on the job scale as well. Globalization gave American businesses access to highly educated, skilled workers from other countries to fill positions in medicine, computer science, engineering, and other professions. Stephen Steinberg noted that this dampened incentives for investing in education and training in the United States. "Despite a dire shortage of nurses, the United States has cut back on the training of nurses, and imported tens of thousands of nurses from the Philippines and the Caribbean where nurses are virtually an export commodity," he wrote. Such policies amounted to a "disinvestment in native workers" that further marginalized black communities already afflicted by inadequate schools and limited economic opportunities.[14]

Increasing immigration after the 1960s added to the problems black people faced in an era of deindustrialization and cuts in social services. African Americans, Latinos, Asians, Africans, and Middle Easterners encountered each other in the context of intense competition over resources. The struggles over access to jobs, housing, public space, and political power generated tensions that sometimes devolved into violence. In South Central

Los Angeles, black residents watched their neighborhood turn from 90 percent African American to 50 percent Latino between 1980 and 1990.[15] In the same period, many small businesses were taken over by Asian immigrants who arrived with modest amounts of capital and could more easily secure loans than African Americans. Rumors circulated among black people that the federal government helped newcomers with financial assistance that was denied to African Americans. For their part, immigrant storekeepers were convinced that laziness or lack of intellectual capacity, not racism, explained the poverty of their black neighbors. African Americans complained of being treated like suspects instead of valued customers when they patronized local businesses. One man stated, "I work for my money, I pay taxes and everything. ... And you walk into a liquor store, and they automatically treat you like you're a criminal and they give you that look, like, 'Ah, what are these kids doing in here?'"[16] In March 1991 Korean grocer Soon Ja Du shot and killed black teenager Latasha Harlins when she tried to steal a bottle of orange juice, and a short while later arsonists firebombed a different Korean store in retaliation. The multiethnic urban uprising that tore South Central apart in 1992 demonstrated that the nation's racial dynamics were more complex than the black–white dichotomy assumed by most analysts before the 1960s. Many of the people arrested during the disturbances were Latinos, and Korean-owned businesses suffered extensive property damage. *Boston Globe* reporter Martin Nolan compared the events in Los Angeles to the "ancient ethnic conflicts" unleashed in Eastern Europe after the collapse of the Soviet Union. "Los Angeles is as balkanized as Yugoslavia," he wrote.[17]

Such analyses made the ethnic tensions that existed in Europe and the United States seem inevitable, as if they resulted from inherent characteristics of human nature that no one could control. Community activists working to encourage interracial understanding and cooperation in distressed urban neighborhoods rejected that view, however. Marsha Chu of the Black-Korean Alliance in Los Angeles stated, "I get really angry when people simplify this as a black-Korean problem, because it's not. We're up against poverty and unemployment and the racism and – and the history of oppression in this country." Similarly, when some commentators accused Latino gangs of engaging in "ethnic cleansing" aimed at driving African Americans out of a South Los Angeles neighborhood, others focused on deeper causes of the violence. "Most of the bloodletting takes place in a dead sea of empty lots created by the deindustrialization of South LA, which lost 70,000 jobs between the Watts and Rodney King riots," noted Roberto Lovato in the *Nation*. Unwilling to consider that gang problems might be "an expression of overcrowded schools, unemployment and the utter failure of urban development policies," city officials adopted a strategy of "militaristic suppression" that intensified instead of reducing gang activity. The rhetoric of "race war" adopted by the police and echoed in the media implied that this was a problem involving black and Latino communities alone, unrelated to the social context that incubated these hostilities and the political decisions that exacerbated them.[18]

Some observers highlighted the international dimensions of such phenomena, noting that the same processes that devastated American cities generated desperate circumstances for poor people all over the world in the late twentieth century. Economic policies that freed capital to seek maximum profits above all other considerations, displaced millions of workers, privatized resources, and decimated public services lay behind the impoverishment of large numbers of citizens in developed and developing countries alike. In some countries where structural adjustment programs undermined the ability of governments to ensure that people's basic needs were met, brutal conflicts resembling the gang violence in the United States broke out as warlords and organized crime rings moved to fill the power vacuum. Western observers attributed the chaos in regions such as Sierra Leone, Somalia, and Rwanda to longstanding tribal rivalries and corrupt political leadership, but the demands of global capitalism also shared some responsibility. Globalization scholar Ankie Hoogvelt pointed out that "all these states imploded when the international community, led by the IMF and the World Bank ... imposed the discipline of the market and sought to combine privatization and liberalization with new forms of political governance in which the state was marginalized." The result was an erosion of government authority that led in many instances to "anarchy and civil wars."[19]

African Americans and the Global South

Black scholars and activists had long recognized African Americans' shared oppression with other nonwhite people around the world. In 1935 W. E. B. Du Bois asserted that the "dark and vast sea of human labor in China and India, the South Seas and all Africa; in the West Indies and Central America and in the United States – that great majority of mankind, on whose bent and broken backs rest today the founding stones of modern industry – shares a common destiny." Participants in the American civil rights movement and the leaders of nationalist independence movements in Africa supported each other's struggles in the mid-twentieth century and worked together on international cooperative efforts.[20] The Student Nonviolent Coordinating Committee included international perspectives in its analyses of racial problems in the 1960s, arguing that African Americans were subject to a form of internal colonialism that mirrored the effects of European imperialism on the inhabitants of the global South. The Black

Women's Alliance within SNCC expanded on these ideas, linking the oppression of women as well as black people to capitalism and critiquing the sexism espoused by some male leaders of black nationalist movements. In 1970 the group expanded to become the Third World Women's Alliance, including Asian, Latin American, and Native American women in an organization that aimed to overcome the triple injustices of racism, imperialism, and sexism.[21] The NCNW engaged in similar work in the post-civil rights era, hosting visits from African women and sending its own members to study the self-help initiatives of poor women in other countries. As in the United States, many communities in the developing world responded to the disruption of their local economies by forming cooperatives and credit unions to provide the means for displaced people to support themselves. Dorothy Height wrote later that her travels to Africa and participation in international conferences convinced her of the interconnectedness of black people's struggles and those of people in other nations. "Women of color around the world have common problems and common dreams," she asserted. "Whether affluent or needy, living in the northern industrialized world or the developing South, educated or illiterate, we all want to improve the quality of life for our loved ones and our communities."[22]

The same premises informed the work of other civil rights groups and social justice organizations as well. ACORN's network of 850 chapters included groups in Canada, the Dominican Republic, India, and Peru that offered assistance to the victims of economic dislocation, encouraged political participation by poor people, and pressured governments to devote more resources to addressing poverty and homelessness. Jesse Jackson frequently highlighted the effects of corporate globalization on workers all over the world and advocated rewriting free trade agreements to ensure minimum standards of conduct regarding labor rights, workplace safety, and environmental practices. "Slave labor anywhere is a threat to organized labor everywhere," he declared during his 1988 presidential campaign. Jackson urged supporters to join him in the fight for "international economic justice" to ensure democracy and prosperity for all people. In the late 1980s Operation PUSH joined with antisweatshop activists to expose the exploitative conditions that existed in factories in developing nations that produced sports apparel for American corporations Nike and Adidas. Environmental justice activists also identified clear links between their fight against policies that turned nonwhite neighborhoods in the United States into toxic waste dumps and parallel developments in poor countries. A group of eight American activists who presented evidence of environmental racism in their communities to the United Nations Commission on Human Rights in 1999 noted that Shell Oil Company displayed the same disregard for the health of black people in the Ogoni region of Nigeria as it did in Norco, Louisiana.[23]

African Americans felt a special connection to the black victims of South African apartheid, a system that closely resembled the Jim Crow regime that they had suffered under themselves before the 1960s. In contrast to the United States, where the civil rights movement successfully pressured national leaders to end legalized discrimination, South Africa's white rulers acted to further curtail the rights of black people in their country in the decades after World War II. A series of laws passed after the racist Nationalist Party gained power in 1948 classified every person by race and restricted access to housing, jobs, education, and public facilities for black South Africans. Black people were confined to reservation "homelands" and had to acquire passes to enter white communities to work. Those who attempted to protest this discrimination faced brutal repression by police. Activists in the African National Congress (ANC) and other organizations that fought the system were frequently imprisoned, beaten, tortured, or killed. In 1961, security forces shot 69 people who took part in a peaceful demonstration outside a police station in Sharpeville. A government ban on the ANC in the wake of the incident and continued state violence against activists forced the South African freedom movement underground. Those who were not imprisoned or exiled turned to armed resistance in an effort to make apartheid untenable. Mass strikes by black workers, consumer boycotts, student protests, and an international campaign to free imprisoned ANC leader Nelson Mandela created more problems for the government in the 1970s and 1980s but resulted in only a few minor reforms.[24]

Civil rights activists in the United States expressed solidarity with black South Africans and joined in the global movement to pressure governments, corporations, and financial institutions to impose sanctions aimed at forcing an end to apartheid (see Figure 8.1). In 1971 workers at Polaroid camera factories in North America who made the equipment used to produce South African identity cards asked their company to stop doing business with the oppressive regime. Anti-apartheid activists also convinced some universities, cities, and states to examine their investment portfolios and avoid buying stock in multinational corporations that operated in South Africa. In November 1984 a broad coalition that included the members of civil rights organizations, black elected officials, churches, and labor unions engaged in several weeks of protest at the South African embassy in Washington, DC, to demand the release of 13 South African labor leaders who had "disappeared" after being taken into police custody. The sit-ins, picketing, and boycotts spread to encompass banks and corporations that were complicit in maintaining apartheid and resulted in the arrests of more than 70 people. The following year Congress voted to limit trade, deny loans, and discourage investments in South Africa, but final passage of the legislation was blocked in a filibuster led by North Carolina senator Jesse Helms. Legislators tried again in 1986, this time managing to pass the measures

Figure 8.1 Singer Harry Belafonte and others at an anti-apartheid protest outside the South African embassy in Washington, DC, 1984
Source: Chas Cancellare/United Press International

over President Reagan's veto. Similar actions by other nations and disinvestment by banks and corporations left South Africa struggling for economic survival by the end of the decade. In February 1990 newly elected president F. W. de Klerk announced plans to release all political prisoners, legalize the ANC, and begin transforming the nation into a democratic, racially integrated society. The dismantling of South African apartheid culminated in April 1994 with the election of Nelson Mandela and the ANC to govern the nation.[25]

The Global Justice Movement

The South African campaign demonstrated that corporate and governmental power were not the only forces at work in the era of globalization. Coordinated action by social justice activists communicating and organizing across national borders shamed international elites into altering their behavior, leaving the white minority in South Africa without the resources they needed to continue the oppression of their black compatriots. The movement's success raised the possibility that other forms of injustice might be targeted the same way. "The warning sounds for the global system of political alliances and economic interests headquartered in Washington," wrote Andrew Kopkind in the *Nation*. "The hope is that a victory against apartheid in South Africa can be shared by others similarly oppressed." The South African model was replicated on a worldwide scale through a system that allowed the planet's white minority to dictate policies that determined the living conditions of "a dark majority of the earth."[26]

Many people in developing nations resisted the economic models imposed on their societies as a condition for international loans and investment. In the decade from 1976 to 1986 some 50 "IMF riots" occurred in 13 countries as citizens protested the loss of subsidies for food and other necessities, cuts in education and health services, and mass unemployment that resulted from structural adjustment programs. These were not the mindless actions of ignorant mobs whose members failed to understand the complexities of the global financial system. The Panamanian workers who shouted "I won't pay the debt! Let the ones who stole the money pay!" at their political leaders in September 1985 understood that they were being forced to accept an unfair burden as the nation struggled to recover from a crisis generated by decisions over which they had no control. According to former World Bank economist Joseph Stiglitz, people in the East Asian nations of Thailand, Malaysia, South Korea, and Indonesia used "IMF" as a synonym for the economic hardships generated by austerity measures adopted after panicked selling by currency speculators brought the region close to financial collapse in the 1990s. "History is dated by 'before' and 'after' the IMF, just as countries that are devastated by an earthquake or some other natural disaster date events by 'before' or 'after' the earthquake," he explained.[27]

The impact of IMF-induced economic disasters fell heavily on women, whose traditional roles as subordinates and caregivers meant they bore most of the responsibility for filling the gaps left by falling incomes and the erosion of public services. In families that could not afford to adequately feed everyone or send every child to school, men received priority while women and girls went without. Women in rich as well as poor nations supplemented male family members' incomes by working long hours in fields, factories, restaurants, hospitals, schools, and offices, returning home each evening to face the cooking, cleaning, and other domestic tasks expected of them. In the absence of government-supported childcare, health care, or retirement programs, women in many societies took care of those who were too young, too sick, or too old to work. Economic theorists and male-dominated governments obsessed with encouraging profit-making activity failed to acknowledge or reward women who performed these essential services. In response, women engaged in transnational collaboration and advocacy efforts to increase awareness of the pressures they faced and push for policies that addressed neglected social needs. Global justice advocates from Barbados, India, and Brazil founded Development Alternatives with Women for a New Era in 1985 and worked with some success to publicize the defects of structural adjustment programs. Activists in Tunisia and Morocco formed organizations that pressed for laws to protect workers' rights and end child labor. Women in developed nations offered support for these efforts through groups such as the Women's International Committee for Economic Justice, a coalition of feminist organizations that lobbied governments to adopt fair labor standards and implement other reforms.[28]

In the 1990s Mexico became a site of intense resistance to free market capitalism and a focal point for global justice efforts. Indigenous people in Chiapas responded to NAFTA by forming the Zapatista National Liberation Army and mounting a campaign of armed resistance against the nation's corrupt government and economic policies that threatened their livelihoods. On January 1, 1994, the day the free trade agreement went into effect, the rebels seized control of several towns and posted notices calling on others to join the fight. The Zapatistas argued that a NAFTA ban on subsidies to indigenous rural cooperatives amounted to a death sentence for 4 million poor people living in Chiapas. "The dictators have been carrying out an undeclared, genocidal war against our people for many years," they stated. "That is why we are asking for your determined participation and support for this decision of the Mexican people, who struggle for work, land, shelter, food, health, education, independence, freedom, democracy, justice and peace."[29] The movement gained support from Mexicans of all social classes who were tired of a government that prioritized the needs of international investors above those of its own people, helping to end the seven-decade rule of the Institutional Revolutionary Party in 2000. Taking advantage of the same modern technologies that facilitated the mobility of capital, activists disseminated news of their protests and impassioned critiques of the global economic order throughout the world. The Zapatista movement, they asserted, was the same struggle being waged by landless peasants, unemployed workers, oppressed religious and ethnic minorities, and political dissenters everywhere. The rebels hosted meetings in Chiapas that drew participants from dozens of nations to discuss how best to ensure freedom, economic security, and meaningful political participation for all the planet's people. By 2002 the internet hosted at least 45,000 Zapatista-themed websites spread across 26 countries. As Naomi Klein observed, reaching out to an international audience enabled the Zapatistas to demonstrate that "what was going on in Chiapas could not be written off as a narrow 'ethnic' struggle, that it was both specific and universal." The movement targeted not only the Mexican government but the broader ideology that lay behind the imposition of free market capitalism on Mexico and other countries.[30]

The global nature of the problems identified by people in developing nations became clearer as the citizens of western democracies realized how the new system affected their own lives. In the United States activists representing views that spanned the political spectrum, from civil rights and labor organizations on the left to anti-immigration groups on the right, tried unsuccessfully to prevent the passage of NAFTA in 1993. Opponents argued that by placing North American workers in competition with each other, with no provisions for ensuring labor rights, the agreement threatened to accelerate job losses and lower wages in the United States and Canada without raising living standards for poor people in Mexico. The SCLC's Joseph Lowery asserted, "We need free trade but only after we have a level playing field. We've got to have wages in Mexico, for example, that will prevent the flight of workers to the North, and we've got to have the kind of sensitivity to that so we can prevent the flight of jobs to the South." Veteran civil rights leader John Lewis, now in Congress, concurred. Lewis told reporters he planned to fight against NAFTA ratification, explaining, "I don't think it is in the best interest of working people in this country. We need to keep those jobs at home and put all of our people to work. We don't need cheap starvation wages in Mexico and to have companies leaving here, crossing the border to hide and support bad working conditions in Mexico."[31]

Labor rights were not the only concerns raised by critics of free trade agreements. In the 1990s international agencies resolved several trade disputes in ways that revealed how the new economic order undermined the ability of national governments to enforce their own laws or protect the health and safety of the people they were supposed to represent. A complaint by Mexico against the United States resulted in the removal of a provision in the Marine Mammal Protection Act that banned imports of tuna caught using methods that endangered dolphins. Similarly, in 1998 the WTO ruled that the United States could not prohibit imports of shrimp from countries that did not use environmentally sound practices. Efforts to impose universal food safety standards were also cause for alarm, since the WTO used guidelines that were not as stringent as those that had been adopted by most developed nations. European laws banning the use of some pesticides, hormones, and genetically modified organisms in food production came under fire from corporations demanding the removal of these barriers to trade. As in the developing world, government services and social programs that kept many citizens of wealthier nations out of poverty were also targeted. Business leaders in the United States who were burdened with responsibility for providing health insurance for their employees argued that Canada's national health system was a form of unfair advantage for manufacturers across the border and asked the federal government to file a challenge under NAFTA. Self-employed lobster fishers who were ineligible for unemployment benefits during the off-season in the United States made the same argument regarding the more generous government assistance enjoyed by their competitors in Canada. United Parcel Service, a private mail delivery company, contended that the Canadian postal service conflicted with NAFTA. The *New York Times* reported in 2001: "Critics worry that if the tribunal upholds the U.P.S. claim, government participation in any service that competes with the private sector will be threatened."[32]

With good reason, global justice advocates perceived trade negotiations and other processes that determined the direction of the international economy as a threat to democracy. Small cliques of government officials, corporate lobbyists, and central bankers made decisions in closed talks with no participation from the masses of people who had to live with the consequences. As Joseph Stiglitz explained, international financial institutions were "dominated not just by the wealthiest industrial countries but by commercial and financial interests in those countries, and the policies of the institutions naturally reflect this. ... The workers who are thrown out of jobs as a result of the IMF programs have no seat at the table; while the bankers, who insist on getting repaid, are well represented through the finance ministers and central bank governors."[33] At the IMF votes were allocated on the basis of how much money each nation contributed to the Fund, giving wealthier countries more power over policy making than poorer ones. The United States, Europe, and Japan dominated the World Bank and WTO as well. In some discussions representatives from the global South were excluded entirely. Meetings of the Group of Seven (G7) initiated in the 1970s included the leaders and finance ministers of only the United States, United Kingdom, France, West Germany, Japan, Italy, and Canada on the assumption that less prominent nations had little to contribute to discussions of the global economy. West German prime minister Helmut Schmidt explained, "We want a private, informal meeting of those who really matter in the world."[34]

Though mostly hidden from public view, the machinations of international financial institutions did not go entirely unnoticed. Social justice activists quietly monitored news accounts of the meetings, analyzed the implications of decisions, and shared interpretations with each other over the internet. Out of these efforts emerged a transnational network of labor organizers, environmentalists, farmers' groups, consumer advocates, antipoverty activists, political dissenters, students, artists, and intellectuals that was able to mount a coordinated challenge to the system at the turn of the century. Protesters in more than 70 cities around the world engaged in several days of demonstrations during the second ministerial meeting of the WTO in Geneva, Switzerland, in May 1998. Peasants and workers in India called for their government to withdraw from the WTO. Ten thousand residents of the Philippines marched on the nation's capital to demand a reorientation of food production "to feed the Filipino people and not aristocrats abroad." A poster advertising events in Berkeley, California, invited participants to a street party to "live, breathe, and dance their defiance to the car, and the capitalist system that spawned it." In Geneva, protesters smashed the windows of some banks and overturned the WTO director-general's Mercedes.[35]

For the next several years no major meeting of global financial or political leaders passed without mass demonstrations aimed at exposing the unequal, undemocratic nature of the international economic order. At the WTO's third ministerial conference in Seattle in November 1999, some 75,000 people representing more than 700 organizations converged on the city. Activists representing diverse ideologies and approaches engaged in a range of activities that included peaceful marches, street theater, civil disobedience, and vandalism. Police responded to the mayhem by arresting and beating people and using tear gas, plastic bullets, and concussion grenades to disperse the crowds (see Figure 8.2). While some analysts blamed protesters for the violence and portrayed them as anarchists and hooligans, independent media activists posted photos and videos on the internet that showed the actual aggressors were the police. The protests unnerved WTO delegates and exposed divisions inside the meeting rooms that echoed the

Figure 8.2　Police and protesters amidst clouds of tear gas during the third ministerial conference of the World Trade Organization in Seattle, 1999
Source: Nick Cobbing/Nick Cobbing

concerns of the people in the streets. Europeans resisted American proposals for eliminating farm subsidies and removing restrictions on food imports containing genetically modified organisms. Representatives from India and Egypt rejected a strong pitch by President Clinton to include fair labor standards in future agreements, viewing it as an attempt by developed nations to obliterate the competitive advantages of poorer countries. The WTO negotiations collapsed after three days, failing to resolve these contentious issues. The *Los Angeles Times* reported: "On the tear gas-shrouded streets of Seattle, the unruly forces of democracy collided with the elite world of trade policy. And when the meeting ended in failure on Friday, the elitists had lost and the debate had changed forever."[36]

Law enforcement agencies watched global justice internet sites to find out what activists were planning and attempted to limit their disruptive influence. In advance of meetings of the World Bank and IMF in April 2000, police in Washington, DC, erected barricades preventing entry into a 50-block area of the city, raided a warehouse that protesters were using to prepare signs and other materials, and preemptively arrested 600 people the day before the meetings opened. Later that year officials in the Czech Republic refused to allow known movement participants into the country during meetings of the same two agencies in Prague. Those who managed to assemble for the protests braved the presence of 11,000 police armed with tear gas and water cannons.[37] In Genoa, Italy, in 2001, police shot and killed demonstrator Carlo Giuliani during a G8 summit (the G7 plus Russia, admitted in 1998). Naomi Klein reported that in the past few years she had "watched with horror as the police have moved from pepper spray to mass tear gas; from tear gas to rubber bullets; rubber bullets to live ammunition." Police and media portrayals of global justice activists as violent, dangerous, and (after September 11, 2001) "terrorists" served to rationalize the repression. Marginalizing critics of global capitalism in this way also exempted political and financial leaders from defending their policies or acknowledging alternative views of how the global economy could be organized. As if to reinforce activists' argument that decisions affecting all the world's people were being made by a tiny cabal with no transparency and no mechanisms for democratic participation, the WTO held its fourth ministerial meeting in Doha, Qatar, a Middle Eastern dictatorship where all political protest was banned.[38]

In addition to the tear gas and bullets, supporters of economic liberalization engaged in a war of words that depicted global justice activists as spoiled, white, flat-earth "protectionists" seeking to deny the benefits of capitalism to poorer, darker-skinned people. "To those who would argue that we should stop our work, I say: Tell that to the poor, to the marginalized around the world who are looking to us to help them," declared WTO head Michael Moore in response to criticisms of the organization. Similarly,

IMF director Stanley Fischer insisted that the protesters did not understand the valuable role the agency played in alleviating poverty. Globalization represented "the only way we are going to raise people around the world to the same level as people in industrialized countries," he stated. Mainstream media analyses echoed these arguments. A December 1999 editorial in *USA Today* asserted, "The global flow of money, goods and workers – the 'globalization' that the WTO has come to symbolize – is among the most powerful forces raising up the world's poor and disenfranchised." Accepting the conventional wisdom that these developments were as natural and uncontrollable as the evolution of species, another report dismissed protesters' actions as futile: "No sane observer believes that the march toward international trade suddenly will halt. In this new millennium, a global economy isn't debatable – it's inevitable." Other commentators noted that the scarcity of nonwhite faces in the crowds that gathered outside international meetings undercut activists' claims to be acting on behalf of the poor and oppressed. One account of the Seattle protests stated that they "had all the egalitarian substance of a whites-mostly garden party."[39]

The notion that the global justice movement was comprised largely of privileged white inhabitants of the world's richest nations ignored three decades of protests in Africa, Asia, and Latin America that predated those in the United States and Europe at the turn of the century. As Naomi Klein pointed out, "When [North American] union members and environmentalists took to the streets … they were playing catch-up with a movement for self-determination that began in the southern nations of the world, where the words 'World Bank' are spat, not said, and where 'IMF' is parodied on protest signs as short for 'I M Fired.'" Moreover, the mass demonstrations in western nations occurred simultaneously with globalized "days of action" in cities like Mumbai (India), Buenos Aires (Argentina), and Johannesburg (South Africa). A collection of first-hand accounts of these events as well as ongoing local acts of resistance titled *We Are Everywhere* contained hundreds of articles and photos testifying to the movement's racially diverse nature and widespread agreement among members regarding the sources of oppression. Filipino demonstrators marched on the United States embassy in Manila in November 2001 with banners urging the world to "Junk WTO!"[40] Black South Africans protested the limits that structural adjustment programs placed on their newfound freedom with street demonstrations and cardboard signs reading: "Stop Profiting from Our Hunger: Capitalism is Unfit for Human Consumption." In townships across the country where poor people could not afford to pay for newly privatized services, neighbors worked together to block evictions and illegally reconnected each other's electricity and water supplies. South African activist Ashwin Desai expressed appreciation for the citizens of the United States and Europe who took to the streets in support of his and other struggles.

"To know that from the beast of the apocalypse people are revolting and inventive is very powerful," he stated.[41]

Seattle activist Grey Filastine's account of a strike by the city's taxi drivers during the WTO conference in 1999 revealed how developments in the world's poorest and richest nations were intertwined. As in many American cities, the drivers were "overwhelmingly poor immigrants" who worked 12-hour shifts, seven days a week without health insurance, workers' compensation, or other benefits. "Many of the African and Indian drivers were familiar with the WTO, World Bank, and IMF because of the activities of those institutions in their home countries," Filastine wrote. Angry at city leaders over "reforms" of the cab companies that emphasized presenting a positive image for tourists rather than improving conditions for workers, the drivers chose November 30, 1999 as an appropriate day to protest phenomena that they had lived with for too long: "People from the global South working too hard for too little. ... Sweatshop hours. A system which caters to the comforts of the wealthy. A popular resistance that gains little ground against a 'business friendly' government."[42]

Global justice activists' collaboration across lines of race, class, gender, religion, and nationality contradicted criticisms that they represented the short-sighted, parochial concerns of people who feared change. Participants in the movement were not trying to prevent globalization but only wanted to ensure the process served wider interests than those of transnational corporations and banks. "The core point of contention ... is over the rules of the global marketplace – and who will set them," explained Jeff Faux. The goal was to create "an economics that serves society, rather than one that is served by society." Indian feminist and environmental activist Vandana Shiva observed that globalization in its current form was "based on reducing every aspect of our lives to commodities and reducing our identities to that of mere consumers in the global marketplace." Human beings were not items to be used or discarded in accordance with the dictates of free markets, she asserted.[43] In January 2001 more than 10,000 global justice advocates who shared such views gathered together at the first World Social Forum in Porto Alegre, Brazil, to discuss and debate alternatives to the existing system. The multiplicity of ethnicities, social classes, and ideologies represented at the meeting demonstrated that this was not a movement of people who were afraid of foreign influences or new ideas. The forum contrasted starkly with the narrow world of global financial elites making decisions based on abstract theories promoted by the world's wealthiest and whitest.

Many global justice activists took inspiration, philosophies, or tactics from the American civil rights movement. An emphasis on participatory democracy and consensus decision-making reminiscent of SNCC and CORE's work in the rural South in the 1960s characterized planning for mass demonstrations and civil disobedience by opponents of free market capitalism in the 1990s. At the 2002 World Social Forum fair trade advocates Joshua Karliner and Karolo Aparicio cited Martin Luther King Jr.'s "Letter from Birmingham Jail" in a discussion of the relative merits of "dialogue versus confrontation" as a means of encouraging socially responsible behavior by corporations. "Negotiation is the purpose of direct action, and confrontations aim to create enough power and tension to force the powerful to negotiate," they argued. The Congress of South African Trade Unions presented proposals for addressing global inequality that were identical to black Americans' calls for sustained government action to end racism and poverty. In place of the IMF's structural adjustment programs, these workers demanded "comprehensive social protection combined with economic development strategies aimed at creating quality jobs, meeting basic needs for food and housing, and improving workers' access to education and training." A manifesto based on a rough consensus of the meeting's 55,000 participants explained the movement's purpose in terms that recognized commonalities among the various freedom movements inspired by the anticolonial and civil rights struggles of the 1960s: "We are diverse – women and men, adults and youth, indigenous peoples, rural and urban, workers and unemployed, homeless, the elderly, students, migrants, professionals, peoples of every creed, colour and sexual orientation. ... We are a global solidarity movement, united in our determination to fight against the concentration of wealth, the proliferation of poverty and inequalities, and the destruction of our earth. ... We are building a large alliance from our struggles and resistance against a system based on sexism, racism and violence, which privileges the interests of capital and patriarchy over the needs and aspirations of people."[44]

Mass protests and the World Social Forums drew attention to defects in the economic order and forced a reassessment of the policies pursued by international financial institutions. By the early twenty-first century many analysts joined with the world's poor people in expressing impatience with those who believed free markets alone could ensure an efficient and fair distribution of the wealth of nations. Ankie Hoogvelt noted that aggregate increases in national and global wealth cited as evidence of globalization's success meant little to the 1.3 billion people living in poverty. "In a world so steeped in social inequality that just three super-billionaires have an amount of wealth exceeding the combined income of all the least developed nations and their 600 million population, and the net worth of another 200 equates to the income of 41 per cent of world population, measures of global growth are simply offensive," she wrote. Most supporters of free trade now acknowledged that the process must be accompanied by mechanisms to cushion the effects of worker displacement and spread the benefits more evenly. A Brookings Institution report viewed such measures as both "a political requirement and a moral obligation." Pressure from activists and consumers persuaded some corporations to pay more attention to social justice concerns. Nike took steps to improve working conditions for laborers in the developing world, and Starbucks began selling a line of fair trade coffee in its stores.[45] Advertising campaigns for these and other companies emphasized values that were gaining popularity among consumers, such as environmental sustainability and protecting human rights.

The reform impulse eventually reached into the highest levels of global economics and policy making. During the Washington, DC, demonstrations in 2000, several former staff members of the World Bank and IMF publicly supported the protesters and confirmed the global justice movement's criticisms of the agencies. In 2002 the collapse of transnational energy giant Enron amidst revelations of fraud and corruption demonstrated the folly of deregulation and generated support for more government oversight of powerful corporations. The same year, Joseph Stiglitz published a highly critical account of the policies pursued by international financial institutions based on his experience serving as chief economist and senior vice president of the World Bank from 1997 to 2000. Stiglitz accused the IMF, especially, of rigidly adhering to economic theories that had little basis in reality, protecting the interests of wealthy banks and investors at the expense of most of humanity, and devastating entire nations with programs that led to hunger, riots, political instability, and capital flight. With the exception of some of his targets at the IMF, Stiglitz's book was well received and the fundamental arguments regarding the deficiencies of the agency's approach were not challenged. Both the IMF and the World Bank were already working to modify their programs to place more emphasis on reducing poverty. World Bank president James Wolfensohn admitted, "At the level of people, the system isn't working." Wolfensohn promoted changes in policy at the agency that encouraged nations to take a more balanced approach to economic growth, including social investments to achieve greater equality. In response to a recession in Bolivia in 2001, the IMF indicated that it was open to allowing alternative approaches to reviving the economy instead of the austerity measures it had imposed in the past. Meanwhile, officials at the WTO avoided making controversial decisions that might spark protest and worked to give representatives of developing nations more influence in shaping trade agreements. In November 2008 a G20 summit held in Washington, DC, significantly expanded the number of countries included in discussions of global economic policy. Participants agreed that the economic practices pushed by the developed nations in past decades bore a heavy responsibility for the worldwide financial meltdown and pledged to cooperate on efforts to solve the immediate crisis, stabilize the system in the long term, and address "other critical challenges" such as climate change, food security, poverty, and disease.[46]

* * * *

As the United States celebrated the inauguration of its first black president in January 2009, the world stood at a crossroads. Political leaders, business people, academics, media analysts, and citizens contemplated the failures of unregulated capitalism and tried to decide which paths might lead to a better future. African Americans were perhaps more qualified than most people to offer insight. The features of the global economy that impoverished millions and resulted in its eventual collapse had shaped black people's experiences since slavery. "Blackness" was historically defined by practices that reduced human beings to commodities whose value was determined by the market, treated them as disposable, and denied them opportunities to participate in decisions that determined the conditions of their lives. In the late twentieth century these processes were extended to encompass numerous other groups: downsized factory workers in the deindustrialized cities of Europe and North America, displaced peasants in the global South, transnational migrant laborers, middle-class homeowners facing foreclosure, even Wall Street bankers whose companies collapsed along with the financial system they helped to create.

By 2008 millions of white Americans who had thought black people's cultural deficiencies explained persistent racial inequality were learning the lessons that African Americans already knew, experiencing little difficulty in identifying the real causes of unemployment, deteriorating neighborhoods, and stresses on families now that they were affected themselves. In Elkhart, Indiana, a town where 18 percent of workers could not find jobs, news reporter Paul Solman encountered some "lifelong Republicans" who were rethinking some of their earlier assumptions about the relationships between the government, citizens, and the economy. Unemployed factory worker Ed Neufeldt stated, "I think I'm slowly sinking from the middle class to the poor class. So it's making me think a little bit different about people that don't have that much. I mean, the hard-working American family that's trying to make it and, through no fault of their own, they're not making it."[47]

Barack Obama's election brought together multiple strands in the historical developments of the previous four decades. The new president was both a beneficiary of and a participant in black Americans' struggles for freedom and equality. Like many other African Americans who held public office in the post-civil rights era, he inherited a pile of economic and social wreckage from the white men who preceded him. Obama's multicultural upbringing within and outside the United States fostered an internationalist perspective that fit well with the new requirements of leadership in a globalized world. The president's proposals for public investments aimed at creating jobs and ending decades of underfunding for education, social services, and infrastructure, along with his willingness to cooperate with other global citizens in meeting the challenges of the twenty-first century, suggested that his priorities differed significantly from those that had prevailed since the 1970s. Resistance to this reform agenda from financial elites, antitax activists, and fiscal conservatives in Congress nonetheless indicated that significant challenges lay ahead. Whatever happened next, the election of a progressive and pragmatic black president imbued with the values of the African American freedom movement opened a new chapter in the story of race in America.

NOTES

INTRODUCTION

1 Stephen Colbert, *The Colbert Report*, Episode 2121, Comedy Central, September 27, 2006, accessed at: http://www.colbertnation.com/the-colbert-report-videos/182287/september-27-2006/tip-wag-george-clooney

2 Julian Bond, "Civil Rights, Now & Then," *Poverty & Race*, August 31, 1998, 1.

3 Stokely Carmichael and Charles V. Hamilton, *Black Power: The Politics of Liberation in America* (New York: Random House, 1967), 4–5 (quotation on p. 4). Two other very useful analyses of racism's systemic nature and white Americans' collective obligation to address it are Beverly Daniel Tatum, "Defining Racism: 'Can We Talk?'" and Peggy McIntosh, "White Privilege: Unpacking the Invisible Knapsack," both in *Race, Class, and Gender in the United States: An Integrated Study*, 7th edn., ed. Paula S. Rothenberg (New York: Worth Publishers, 2007), 123–30 (Tatum) and 177–82 (McIntosh). Eduardo Bonilla-Silva offers additional insight into the ways institutional racism persisted into the civil rights era and the role of colorblind ideology in perpetuating racial disparities in *White Supremacy and Racism in the Post-Civil Rights Era* (Boulder, CO: Lynne Rienner Publishers, 2001) and *Racism Without Racists: Color-Blind Racism and the Persistence of Racial Inequality in the United States*, 2nd edn. (Lanham, MD: Rowman & Littlefield, 2006).

4 Richard Viguerie and Mark Fitzgibbons, "What about Liberal Bigots?" *Washington Times*, November 23, 2008, B3.

5 Gary Younge, "White History 101," *Nation*, March 5, 2007, 10.

CHAPTER 1: THE NEVER ENDING STORY

1 Malcolm X quoted in George Lipsitz, *The Possessive Investment in Whiteness: How White People Profit from Identity Politics* (Philadelphia, PA: Temple University Press, 1998), 182.

2 William J. Simmons, filmed interview footage in *Eyes on the Prize: America's Civil Rights Movement, Episode 5: Is This America?*, produced and directed by Orlando Bagwell, Blackside, Inc., 1986, DVD video recording.

3   Audrey Smedley, *Race in North America: Origin and Evolution of a Worldview*, 3rd edn. (Boulder, CO: Perseus Books, Westview Press, 2007), 47–9.

4   Edmund S. Morgan, *American Slavery, American Freedom: The Ordeal of Colonial Virginia* (New York: W. W. Norton & Company, 1975), 77; Audrey Smedley, *Race in North America*, 47–51, 113.

5   Edward Countryman, "The Beginnings of American Slavery," in *How Did American Slavery Begin?*, ed. Edward Countryman (Boston, MA: Bedford/St. Martin's, 1999), 7; Betty Wood, *Slavery in Colonial America, 1619–1776* (Lanham, MD: Rowman & Littlefield, 2005), 4–5.

6   Ira Berlin, *Many Thousands Gone: The First Two Centuries of Slavery in North America* (Cambridge, MA: Belknap Press of Harvard University Press, 1998), 29–46; Theodore W. Allen, *The Invention of the White Race, Vol. II: The Origin of Racial Oppression in Anglo-America* (London: Verso, 1997), 180–3.

7   Theodore W. Allen, *Invention of the White Race*, 179–80, 188; Betty Wood, *Slavery in Colonial America*, 9–10; Edmund S. Morgan, *American Slavery, American Freedom*, 155, 327, 333–4.

8   Edmund S. Morgan, *American Slavery, American Freedom*, 123–9.

9   Theodore W. Allen, *Invention of the White Race*, 189 (Baptista); Anthony S. Parent Jr., *Foul Means: The Formation of a Slave Society in Virginia, 1660–1740* (Chapel Hill: University of North Carolina Press, 2003), 110–12, 115 (Key).

10 Theodore W. Allen, *Invention of the White Race*, 151–6.

11 Virginia Assembly quoted in Theodore W. Allen, *Invention of the White Race*, 150; Edmund S. Morgan, *American Slavery, American Freedom*, 215–24; 235–70; Audrey Smedley, *Race in North America*, 111–12.

12 Observers, Virginia House of Burgesses, and Francis Nicholas quoted in Theodore W. Allen, *Invention of the White Race*, 217–19.

13 Theodore W. Allen, *Invention of the White Race*, 171–2 (Governor Thomas Lord Culpeper quoted on p. 172); Anthony S. Parent, *Foul Means*, 60 (Spencer), 55–70.

14 Anthony S. Parent, *Foul Means*, 105–34.

15 Theodore W. Allen, *Invention of the White Race*, 187 (exemptions quotation), 241–2, 250–1.

16 Anthony S. Parent, *Foul Means*, 118, 121, 147; Theodore W. Allen, *Invention of the White Race*, 250–3; Edmund S. Morgan, *American Slavery, American Freedom*, 332.

17 Edmund S. Morgan, *American Slavery, American Freedom*, 346, 386; Anthony Benezet quoted in Winthrop Jordan, *White Over Black: American Attitudes toward the Negro, 1550–1812* (Chapel Hill: University of North Carolina Press, 1968), 275.

18 Emanual Downing to John Winthrop, 1645, in *Documents Illustrative of the History of the Slave Trade to America, Vol. III: New England and the Middle Colonies*, ed. Elizabeth Donnan (Washington, DC: Carnegie Institution of Washington, 1932), 8; Audrey Smedley, *Race in North America*, 224.

19 Larry E. Tise, *Proslavery: A History of the Defense of Slavery in America, 1701–1840* (Athens: University of Georgia Press, 1987), 12–40; Donald L.

Robinson, *Slavery in the Structure of American Politics, 1765–1820* (New York: Harcourt Brace Jovanovich, 1971), 54–97.

20   Winthrop Jordan, *White Over Black*, 81, 134; Edmund S. Morgan, *American Slavery, American Freedom*, 4 (quotation), 363–87; Audrey Smedley, *Race in North America*, 197, 200, 218, 232; Michael Goldfield, *The Color of Politics: Race and the Mainsprings of American Politics* (New York: New Press, 1997), 70–3.

21   Donald L. Robinson, *Slavery in the Structure of American Politics*, 71–97; Ira Berlin, *Many Thousands Gone*, 228–39.

22   "The Tailors' Strike of 1836," in *A Documentary History of American Industrial Society, Vol. V: Labor Movement*, eds. John R. Commons, Ulrich B. Phillips, Eugene A. Gilmore, John B. Andrews and Helen L. Sumner (New York: Russell & Russell, 1958), 317.

23   David Roediger, *The Wages of Whiteness: Race and the Making of the American Working Class*, rev. edn. (London: Verso, 2007), 65–92.

24   W. E. B. Du Bois, *Black Reconstruction in America: An Essay Toward a History of the Part Which Black Folk Played in the Attempt to Reconstruct Democracy in America, 1860–1880* (New York: Russell & Russell, 1962; 1935), 17–31; David Roediger, *Wages of Whiteness*, 140–4.

25   Thomas F. Gossett, *Race: The History of an Idea in America* (New York: Oxford University Press, 1997; 1963), 73–4; Robert W. Gibbes quoted in William Stanton, *The Leopard's Spots: Scientific Attitudes Toward Race in America, 1815–59* (Chicago: University of Chicago Press, 1960), 144.

26   Audrey Smedley, *Race in North America*, 170–4.

27   Eric Foner, *Nothing but Freedom: Emancipation and Its Legacy* (Baton Rouge, LA: Louisiana State University Press, 1983), 39–47.

28   Eric Foner, *Reconstruction: America's Unfinished Revolution, 1863–1877* (New York: Harper & Row, 1988), 170–5, 282–91, 412–44, 569–75; Paul Ortiz, *Emancipation Betrayed: The Hidden History of Black Organizing and White Violence in Florida from Reconstruction to the Bloody Election of 1920* (Berkeley, CA: University of California Press, 2005), 9–32.

29   Grace Elizabeth Hale, *Making Whiteness: The Culture of Segregation in the South, 1890–1940*, reprint (New York: Vintage Books, 1999; Pantheon Books, 1998), 121–97.

30   All quoted in C. Vann Woodward, *The Strange Career of Jim Crow*, 3rd rev. edn. (New York: Oxford University Press, 1974), 37 (English visitor George Campbell); 40 (Stewart); 37–8 (Charleston editor).

31   C. Vann Woodward, *Strange Career*, 33.

32   C. Vann Woodward, *Origins of the New South, 1877–1913*, 2nd edn. (Baton Rouge, LA: Louisiana State University Press, 1971), 51–74, 107–41, 175–204; Harold D. Woodman, *New South–New Law: The Legal Foundations of Credit and Labor Relations in the Postbellum Agricultural South* (Baton Rouge, LA: Louisiana State University Press, 1995), 28–66; Thomas E. Watson, "The Negro Question in the South," *Arena*, October 1892, 548.

33   William Ivy Hair, *Bourbonism and Agrarian Protest: Louisiana Politics, 1877–1900* (Baton Rouge, LA: Louisiana State University Press, 1969), 234–67; C. Vann Woodward, *Tom Watson: Agrarian Rebel* (London: Oxford

University Press, 1963; 1938), 370–80; Paul Ortiz, *Emancipation Betrayed*, 33–60.

34   Pete Daniel, *The Shadow of Slavery: Peonage in the South, 1901–1969*, Illini Books edn. (Urbana: University of Illinois Press, 1990; 1972), 19–42; Jessie Parkhurst Guzman, *Negro Yearbook: A Review of Events Affecting Negro Life, 1941–1946* (Tuskegee, AL: Tuskegee Institute Department of Records and Research, 1947), 308 (lynching statistics); W. Fitzhugh Brundage, *Lynching in the New South: Georgia and Virginia, 1880–1930* (Urbana, IL: University of Illinois Press, 1993), 17–48; Neil R. McMillen, *Dark Journey: Black Mississippians in the Age of Jim Crow* (Urbana, IL: University of Illinois Press, 1989), 224–53.

35   Mamie Garvin Fields with Karen Fields, *Lemon Swamp and Other Places: A Carolina Memoir* (New York: Free Press, Macmillan, 1983), 47–9.

36   Plantation owner in Minter City, Mississippi quoted in William H. Holtzclaw, *The Black Man's Burden* (New York: Negro Universities Press, 1970; Neale Publishing Company, 1915), 75–6; Thomas Pearce Bailey, *Race Orthodoxy in the South and Other Aspects of the Negro Question* (New York: Negro Universities Press, 1969; 1914), 278. Neil R. McMillen's *Dark Journey* offers one of the best and most detailed analyses of the political and economic functions served by the Jim Crow system and its impact on black Americans. Also helpful is Leon Litwack, *Trouble in Mind: Black Southerners in the Age of Jim Crow* (New York: Alfred A. Knopf, 1998).

37   C. Vann Woodward, *Origins of the New South*, 205–34, 342–6; Stanley B. Greenberg, *Race and State in Capitalist Development: Comparative Perspectives* (New Haven, CT: Yale University Press, 1980), 385–410; V. O. Key Jr., *Southern Politics in State and Nation*, new edn. (Knoxville, TN: University of Tennessee Press, 1984; 1949), 131.

38   C. Vann Woodward, *Strange Career*, 17–21, 70–4, 113–15; James R. Grossman, *Land of Hope: Chicago, Black Southerners, and the Great Migration* (Chicago: University of Chicago Press, 1989), 123–8, 251–8; Grace Elizabeth Hale, *Making Whiteness*, 167–8, 281–4.

39   Harvard Sitkoff, *A New Deal for Blacks: The Emergence of Civil Rights as a National Issue, Vol. I: The Depression Decade* (New York: Oxford University Press, 1978), 58–83, 190–215; Patricia Sullivan, *Days of Hope: Race and Democracy in the New Deal Era* (Chapel Hill, NC: University of North Carolina Press, 1996), 41–67.

40   Ira Katznelson, *When Affirmative Action Was White: An Untold History of Racial Inequality in Twentieth-Century America* (New York: W. W. Norton & Company, 2005), 20–2, 36–8; Charles Houston quoted in Michael K. Brown, Martin Carnoy, Elliott Currie and Troy Duster, *Whitewashing Race: The Myth of a Color-Blind Society* (Berkeley, CA: University of California Press, 2003), 28; Jill Quadagno, *The Color of Welfare: How Racism Undermined the War on Poverty* (New York: Oxford University Press, 1994), 19–21.

41   Douglas S. Massey and Nancy A. Denton, *American Apartheid: Segregation and the Making of the Underclass* (Cambridge, MA: Harvard University Press, 1993), 10–23; New Orleans man quoted in Juliette Landphair, " 'The Forgotten

People of New Orleans': Community, Vulnerability, and the Lower Ninth Ward," *Journal of American History* 94 (December 2007): 839.

42 Douglas S. Massey and Nancy A. Denton, *American Apartheid*, 33–6.

43 Gary Orfield, "Segregated Housing and School Resegregation," in *Dismantling Desegregation: The Quiet Reversal of Brown v. Board of Education*, eds. Gary Orfield and Susan E. Eaton (New York: New Press, 1996), 304–5; NAREB code of ethics quoted in Rose Helper, *Racial Policies and Practices of Real Estate Brokers* (Minneapolis: University of Minnesota Press, 1969), 201.

44 Kenneth Jackson, *Crabgrass Frontier: The Suburbanization of the United States* (New York: Oxford University Press, 1985), 195–215.

45 Ira Katznelson, *When Affirmative Action Was White*, 113 (GI bill statistics); Michael K. Brown et al., *Whitewashing Race*, 74–8.

46 Andrew Wiese, " 'The House I Live In': Race, Class, and African American Suburban Dreams in the Postwar United States," in *The New Suburban History*, eds. Kevin Kruse and Thomas J. Sugrue (Chicago, IL: University of Chicago Press, 2006), 99–100 (realtor quoted on p. 99), 111 (engineer).

47 Gary Orfield, "Segregated Housing," 55–7.

48 Douglas S. Massey and Nancy A. Denton, *American Apartheid*, 131–40.

49 David M. Freund, "Marketing the Free Market: State Intervention and the Politics of Prosperity in Metropolitan America," in *New Suburban History*, eds. Kevin M. Kruse and Thomas J. Sugrue, 12.

50 The following studies of the civil rights movement provide good overviews of the activities of major organizations and activists in the 1960s: August Meier and Elliott Rudwick, *CORE: A Study in the Civil Rights Movement, 1942–1968* (New York: Oxford University Press, 1973); Clayborne Carson, *In Struggle: SNCC and the Black Awakening of the 1960s* (Cambridge, MA: Harvard University Press, 1981); Aldon Morris, *The Origins of the Civil Rights Movement: Black Communities Organizing for Change* (New York: Free Press, 1984); Adam Fairclough, *To Redeem the Soul of America: The Southern Christian Leadership Conference and Martin Luther King, Jr.* (Athens: University of Georgia Press, 1987); Charles M. Payne, *I've Got the Light of Freedom: The Organizing Tradition and the Mississippi Freedom Struggle* (Berkeley, CA: University of California Press, 1995).

CHAPTER 2: FROM THE FREEDOM MOVEMENT TO FREE MARKETS

1 Walter Fauntroy, speech to the Annual Convention of the SCLC, 1976, quoted in Mary R. Warner, *The Dilemma of Black Politics: A Report on Harassment of Black Elected Officials* (Sacramento, CA: National Association of Human Rights Workers, 1977), 211.

2 Christopher B. Strain, *Pure Fire: Self-Defense as Activism in the Civil Rights Era* (Athens, GA: University of Georgia Press, 2005), 129–35.

3 Mervyn Dymally quoted in Gladwin Hill, "Isolation of the Poorer Negroes Called Key to Los Angeles Riots," *New York Times*, August 29, 1965, 54.

4 U.S. Bureau of the Census, *1946 Statistical Abstract*, 172 (Table 195) and *1965*, 218 (Table 300), U.S. Census Bureau website, accessed at: http://www.

census.gov/compendia/statab/past_years.html; Michael B. Katz, Mark J. Stern, and Jamie J. Fader, "The New African American Inequality," *Journal of American History* 92 (June 2005): 81–2, 85–8; Greta de Jong, "Staying in Place: Black Migration, the Civil Rights Movement, and the War on Poverty in the Rural South," *Journal of African American History* 90 (fall 2005) 388–95; Bayard Rustin quoted in Dona Cooper Hamilton and Charles V. Hamilton, *The Dual Agenda: Race and the Social Welfare Policies of Civil Rights Organizations* (New York: Columbia University Press, 1997), 124.

5   Lyndon B. Johnson, "State of the Union Message to Congress," January 8, 1964, in *A Time for Action: A Selection of Speeches and Writings of Lyndon B. Johnson, 1953–64* (New York: Atheneum, 1964), 164–79 (quotation on p. 174).

6   Robert Levine, *The Poor Ye Need Not Have With You: Lessons from the War on Poverty* (Cambridge, MA: MIT Press, 1970), 48; Robert F. Clark, *The War on Poverty: History, Selected Programs and Ongoing Impact* (Lanham, MD: University Press of America, 2002), 26–8; Gareth Davies, *From Opportunity to Entitlement: The Transformation and Decline of Great Society Liberalism* (Lawrence, KA: University Press of Kansas, 1996), 30, 37; Susan Youngblood Ashmore, *Carry It On: The War on Poverty and the Civil Rights Movement in Alabama, 1964–1972* (Athens, GA: University of Georgia Press, 2008), 25–6; Whitney Young quoted in Marjorie Hunter, "Negro Ties Rights to Poverty Plans," *New York Times*, April 15, 1964, 20.

7   Robert F. Clark, *The War on Poverty*, 31; *Congressional Record*, 88th Cong., 2nd sess., 1964, 110, pt. 4, 5287–8; Daniel P. Moynihan, *Maximum Feasible Misunderstanding: Community Action in the War on Poverty* (New York: Free Press, 1969), 81–6, 90, 97; Jill Quadagno, *The Color of Welfare: How Racism Undermined the War on Poverty* (New York: Oxford University Press, 1994), 30–3.

8   John Dittmer, *Local People: The Struggle for Civil Rights in Mississippi* (Urbana, IL: University of Illinois Press, 1994), 368–71.

9   Susan Youngblood Ashmore, *Carry It On*, 254; Jill Quadagno, *Color of Welfare*, 49–52.

10 John Dittmer, *Local People*, 370–1; Joseph A. Loftus, "South Is Lagging in Requests for Federal Antipoverty Money," *New York Times*, January 2, 1966, 48.

11 Robert Sherrill, "It Isn't True That Nobody Starves in America," *New York Times Sunday Magazine*, June 4, 1967, 102, 104; Ellett Lawrence to Friend, n.d., [1960s], 1, file 2, box 105, Walter Sillers Jr. Papers, Charles W. Capps Jr. Archives and Museum, Delta State University, Cleveland, MS.

12 Hamner Cobbs quoted in Susan Youngblood Ashmore, *Carry It On*, 131; Donald C. Mosley and D. C. Williams Jr., "An Analysis and Evaluation of a Community Action Anti-Poverty Program in the Mississippi Delta," July 1967, 26–7, 31, file "Community Action Program [1 of 6]," box 150, Grant Files, 1966–71, Migrant Division, Office of Operations, Office of Economic Opportunity, Record Group 381, National Archives, Washington, DC (RG 381).

13 Unita Blackwell quoted in National Advisory Council on Economic Opportunity, "Perspectives on Poverty: First Draft of the 1968 Report to the President,"

January 5, 1967, file "National Advisory Council (1 of 2)," box 3, Deputy Director Files, 1965–70, RG 381; Jon Nordheimer, "'The Dream,' 1973: Blacks Move Painfully Toward Full Equality," *New York Times*, August 26, 1973, 1, 44.

14 John Dittmer, *Local People*, 371–82.

15 Theodore McKeldin quoted in Nicholas Lemann, *The Promised Land: The Great Migration and How It Changed America* (New York: Alfred A. Knopf, 1991), 165; Walter H. Waggoner, "Newark Stirred Over Poverty Aid," *New York Times*, December 12, 1965, 81; Martin Arnold, "Newark Demands a Poverty Study," July 25, 1967, *New York Times*, 22; Noel A. Cazenave, *Impossible Democracy: The Unlikely Success of the War on Poverty Community Action Programs* (Albany, NY: State University of New York Press, 2007), 146–9, 150–3.

16 Strom Thurmond, "'Poor' Excuse for Revolution," *Citizen*, December 1967, 14; "Commission on Riots," *Citizen*, April 1968, 2.

17 Citizens' Council newsletter quoted in "The Quiet Revolution of a Parish Priest," *Ebony*, May 1968, 57; William Lowndes, "Forgotten Man, 1968 Style," *Citizen*, May 1968, 14; "Integration in Housing," *Citizen*, November 1972, 2.

18 Nick Kotz, "In the Deep South, the Enemy is Poverty," *Minneapolis Tribune*, May 14, 1967, 1B; Kenneth T. Andrews, "Social Movements and Policy Implementation: The Mississippi Civil Rights Movement and the War on Poverty, 1965 to 1971," *American Sociological Review* 66 (February 2001): 84.

19 Kevin Kruse's *White Flight: Atlanta and the Making of Modern Conservatism* (Princeton, NJ: Princeton University Press, 2005) and Matthew D. Lassiter's *The Silent Majority: Suburban Politics in the Sunbelt South* (Princeton, NJ: Princeton University Press, 2006) both provide detailed and insightful analyses of how segregationists and middle-class homeowners deployed colorblind rhetoric to defend actions aimed at preserving racial hierarchies after the mid-1960s.

20 Gary Orfield and Susan E. Eaton, "Leading Decisions on Desegregation 1896–1995," in *Dismantling Desegregation: The Quiet Reversal of Brown v. Board of Education*, eds. Gary Orfield and Susan E. Eaton (New York: New Press, 1996), xxii.

21 Kenneth O'Reilly, *Nixon's Piano: Presidents and Racial Politics from Washington to Clinton* (New York: Free Press, 1995), 297; Orfield and Eaton, "Leading Decisions," xxii.

22 Donald Janson, "Bomb Mars Start of Chicago Busing," *New York Times*, March 12, 1968, 27; "Explosions Damage 36 Buses in Eastern Texas," *New York Times*, July 6, 1970, 31; Tracy Price Thompson, "Bensonhurst: Black and Then Blue," in *Children of the Dream: Our Own Stories of Growing Up Black in America*, ed. Laurel Holliday (New York: Pocket Books, 1999), 179; Howard Husock, "No More Mileage in Busing," *Nation*, December 31, 1977, 710–12 (Boston).

23 Mr. and Mrs. D. Long to Russell B. Long, February 20, 1967, 3–4, file 5, box 103, Russell B. Long Papers, Hill Memorial Library, Louisiana State University,

Baton Rouge, LA (Long Papers); Louise Day Hicks quoted in "Mrs. Hicks to Seek McCormack's Seat; Will Stress Crime," *New York Times*, June 9, 1970, 33.

24 U.S. Commission on Civil Rights quoted in Donald Janson, "School Busing a U.S. Tradition," *New York Times*, May 24, 1970, 49; Jon Hillson, *The Battle of Boston* (New York: Pathfinder Press, 1977), 60, 110 (Boston man).

25 Medford Evans, "The Future of Private Education," *Citizen*, April 1966, 14–18; William J. Simmons, "Council Schools 'Wave of the Future,'" *Citizen*, July–August 1972, 20–3; "Notes from the State Office," *The Council Newsletter*, January 1971, 3, file "Mississippi Council on Human Relations – Newsletters, 1970–1972," box 4, Tombigbee Council on Human Relations Collection, Special Collections, Mitchell Library, Mississippi State University, Starkville. For some scholarly analyses of the links between segregationist sentiments and the rise of private, Christian academies in the South after the 1960s see Thomas Byrne Edsall with Mary D. Edsall, *Chain Reaction: The Impact of Race, Rights, and Taxes on American Politics* (New York: W. W. Norton & Company, 1992), 131–4 and Kevin Kruse, *White Flight*, 170–8.

26 Kevin Kruse, *White Flight*, 114–25, 169.

27 Kevin Kruse, *White Flight*, 107, 125–30; Thomas Byrne Edsall with Mary D. Edsall, *Chain Reaction*, 18, 130–1; Paul Street, *Segregated Schools: Educational Apartheid in Post-Civil Rights America* (New York: Routledge, 2005), 90, 94.

28 Gerald Frug, "The Legal Technology of Exclusion in Metropolitan America," in *New Suburban History*, eds. Kevin Kruse and Thomas J. Sugrue (Chicago, IL: University of Chicago Press, 2006), 205–7; Roger Samson to Russell B. Long, October 3, 1966, 2, file 46, box 97, Long Papers.

29 Matthew D. Lassiter, *Silent Majority*, 1.

30 Alabama politician quoted in Marshall Frady, *Wallace* (New York: New American Library with World Publishing Company, 1968), 6–7. Dan Carter analyzes Wallace's political career, his use of racial code words after 1965, and his role in shaping late twentieth-century American political discourse in *The Politics of Rage: George Wallace, the Origins of the New Conservatism, and the Transformation of American Politics* (Baton Rouge, LA: Louisiana State University Press, 1996), esp. 10–12, 195–225, 324–70.

31 Thomas Byrne Edsall with Mary D. Edsall, *Chain Reaction*, 42; Kevin P. Phillips, *The Emerging Republican Majority* (New Rochelle, NY: Arlington House, 1969), 33; Richard H. Rovere, *The Goldwater Caper* (New York: Harcourt, Brace & World, 1965), 134–44 (quotation on p. 143).

32 Robert D. Novak, *The Agony of the G.O.P. 1964* (New York: Macmillan, 1965), 179, 201; "Thurmond to Bolt Democrats Today," *New York Times*, September 16, 1964, 1; Roy V. Harris, "What Does the Election Prove?" *Citizen*, November 1964, 6–7; "Address of Charles H. Percy to the Mississippi Council on Human Relations," Jackson, MS, February 17, 1966, file 1, box 3A, Allen Eugene Cox Collection, Special Collections, Mitchell Library, Mississippi State University, Starkville.

33 Kenneth O'Reilly, *Nixon's Piano*, 282–283; Robert B. Semple Jr., "The Nixon Strategy: Unity and Caution," *New York Times*, August 11, 1968, 1, 56.

34 Kevin P. Phillips, *Emerging Republican Majority*, 286; Kenneth O'Reilly, *Nixon's Piano*, 279, 284–6, 308 (Buchanan quotation); Nixon quoted in Matthew D. Lassiter, "'Socioeconomic Integration' in the Suburbs: From Reactionary Populism to Class Fairness in Metropolitan Charlotte," in *New Suburban History*, eds. Kevin Kruse and Thomas J. Sugrue, 121, 129.

35 John Ehrlichman, *Witness to Power: The Nixon Years* (New York: Simon and Schuster, 1982), 227–8; Robert F. Clark, *War on Poverty*, 60–8, 133–5.

36 Robert K. Schaeffer, *Understanding Globalization: The Social Consequences of Political, Economic, and Environmental Change* (Lanham, MD: Rowman & Littlefield, 2003), 53–6; William C. Berman, *America's Right Turn: From Nixon to Clinton*, 2nd edn. (Baltimore, MD: Johns Hopkins University Press, 1998), 14, 21.

37 Saskia Sassen, *The Global City: New York, London, Tokyo* (Princeton, NJ: Princeton University Press, 1991), 221.

38 Saskia Sassen, *Global City*, 8–13, 197–8; William C. Berman, *America's Right Turn*, 14, 19, 23, 39; Bureau of the Census, *1990 Statistical Abstract*, 407 (Table 666) (average weekly earnings) and 383 (Table 633) (unemployment).

39 Thomas I. Palley, *Plenty of Nothing: The Downsizing of the American Dream and the Case for Structural Keynesianism* (Princeton, NJ: Princeton University Press, 1998), 57 (CEO pay); Saskia Sassen, *Global City*, 249.

40 Ronald Reagan, "Building a Prosperous America," speech to the American Trucking Association Board of Directors, October 16, 1974, in *A Time for Choosing: The Speeches of Ronald Reagan, 1961–1982*, ed. Alfred Balitzer (Chicago: Regnery Gateway, 1983), 154, 156.

41 Ronald Reagan, "Government and the Family," national television address, July 6, 1976, in *Time For Choosing*, ed. Alfred Balitzer, 171; Jon Nordheimer, "Reagan is Picking His Florida Spots," *New York Times*, February 5, 1976, 29; "'Welfare Queen' Becomes Issue in Reagan Campaign," *New York Times*, February 15, 1976, 51; Kenneth O'Reilly, *Nixon's Piano*, 360.

42 Lee Atwater quoted in Alexander P. Lamis, "The Two-Party South: From the 1960s to the 1990s," in *Southern Politics in the 1990s*, ed. Alexander P. Lamis (Baton Rouge, LA: Louisiana State University Press, 1999), 8; Hastings Wyman Jr., Review of *The Two-Party South*, by Alexander P. Lamis, *Election Politics: A Journal of Political Campaigns and Elections* 2 (summer 1985): 30–1.

43 William C. Berman, *America's Right Turn*, 21–2.

44 Thomas Byrne Edsall with Mary D. Edsall, *Chain Reaction*, 6 (Donahue), 182 (Macomb County study).

45 Ankie Hoogvelt, *Globalization and the Postcolonial World: The New Political Economy of Development*, 2nd edn. (Baltimore, MD: Johns Hopkins University Press, 2001), 5; Joseph Stiglitz, *Globalization and Its Discontents* (New York: W. W. Norton & Company, 2002), 73, 195, 208.

46 Thomas Byrne Edsall with Mary D. Edsall, *Chain Reaction*, 23, 159, 168, 193–4, 219–20 (quotation on p. 23); William C. Berman, *America's Right Turn*, 149.

47 Ronald Reagan, "A Time for Choosing," in *Time for Choosing*, ed. Alfred Balitzer, 43; Saskia Sassen, *Global City*, 240.

48 Thomas R. Peake, *Keeping the Dream Alive: A History of the Southern Christian Leadership Conference from King to the Nineteen-Eighties* (New York: Peter Lang, 1987), 343–5; Philip A. Klinkner and Rogers M. Smith, *The Unsteady March: The Rise and Decline of Racial Equality in America* (Chicago: University of Chicago Press, 1999), 297–8; Kenneth O'Reilly, *Nixon's Piano*, 336–44.

49 Phil Gailey, "Dissidents Defy Top Democrats," *New York Times*, March 1, 1985, A1.

50 Kenneth O'Reilly, *Nixon's Piano*, 410.

51 Democratic Party Platform quoted in Robert Pear, "In a Final Draft, Democrats Reject a Part of Their Past," *New York Times*, June 26, 1992, A13.

52 Iwan Morgan, "Reaganomics and its Legacy," in *Ronald Reagan and the 1980s: Perceptions, Policies, Legacies*, eds. Cheryl Hudson and Gareth Davies (New York: Palgrave Macmillan, St. Martin's Press, 2008), 112–14; William Julius Wilson, *More than Just Race: Being Black and Poor in the Inner City* (New York: W. W. Norton & Company, 2009), 11–13, 37; Paul Street, *Segregated Schools*, 31, 43, 81–5; Robert D. Bullard, Introduction to *The Quest for Environmental Justice: Human Rights and the Politics of Pollution*, ed. Robert D. Bullard (San Francisco, CA: Sierra Club Books, 2005), 12; William Greider, "Establishment Disorder," *Nation*, November 17, 2008, 16–20.

CHAPTER 3: A SYSTEM WITHOUT SIGNS

1 Thomas C. Holt, *The Problem of Race in the Twenty-First Century* (Cambridge, MA: Harvard University Press, 2000), 121.

2 Rick Bragg, "Killings Jolt Fort Bragg Area, Recalling Angry, Ugly Past," *New York Times*, December 11, 1995, A1, B6.

3 U.S. Bureau of the Census, *2008 Statistical Abstract*, 145 (Table 217) (high school graduation rate and college education); *2009*, 442 (Table 668) (income over $75,000); *1970*, 325, (Table 499) and *2001*, 475 (Table 754) (poverty); *1970*, 55 (Table 69) and *2009*, 81 (Table 110) (infant mortality); *2009*, 74, (Table 100) (life expectancy), U.S. Census Bureau website, accessed at: http://www.census.gov/compendia/statab/past_years.html

4 U.S. Bureau of the Census, *2008 Statistical Abstract*, 374 (Table 571) (unemployment); *2008*, 458 (Table 689) (poverty) and 449 (Table 674) (median income); *2009*, 442 (Table 668) (income over $75,000); *2008*, 463 (Table 699) (net worth); *2008*, 145 (Table 217) (college education) and 107 (Table 146) (health insurance); *2008*, 81 (Table 108) (infant mortality).

5 U.S. Bureau of the Census, *1990 Statistical Abstract*, 380 (Table 628) (overall unemployment) and *1990*, 383 (Table 633) (education and employment).

6 Fred P. Graham, "Mitchell Vows 'Vigorous' Law Enforcement in U.S.," *New York Times*, January 22, 1969, 28; Thomas Byrne Edsall with Mary D. Edsall, *Chain Reaction: The Impact of Race, Rights, and Taxes on American Politics* (New York: W. W. Norton & Company, 1992), 187–8; Charles M. Lamb,

"Education and Housing," in *The Reagan Administration and Human Rights*, ed. Tinsley E. Yarbrough (New York: Praeger, 1985), 98–9.

7   Fred P. Graham, "Chipping Away at Decisions of Warren Era," *New York Times*, February 28, 1971, E7 (judicial activists); James N. Naughton, "Nixon Names 2 to Supreme Court," *New York Times*, October 22, 1971, 1, 25 (Nixon quotation); Paul Delaney, "Civil Rights Slowdown," *New York Times*, August 3, 1974, 26; Philip A. Klinkner and Rogers M. Smith, *The Unsteady March: The Rise and Decline of Racial Equality in America* (Chicago: University of Chicago Press, 1999), 297; Kenneth O'Reilly, *Nixon's Piano: Presidents and Racial Politics from Washington to Clinton* (New York: Free Press, 1995), 368; Thomas Byrne Edsall with Mary D. Edsall, *Chain Reaction*, 217–18.

8   Douglas S. Massey and Nancy A. Denton, *American Apartheid: Segregation and the Making of the Underclass* (Cambridge, MA: Harvard University Press, 1993), 150.

9   Douglas S. Massey and Nancy A. Denton, *American Apartheid*, 189–94, 204–5.

10 Douglas S. Massey and Nancy A. Denton, *American Apartheid*, 195–200.

11 George Romney quoted in Douglas S. Massey and Nancy A. Denton, *American Apartheid*, 204; Matthew D. Lassiter, *The Silent Majority: Suburban Politics in the Sunbelt South* (Princeton, NJ: Princeton University Press, 2006), 305–6 (Nixon quoted on p. 305).

12 Gary Orfield, "Segregated Housing and School Resegregation," in *Dismantling Desegregation: The Quiet Reversal of Brown v. Board of Education*, eds. Gary Orfield and Susan E. Eaton (New York: New Press, 1996), 306; Douglas S. Massey and Nancy A. Denton, *American Apartheid*, 97–9; Eduardo Bonilla-Silva, *White Supremacy and Racism in the Post-Civil Rights Era* (Boulder, CO: Lynne Rienner Publishers, 2001), 95–6; Michael K. Brown, Martin Carnoy, Elliott Currie and Troy Duster, *Whitewashing Race: The Myth of a Color-Blind Society* (Berkeley: University of California Press, 2003), 14.

13 Robert D. Bullard, *Dumping in Dixie: Race, Class, and Environmental Quality*, 3rd edn. (Boulder, CO, Westview Press, 2000), 30–2, 43, 81, 102 (EPA official William Sanjour quoted on p. 32); Commission for Racial Justice, United Church of Christ, *Toxic Wastes and Race in the United States: A National Report on the Racial and Socio-Economic Characteristics of Communities with Hazardous Waste Sites* (New York: United Church of Christ Commission for Racial Justice, 1987), 15.

14 Robert D. Bullard, *Dumping in Dixie*, 27–9, 55, 134.

15 Beverly Wright, "Living and Dying in Louisiana's Cancer Alley," in *The Quest for Environmental Justice: Human Rights and the Politics of Pollution*, ed. Robert D. Bullard (San Francisco, CA: Sierra Club Books, 2005), 88, 91–2.

16 Robert D. Bullard, *Dumping in Dixie*, 52–5, 60–2 (*Sumter County Record* quoted on p. 60; Wendell Paris quoted on p. 62).

17 James Dailey quoted in Andre Carothers, "The Coming of Age of Sumter County," *Greenpeace* 12 (1987), 13; Robert D. Bullard, *Dumping in Dixie*, 88 (Houston resident), 132–5.

18 Robert D. Bullard, *Dumping in Dixie*, 6, 99.

19 Thomas Byrne Edsall with Mary D. Edsall, *Chain Reaction*, 82; Russell B. Long to Mercedes Lago, July 18, 1969, file 5, box 117, Russell B. Long Collection, Hill Memorial Library, Louisiana State University, Baton Rouge, Louisiana.

20 Barney Sellers, "Civil Rights, the Nixon Fiddle," *Nation*, October 6, 1969, 346; Charles T. Clotfelter, *After Brown: The Rise and Retreat of School Desegregation* (Princeton, NJ: Princeton University Press, 2004), 75–6; James T. Patterson, *Brown v. Board of Education: A Civil Rights Milestone and Its Troubled Legacy* (Oxford, UK: Oxford University Press, 2001), 158 (Charlotte); Jon Hillson, *The Battle of Boston* (New York: Pathfinder Press, 1977), 180, 187.

21 Cynthia Griggs Fleming, *In the Shadow of Selma: The Continuing Struggle for Civil Rights in the Rural South* (Lanham, MD: Rowman & Littlefield, 2004), 200–1 (Threadgill), 203 (Ray).

22 Stokely Carmichael and Charles V. Hamilton, *Black Power: The Politics of Liberation in America* (New York: Random House, 1967), 54; Gary Orfield, "Toward an Integrated Future: New Directions for Courts, Educators, Civil Rights Groups, Policymakers, and Scholars," in *Dismantling Desegregation*, eds. Gary Orfield and Susan E. Eaton, 343.

23 Susan E. Eaton, Joseph Feldman, and Edward Kirby, "Still Separate, Still Unequal: The Limits of *Milliken II*'s Monetary Compensation to Segregated Schools" in *Dismantling Desegregation*, eds. Gary Orfield and Susan E. Eaton, 143–4, 158–61 (observer Melissa Guldin quoted on p. 161).

24 Susan E. Eaton and Christina Meldrum, "Broken Promises: Resegregation in Norfolk, Virginia," in *Dismantling Desegregation*, eds. Gary Orfield and Susan E. Eaton, 115–19.

25 Gary Orfield, "Turning Back to Segregation," in *Dismantling Desegregation*, eds. Gary Orfield and Susan E. Eaton, 1–4.

26 Gary Orfield, "Plessy Parallels," in *Dismantling Desegregation*, eds. Gary Orfield and Susan E. Eaton, 34–5.

27 Gary Orfield, "The Growth of Segregation," in *Dismantling Desegregation*, eds. Gary Orfield and Susan E. Eaton, 53–54; Paul Street, *Segregated Schools: Educational Apartheid in Post-Civil Rights America* (New York: Routledge, 2005), 4, 72–3, 125–6; Gary Orfield, "Unexpected Costs and Uncertain Gains of Dismantling Desegregation," in *Dismantling Desegregation*, eds. Gary Orfield and Susan E. Eaton, 81–92.

28 Alison Morantz, "Money and Choice in Kansas City: Major Investments With Modest Returns," in *Dismantling Desegregation*, eds. Gary Orfield and Susan E. Eaton, 244; Barbara B. Underwood to Bill Nichols, August 19, 1982, 1, file "32-C-2 Tax Exempt Schools," box 22, ser. 87–4, William F. Nichols Papers, Special Collections and Archives Department, Draughon Library, Auburn University, Alabama.

29 Antoine P. Reddick, "All the Black Children," in *Children of the Dream: Our Own Stories of Growing Up Black in America*, ed. Laurel Holliday (New York: Pocket Books, 1999), 272–7.

30 Marc Mauer, *Race to Incarcerate*, 2nd edn. (New York: New Press, 2006), 1, 20; Pew Center on the States, *One in 100: Behind Bars in America 2008* (Washington, DC: Pew Charitable Trusts, 2008), 5, 34.

31 Marc Mauer, *Race to Incarcerate*, 51–2; Richard Nixon, "If Mob Rule Takes Hold in the U.S.," *U.S. News & World Report*, August 15, 1966, 64–5; Richard Nixon quoted in Arnold S. Trebach, "Nixon: Soft on Crime?" *Justice Magazine* (June/July 1972), 20.

32 Marion Orr, "Congress, Race, and Anticrime Policy," in *Black and Multiracial Politics in America*, eds. Yvette Alex-Assensoh and Lawrence J. Hanks (New York: New York University Press, 2000), 8, 234; Thomas Byrne Edsall with Mary D. Edsall, *Chain Reaction*, 112; Marc Mauer, *Race to Incarcerate*, 56–8, 155.

33 Philip M. Boffey, "U.S. Attacks Drug Suppliers but Loses Battle of the Users," *New York Times*, April 12, 1988, A1, A10 (drug law enforcement expenditures); Alfonse M. D'Amato, "Continuing the War on Drugs," *New York Times*, October 28, 1986, A35; Ronald Reagan quoted in Gerald M. Boyd, "Reagan Signs Anti-Drug Measure," *New York Times*, October 28, 1986, B19.

34 Marc Maur, *Race to Incarcerate*, 150; Andrew L. Barlow, *Between Fear and Hope: Globalization and Race in the United States* (Lanham, MD: Rowman & Littlefield, 2003), 125.

35 Christian Parenti, *Lockdown America: Police and Prisons in the Age of Crisis*, new edn. (London: Verso, 2008), 47; Marc Mauer, *Race to Incarcerate*, 158–60, 167 (drug arrest statistics).

36 Michael K. Brown, Martin Carnoy, Elliott Currie and Troy Duster, *Whitewashing Race*, 147–152.

37 Marc Mauer, *Race to Incarcerate*, 158, 163, 169–71.

38 Marc Mauer, *Race to Incarcerate*, 134, 137, 199–200; Michael K. Brown, Martin Carnoy, Elliott Currie and Troy Duster, *Whitewashing Race*, 135.

39 Michael K. Brown, Martin Carnoy, Elliott Currie and Troy Duster, *Whitewashing Race*, 158; Jennifer E. Smith, "Onamove: African American Women Confronting the Prison Crisis," in *Still Lifting, Still Climbing: Contemporary African American Women's Activism*, ed. Kimberly Springer (New York: New York University Press, 1999), 223–4; Marc Mauer, *Race to Incarcerate*, 202–4.

40 Christian Parenti, *Lockdown America*, 112–18, 135; Loïc Wacquant, "Deadly Symbiosis: When Ghetto and Prison Meet and Mesh," *Punishment and Society* 3 (January 2001): 95; Jennifer E. Smith, "Onamove," 234.

41 U.S. Bureau of the Census, *1995 Statistical Abstract*, 338 (Table 522); Mike Davis, "In L.A., Burning All Illusions," *Nation*, June 1, 1992, 743–6; Marc Mauer, *Race to Incarcerate*, 68–81, 185.

42 Marc Mauer, *Race to Incarcerate*, 10–11 (World Research Group quoted on p. 11); Christian Parenti, *Lockdown America*, 212, 223–31 (Crescent City); Jennifer E. Smith, "Onamove," 224 (corporations); Lani Guinier and Gerald Torres, *The Miner's Canary: Enlisting Race, Resisting Power, Transforming Democracy* (Cambridge, MA: Harvard University Press, 2003), 265.

43 Eduardo Bonilla-Silva, *Racism Without Racists: Color-Blind Racism and the Persistence of Racial Inequality in the United States*, 2nd edn. (Lanham, MD:

Rowman and Littlefield, 2006), 28–9; Thomas Byrne Edsall with Mary D. Edsall, *Chain Reaction*, 283.

44 Charles Murray, *Losing Ground: American Social Policy, 1950–1980* (New York: Basic Books, 1984), 18–20, 71–82, 154–66; Dinesh D'Souza, *The End of Racism: Principles for a Multiracial Society* (New York: Free Press, 1995), 15, 24; Shelby Steele, "Wresting with Stigma" and Ward Connerly, "One Nation, Indivisible," both in *Beyond the Color Line: New Perspectives on Race and Ethnicity in America*, eds. Abigail Thernstrom and Stephan Thernstrom (Stanford, CA: Hoover Institution Press, 2002), 69–80, 415–23 (Connerly quotation on p. 421).

45 Kevin Kruse, *White Flight: Atlanta and the Making of Modern Conservatism* (Princeton, NJ: Princeton University Press, 2005), 246–50 (legislator Mike Barnett quoted on pp. 249–50).

46 Dorothy Height, *Open Wide the Freedom Gates: A Memoir* (New York: PublicAffairs, Perseus Books, 2003), 269.

47 South End Press Collective, Preface, and Kalamu Ya Salaam, Introduction to *What Lies Beneath: Katrina, Race, and the State of the Nation*, ed. South End Press Collective (Cambridge, MA: South End Press, 2007), vii–viii, ix–xi; Kenneth B. Nunn, "Still Up on the Roof: Race, Victimology, and the Response to Hurricane Katrina," in *Hurricane Katrina: America's Unnatural Disaster*, eds. Jeremy I. Levitt and Matthew C. Whitaker (Lincoln: University of Nebraska Press, 2009), 183–91.

48 Leah Hodges, Written Testimony for the Record, in U.S. House of Representatives, Select Bipartisan Committee to Investigate the Preparation for and Response to Hurricane Katrina, *Hurricane Katrina: Voices from Inside the Storm*, December 6, 2005, accessed at: http://katrina.house.gov/hearings/12_06_05/witness_list_120605.htm

49 Testimony of Barbara R. Arnwine, in U.S. House, *Hurricane Katrina*, 2.

50 Center for American Progress, "Who Are Katrina's Victims?" September 6, 2005, 1, 4, Center for American Progress website, accessed at: http://www.americanprogress.org/kf/katrinavictims.pdf (statistics); Demond Shondell Miller and Jason David Rivera, "Setting the Stage: Roots of Social Inequity and the Human Tragedy of Hurricane Katrina," in *Through the Eye of Katrina: Social Justice in the United States*, eds. Kristin A. Bates and Richelle S. Swan (Durham, NC: Carolina Academic Press, 2007), 17–21; Jeremy I. Levitt and Matthew C. Whitaker, " 'Truth Crushed to Earth Will Rise Again': Katrina and Its Aftermath," in *Hurricane Katrina*, eds. Jeremy I. Levitt and Matthew C. Whitaker, 1–10.

51 Statement of Attorney Ishmael Muhammad, in U.S. House, *Hurricane Katrina*, 1; Nunn, "Still Up on the Roof," 199–200; Lizzy Ratner, "New Orleans Redraws Its Color Line," *Nation*, September 15, 2008, 22; Leah Hodges, Written Testimony.

52 Leah Hodges, Written Testimony; Charmaine Neville, "How We Survived the Flood," in *What Lies Beneath*, ed. South End Press Collective, 28–30; Sue Hilderbrand, Scott Crow, and Lisa Fithian, "Common Ground Relief," in *What Lies Beneath*, ed. South End Press Collective, 80–98.

CHAPTER 4: FIGHTING JIM CROW'S SHADOW

1   Martin Luther King Jr., "The Birth of a New Nation," sermon delivered at Dexter Avenue Baptist Church, April 7, 1957, in *The Papers of Martin Luther King, Jr., Vol. 4: Symbol of the Movement, January 1957-December 1958*, ed. Clayborne Carson, Susan Carson, Adrienne Clay, Virginia Shadron, and Kieran Taylor (Berkeley, CA: University of California Press, 2000), 161.

2   Fred Powledge, *Free At Last? The Civil Rights Movement and the People Who Made It* (Boston: Little, Brown & Company, 1991), xiv.

3   Dinesh D'Souza, *The End of Racism: Principles for a Multiracial Society* (New York: Free Press, 1995), 166, 198, 201–2, 232–4 (quotation on p. 234); Martin Luther King Jr., "I Have a Dream," address delivered at the March on Washington for Jobs and Freedom, Washington, DC, August 28, 1963, Martin Luther King, Jr. Research and Education Institute website, accessed at: http:// mlk-kpp01.stanford.edu/kingweb/publications/speeches/address_at_march_ on_washington.pdf; Abigail Thernstrom and Stephan Thernstrom, Introduction to *Beyond the Color Line: New Perspectives on Race and Ethnicity in America*, eds. Abigail Thernstrom and Stephan Thernstrom (Stanford, CA: Hoover Institution Press, 2002), 2–3; Shelby Steele, "Wrestling with Stigma," in Abigail Thernstrom and Stephan Thernstrom, eds. *Beyond the Color Line*, 74–6.

4   Martin Luther King Jr., *Where Do We Go from Here: Chaos or Community?* (New York: Harper & Row, 1967), 5–7, 90.

5   Timothy J. Minchin, "Black Activism, the 1964 Civil Rights Act, and the Racial Integration of the Southern Textile Industry," *Journal of Southern History* 65 (November 1999): 670–5.

6   Thomas R. Peake, *Keeping the Dream Alive: A History of the Southern Christian Leadership Conference from King to the Nineteen-Eighties* (New York: Peter Lang, 1987); Carl F. Walton, "Southern Christian Leadership Conference," in *Black Political Organizations in the Post-Civil Rights Era*, eds. Ollie A. Johnson III and Karin L. Stanford (New Brunswick, N.J.: Rutgers University Press, 2002), 145–7.

7   Robert C. Smith, *We Have No Leaders: African Americans in the Post-Civil Rights Era* (Albany: State University of New York Press, 1996), 95–7; Jennifer A. Wade and Brian N. Williams, "The National Urban League: Reinventing Service for the Twenty-First Century," in *Black Political Organizations*, eds. Ollie A. Johnson III and Karin L. Stanford, 40–8.

8   Clayborne Carson, *In Struggle: SNCC and the Black Awakening of the 1960s* (Cambridge, MA: Harvard University Press, 1981), 287–303; Charles E. Jones, "From Protest to Black Conservatism: The Demise of the Congress of Racial Equality," in *Black Political Organizations*, eds. Ollie A. Johnson III and Karin L. Stanford, 80–98; Maureen Dowd, "Dunces of Confederacy," *New York Times*, December 15, 2002, C15.

9   Greta de Jong, "The Scholarship, Education and Defense Fund for Racial Equality and the Freedom Struggle in the Post-Civil Rights Era," paper presented at the 91st Annual Convention of the Association for the Study of African American Life and History, September 29, 2006; Felicia Kornbluh, *The Battle for Welfare Rights: Politics and Poverty in Modern America* (Philadelphia:

University of Pennsylvania Press, 2007), 37–8; 168–9; Karin L. Stanford, "Reverend Jesse Jackson and the Rainbow/PUSH Coalition," in *Black Political Organizations*, eds. Ollie A. Johnson III and Karin L. Stanford, 150–69; Greta de Jong, "The Federation of Southern Cooperatives and African American Responses to Agricultural Modernization in the U.S. South, 1960–1980," paper presented at the Biennial Conference of the Collegium for African-American Research, Madrid, Spain, April 20, 2007.

10 Manning Marable, "Black (Community) Power!" *Nation*, December 22, 1997, 21–4.

11 Robert D. Bullard, *Dumping in Dixie: Race, Class, and Environmental Quality*, 3rd edn. (Boulder, CO: Westview Press, 2000), xiii.

12 Robert D. Bullard, *Dumping in Dixie*, xiv (quotation), 43–5, 128.

13 Robert D. Bullard, *Dumping in Dixie*, 30–5 (Charles Cobb quoted on p. 31); Eileen McGurty, *Transforming Environmentalism: Warren County, PCBs, and the Origins of Environmental Justice* (New Brunswick: Rutgers University Press, 2007), 1–10; Manuel Pastor Jr., James L. Sadd and Rachel Morello-Frosch, "Environmental Inequity in Metropolitan Los Angeles," in *The Quest for Environmental Justice: Human Rights and the Politics of Pollution*, ed. Robert D. Bullard (San Francisco, CA: Sierra Club Books, 2005), 109–21; Luther Brown quoted in Dale Russakoff, "As in the 60s, Protesters Rally," *Washington Post*, October 11, 1982, A1.

14 Robert D. Bullard, "Environmental Justice in the Twenty-first Century," in *Quest for Environmental Justice*, ed. Robert D. Bullard, 26 (California); Robert D. Bullard, *Dumping in Dixie*, 106–8 (St. John the Baptist Parish).

15 Robert D. Bullard, *Dumping in Dixie*, 134; Robert D. Bullard and Damu Smith, "Women Warriors of Color on the Front Line," in *Quest for Environmental Justice*, ed. Robert D. Bullard, 70–3.

16 Robert D. Bullard, *Dumping in Dixie*, 113–14; Eileen McGurty, *Transforming Environmentalism*, 142–5; Robert D. Bullard, Introduction to *Quest for Environmental Justice*, ed. Robert D. Bullard, 3, 7.

17 Robert D. Bullard, Introduction to *Quest for Environmental Justice*, ed. Robert D. Bullard, 8–10.

18 Robert D. Bullard, "Environmental Justice," 20, 22; Peggy Morrow Shepard, Preface to *Quest for Environmental Justice*, ed. Robert D. Bullard, xvi.

19 "Ella Baker Center: A Brief History," Ella Baker Center website, accessed at: http://www.ellabakercenter.org/page.php?pageid=19&contentid=152; Van Jones, "Working Together for a Green New Deal," *Nation*, November 17, 2008, 14; "Van Jones to Join White House," Green For All press release, March 10, 2009, Green For All website, accessed at: http://www.greenforall. org/media-room/statements/van-jones-to-join-white-house-phaedra-ellis-lamkins-to-lead-green-for-all

20 Thomas R. Peake, *Keeping the Dream Alive*, 342; "Klan and Foes March in Alabama," *New York Times*, March 12, 1978, 26.

21 Manning Marable, "Black (Community) Power!" 22.

22 Christian Parenti, *Lockdown America: Police and Prisons in the Age of Crisis*, new edn. (London: Verso, 2008), 81, 83; Manning Marable, "Black (Community) Power!" 22.

23 David Cole, "The Color of Justice," *Nation*, October 11, 1999, 12–13; David Kocieniewski, "New Jersey Adopts Ban on Racial Profiling," *New York Times*, March 14, 2003, B5; Eric Lichtblau, "Bush Issues Racial Profiling Ban but Exempts Security Inquiries," *New York Times*, June 18, 2003, A1.

24 "About Us," Southern Center for Human Rights website, accessed at: http://www.schr.org/about; Christian Parenti, *Lockdown America*, 164–166, 243–245; Citizens United and Ramona Africa quoted in Jennifer E. Smith, "Onamove: African American Women Confronting the Prison Crisis" in *Still Lifting, Still Climbing: Contemporary African American Women's Activism*, ed. Kimberly Springer (New York: New York University Press, 1999), 226, 230.

25 Marc Mauer, *Race to Incarcerate*, 2nd edn. (New York: New Press, 2006), xiii, 105, 212; Pew Center on the States, *One in 100: Behind Bars in America 2008* (Washington, DC: Pew Charitable Trusts, 2008), 17–18 (Whitmire quoted on p. 18).

26 Cynthia Griggs Fleming, *In the Shadow of Selma: The Continuing Struggle for Civil Rights in the Rural South* (Lanham, MD: Rowman and Littlefield, 2004), 195–7, 206, 210, 212–69, 292 (quotations on p. 197 (school board), 206 (Nettles), 292 (white youth). Similar accounts of white intransigence and long drawn out struggles over school desegregation in the South appear in J. Todd Moye, *Let the People Decide: Black Freedom and White Resistance Movements in Sunflower County, Mississippi, 1945–1986* (Chapel Hill: University of North Carolina Press, 2004), 172–99 and Emilye Crosby, *A Little Taste of Freedom: The Black Freedom Struggle in Claiborne County, Mississippi* (Chapel Hill: University of North Carolina Press, 2007), 235–7, 261.

27 Boston School Committee member quoted in Jon Hillson, *The Battle of Boston* (New York: Pathfinder Press, 1977), 54; Jeanne Theoharis, " 'They Told Us Our Kids Were Stupid': Ruth Batson and the Educational Movement in Boston," in *Groundwork: Local Black Freedom Movements in America*, eds. Jeanne Theoharis and Komozi Woodard (New York: New York University Press, 2005), 19–22.

28 Jeanne Theoharis, "They Told Us Our Kids Were Stupid," 17–44; Robert Reinhold, "Boston's Schools Held Segregated," *New York Times*, June 22, 1974, 13.

29 Jon Hillson, *Battle of Boston*, 180–95; Matthew J. Wald, "After Years of Turmoil, Judge Is Yielding Job of Integrating Boston Schools," *New York Times*, August 22, 1985, A16.

30 Evelyn Morash quoted in Jon Hillson, *Battle of Boston*, 115.

31 Jim Hill quoted in Larry Tye, "U.S. Sounds Retreat in School Integration," *Boston Globe*, January 5, 1992, 14; Gary Orfield and Susan E. Eaton, Introduction to *Dismantling Desegregation: The Quiet Reversal of Brown v. Board of Education*, eds. Gary Orfield and Susan E. Eaton (New York: New Press, 1996), xv.

32 Charles T. Clotfelter, *After Brown: The Rise and Retreat of School Desegregation* (Princeton, NJ: Princeton University Press, 2004), 126–39 (quotations on p. 131 (New York) and p. 139 (trade off)).

33 Ronald Smothers, "In Pupil 'Tracks,' Many See a Means of Resegregation," *New York Times*, February 18, 1990, E5; Patricia J. Williams, "The Theft of Education," *Nation*, May 19, 1997, 10 (Rockford).

34 Mari Matsuda, contribution to "Forum: Beyond Black, White and *Brown*," *Nation*, May 3, 2004, 18–19.

35 David L. Kirp, "New Hope for Failing Schools, *Nation*, June 1, 1998, 20–2; Peter Schrag, "What's Good Enough?" *Nation*, May 3, 2004, 41–4.

36 Jonathan Kozol, contribution to "Forum: Beyond Black, White and *Brown*," *Nation*, May 3, 2004, 23–4.

37 Martin Luther King Jr., speech delivered at Ohio Northern University, January 11, 1968, Heterick Memorial Library, Ohio Northern University website, accessed at: http://www.onu.edu/library/onuhistory/king/; Thomas R. Peake, *Keeping the Dream Alive*, 207–12 (King quoted on pp. 208 and 209).

38 Juliet Z. Saltman, *Open Housing as a Social Movement: Challenge, Conflict and Change* (Lexington, MA: D. C. Heath and Company, 1971), 25–53; Nina Mjagkij, *Organizing Black America: An Encyclopedia of African American Associations* (New York: Garland, 2001), 433–5; Douglas S. Massey and Nancy A. Denton, *American Apartheid: Segregation and the Making of the Underclass* (Cambridge, MA: Harvard University Press, 1993), 199.

39 Charles M. Lamb, "Education and Housing," in *The Reagan Administration and Human Rights*, ed. Tinsley E. Yarbrough (New York: Praeger, 1985), 98–9; Charles M. Lamb, Brandon M. Potryrala and Eric M. Wilk, "The Presidency, the Justice Department, and Fair Housing Litigation: A Preliminary Examination," 8–9, paper presented at the Annual Meeting of the Midwest Political Science Association, Chicago, Ill., April 3–6, 2008, All Academic Research website, accessed at: http://www.allacademic.com/meta/p_mla_apa_research_citation/2/6/6/7/8/p266787_index.html; "House Backs Move to Strengthen Enforcement of Housing Rights," *New York Times*, June 30, 1988, A20.

40 Statement of Barbara Arnwine and Written Testimony of Shanna L. Smith, U.S. Congress, House Committee on Financial Services, Subcommittee on Housing and Community Opportunity and Subcommittee on Oversight and Investigations, *Fighting Discrimination against the Disabled and Minorities through Fair Housing Enforcement*, 107th Cong., 2nd sess., June 25, 2002, 42–52, 121–38 (Smith quotation on p. 49), accessed at: mhttp://frwebgate. access.gpo.gov/cgi-bin/getdoc.cgi?dbname=107_house_hearings&docid=f: 82683.pdf

41 "Protest March Set in Colonial Heights," *Washington Post*, March 18, 1987, D4; Donald P. Baker and Sandra R. Gregg, "SCLC March Draws Jeers in Va. City," *Washington Post*, April 5, 1987, B1; Donald P. Baker, "Va. City Rejects SCLC Wishes," *Washington Post*, April 16, 1987, A22.

42 Bill Peterson, "Head of SCLC Urged to Run for President," *Washington Post*, August 27, 1983, A10.

43 Richard Celeste quoted in Karl Vick, "Thousands Rally at Capitol in Support of Homeless," *St. Petersburg Times* (Fla.), October 8, 1989, 1A; "Kemp Promises Action to House Homeless," *New York Times*, October 7, 1989, 6.

44 ACORN, "History," Association of Community Organizations for Reform Now website, accessed at: http://acorn.org/index.php?id=12377; Peter Dreier and John Atlas, "The GOP's Blame-ACORN Game," *Nation*, November 10, 2008, 21.

45 Michael S. Barr and Gene Sperling, "Poor Homeowners, Good Loans," *New York Times*, October 18, 2008, 23; Peter Dreier and John Atlas, "GOP's Blame-ACORN Game," 20, 22; ACORN Fair Housing, *The Impending Rate Shock: A Study of Home Mortgages in 130 American Cities* (Washington, DC: Association of Community Organizations for Reform Now, 2006), 3, 6, 11, 28.

46 Kai Wright, "The Subprime Swindle," *Nation*, July 14, 2008, 11–22 (Mitchell's daughter Chandra Chavis quoted on p. 17).

47 Kai Wright, "The Subprime Swindle," 18; Jack Kemp and Henry Cisneros to Christopher Dodd, Barney Frank, Richard Shelby, and Spencer Bachus, September 24, 2008, National Commission on Fair Housing and Equal Opportunity website, accessed at: http://www.nationalfairhousing.org/Portals/33/Commission%20letter%20final.pdf; Patricia J. Williams, "Movin' On Down," *Nation*, July 14, 2008, 9.

CHAPTER 5: TO SEE OR NOT TO SEE

1 Eva Paterson, President, Equal Justice Society, quoted in Carmina Ocampo, "Prop 209: Ten Long Years," *Nation*, December 11, 2006, 8.

2 Aldon D. Morris, *The Origins of the Civil Rights Movement: Black Communities Organizing for Change* (New York: Free Press, 1984), 53, 250–1; August Meier and Elliott Rudwick, *CORE: A Study in the Civil Rights Movement, 1942–1968* (New York: Oxford University Press, 1973), 124, 191–2 (Gordon Carey quoted on pp. 191–2). Nancy MacLean highlights the centrality of employment and economic inclusion in black Americans' struggles for equality in *Freedom Is Not Enough: The Opening of the American Workplace* (New York: Russell Sage Foundation, 2006), esp. 3–10, 76–113.

3 "Employment Aid to Negroes Asked," *New York Times*, September 12, 1962, 40; Whitney M. Young Jr., "Domestic Marshall Plan," *New York Times*, October 6, 1963, 43, 129.

4 Kyle Haselden, "Parity, Not Preference," *New York Times*, October 6, 1963, 43, 128; James Reston, "The White Man's Burden and All That," *New York Times*, August 28, 1963, 32; M. S. Handler, "Rustin Sees Losses," *New York Times*, December 2, 1963, 1.

5 Allen Ellender quoted in Jack Raymond, "Tower Attacks Rights Proposal," *New York Times*, July 7, 1963, 44; MacLean, *Freedom Is Not Enough*, 67–8; "Civil Rights Bill–V," *New York Times*, May 8, 1964, 32; "Forced Hiring of Negroes – How It Would Work," *U.S. News & World Report*, July 29, 1963, 83–4.

6 *Congressional Record*, 88th Cong., 2nd sess., 1964, 110, pt. 5: 6549; *Civil Rights Act of 1964, U.S. Statutes at Large* 78 (1964): 253–66 (quotations on pp. 255 and 257).

7   Timothy J. Minchin, *Hiring the Black Worker: The Racial Integration of the Southern Textile Industry, 1960–1980* (Chapel Hill: University of North Carolina Press, 1999), 168–71 (quotations on pp. 168 (Tinnin), 170 (Pinnix), and 171 (Jennings)).

8   Timothy J. Minchin, *Hiring the Black Worker*, 67–80, 127–41, 224 (quotations on pp. 69 (Smyka), 131 (EEOC complaint), 224 (McLean)).

9   John David Skrentny, *The Ironies of Affirmative Action: Politics, Culture, and Justice in America* (Chicago, IL: University of Chicago Press, 1996), 121–4; Everett Crosson quoted in *Making a Right a Reality: An Oral History of the Early Years of the EEOC, 1965–1972*, ed. Sylvia Eisner Danovitch (Equal Employment Opportunity Commission: Washington, DC, 1990), 15.

10 Robert B. Semple, "Wirtz Finds Lag in Hiring Negroes," *New York Times*, May 5, 1967, 20; Prepared statement of Whitney M. Young Jr., in U.S. Senate, Subcommittee on Employment, Manpower, and Poverty of the Committee on Labor and Public Welfare, *Equal Employment Opportunity: Hearings on S. 1308 and S. 1667*, 90th Cong., 1st sess., May 4–5, 1967, 117.

11 Daniel Patrick Moynihan quoted in Gareth Davies, *From Opportunity to Entitlement: The Transformation and Decline of Great Society Liberalism* (Lawrence: University Press of Kansas, 1996), 66–7; Lyndon B. Johnson, "Commencement Address at Howard University: 'To Fulfill These Rights,'" June 4, 1965, in *Public Papers of the Presidents of the United States: Lyndon B. Johnson, 1965, Book II* (Washington, DC: Government Printing Office, 1966), 634.

12 Terry H. Anderson, *The Pursuit of Fairness: A History of Affirmative Action* (New York: Oxford University Press, 2004), 92.

13 John David Skrentny, *Ironies of Affirmative Action*, 119–20, 128, 131–2.

14 Edward Sylvester quoted in Richard P. Nathan, *Jobs and Civil Rights: The Role of the Federal Government in Promoting Equal Opportunity in Employment and Training* (Washington, DC: Brookings Institution, 1969), 93; John David Skrentny, *Ironies of Affirmative Action*, 136–7.

15 Terry H. Anderson, *Pursuit of Fairness*, 105; John David Skrentny, *Ironies of Affirmative Action*, 137–8, 193–209.

16 Hugh Davis Graham, *The Civil Rights Era: Origins and Development of National Policy, 1960–1972* (New York: Oxford University Press, 1990), 412–13; Thomas Byrne Edsall with Mary D. Edsall, *Chain Reaction: The Impact of Race, Rights, and Taxes on American Politics* (New York: W. W. Norton & Company, 1992), 124; Terry H. Anderson, *Pursuit of Fairness*, 124–5, 134–6, 140–4.

17 Arthur Fletcher, *The Silent Sell-Out: Government Betrayal of Blacks to the Craft Unions* (New York: The Third Press, Joseph Okpaku Publishing Company, 1973), 65 (targets); Arthur A. Fletcher, "A Personal Footnote in History," in *The Affirmative Action Debate*, ed. George E. Curry (Reading, MA: Addison-Wesley Publishing Company, 1996), 27 (unions); George Shultz quoted in Graham, *Civil Rights Era*, 323. For a detailed discussion of the role that "administrative pragmatism" played in the evolution of affirmative action, see John David Skrentny, *Ironies of Affirmative Action*, 111–44.

18 John David Skrentny, *Ironies of Affirmative Action*, 193, 204–9 (Nixon quoted on pp. 204–5); John Ehrlichman, *Witness to Power: The Nixon Years* (New York: Simon and Schuster, 1982), 228.

19 John David Skrentny, *Ironies of Affirmative Action*, 197–8, 207, 209–10; *Congressional Record*, 91st Cong., 1st sess., 1969, 115, pt. 30: 40917 (Hawkins).

20 Gareth Davies, *From Opportunity to Entitlement*, 113–14; John David Skrentny, *Ironies of Affirmative Action*, 77, 99; Kevin L. Yuill, *Richard Nixon and the Rise of Affirmative Action: The Pursuit of Racial Equality in an Era of Limits* (Lanham, Md.: Rowman & Littlefield, 2006), 66.

21 Christian Parenti, *Lockdown America: Police and Prisons in the Age of Crisis*, new edn. (London: Verso, 2008), 35, 42; Walter Feinberg, *On Higher Ground: Education and the Case for Affirmative Action* (New York: Teachers College, Columbia University, 1998), 2; Michael Goldfield, *The Color of Politics: Race and the Mainsprings of American Politics* (New York: New Press, 1997), 344.

22 Roy Reed, "New U.S. Job Plan for Negroes Set," *New York Times*, July 18, 1969, 10; George Shultz quoted in John David Skrentny, *Ironies of Affirmative Action*, 200.

23 Construction worker quoted in Quadango, *Color of Welfare*, 65; James Henson quoted in Stuart Taylor Jr., "Second Class Citizens," *American Lawyer* 11 (September 1989): 44.

24 Carl Cook quoted in Taylor, "Second Class Citizens," 44.

25 John David Skrentny, *Ironies of Affirmative Action*, 161–162.

26 Terry H. Anderson, *Pursuit of Fairness*, 127–129.

27 John David Skrentny, *Ironies of Affirmative Action*, 102–103, 165.

28 Terry H. Anderson, *Pursuit of Fairness*, 152–155.

29 Robin D. G. Kelley, "Into the Fire: 1970 to the Present," in *To Make Our World Anew: A History of African Americans*, eds. Robin D. G. Kelley and Earl Lewis (New York: Oxford University Press, 2000), 567; Stephen Steinberg, *Turning Back: The Retreat from Racial Justice in American Thought and Policy* (Boston, MA: Beacon Press, 1995), 167; Terry H. Anderson, *Pursuit of Fairness*, 159; MacLean, *Freedom Is Not Enough*, 317.

30 Robert Earl Holmes and Felder Holmes to William M. Colmer, February 24, 1969, file "Farmers Home Administration–General, 1969," box 2, ser. 8, John C. Stennis Collection, Congressional and Political Research Center, Mitchell Library, Mississippi State University, Starkville; George R. Thomas to John J. Sparkman, September 19, 1969, cons. with Sparkman to Thomas, September 26, 1969, file "CR," box 1, 1969 series, John J. Sparkman Senate Papers, Special Collections, Hoole Library, University of Alabama, Tuscaloosa; "Whites' Rights at Stake," *Citizen*, September 1977, 2; "Bakke In, Quotas Out: Whites' Rights Upheld," *Citizen*, August 1978, 10–11.

31 Richard Nixon quoted in John David Skrentny, *Ironies of Affirmative Action*, 217; Ronald Reagan, "Government and the Family," national television address, July 6, 1976, in *A Time for Choosing: The Speeches of Ronald Reagan, 1961–1982*, ed. Alfred Balitzer (Chicago: Regnery Gateway, 1983), 169; Terry H. Anderson, *Pursuit of Fairness*, 164; Republican Party platform

quoted in Gary L. McDowell, "Affirmative Inaction: The Brock-Meese Standoff on Federal Racial Quotas," *Policy Review* 48 (spring 1989), 32.

32 Ronald Reagan quoted in Gary L. McDowell, "Affirmative Inaction," 32; Ronald Reagan, "Radio Address to the Nation on Civil Rights," June 15, 1985, in *Public Papers of the Presidents of the United States: Ronald Reagan, 1985, Book I* (Washington, DC: Government Printing Office, 1988) 733.

33 Philip Shabecoff, "Hatch Plans Inquiry into Corruption," *New York Times*, January 25, 1981, 18; "After 15 Years Affirmative Action Debate Still Heated," *New York Times*, October 4, 1981, E20; Terry H. Anderson, *Pursuit of Fairness*, 186.

34 National Association of Manufacturers president Alexander L. Trowbridge quoted in Nicholas Laham, *The Reagan Presidency and the Politics of Race: In Pursuit of Colorblind Justice and Limited Government* (Westport, CT: Praeger Publishers, 1998), 98–9; Daniel Seligman, "Affirmative Action Is Here to Stay," *Fortune*, April 19, 1982, 156, 160.

35 William Bradford Reynolds quoted in Kenneth O'Reilly, *Nixon's Piano: Presidents and Racial Politics from Washington to Clinton* (New York: Free Press, 1995), 363; Robert Pear, "U.S. Agencies Vary on Rights Policy," *New York Times*, November 16, 1981, A1, A16.

36 Terry H. Anderson, *Pursuit of Fairness*, 169, 177–8; "E.E.O.C. Chief Cites Trouble in Resolving Some Job Bias Cases," *New York Times*, June 2, 1982, B9.

37 Terry H. Anderson, *Pursuit of Fairness*, 201–6; John David Skrentny, *Ironies of Affirmative Action*, 227.

38 "Split Down the Right," *Nation*, July 20, 1998, 3.

39 Martin Luther King Jr., *Where Do We Go from Here: Chaos or Community?* (New York: Harper & Row, 1967), 144–5.

40 Karin L. Stanford, "Reverend Jesse Jackson and the Rainbow/PUSH Coalition," in *Black Political Organizations in the Post-Civil Rights Era*, eds. Ollie A. Johnson III and Karin L. Stanford (New Brunswick, NJ: Rutgers University Press, 2002), 155, 159; Thomas R. Peake, *Keeping the Dream Alive: A History of the Southern Christian Leadership Conference from King to the Nineteen-Eighties* (New York: Peter Lang, 1987), 289; "Chicagoans Can't Be Neutral about Jackson," *New York Times*, March 20, 1984, B13.

41 "At Last the Urban League Takes Off Its Gloves," *Journal of Blacks in Higher Education* 9 (autumn 1995): 23; Kurt Eichenwald, "Calls Issued for Boycott of Texaco," *New York Times*, November 13, 1996, D1, 19; Kurt Eichenwald, "Texaco Plans Wide Program for Minorities," *New York Times*, December 19, 1996, D1, 6 (Cleaver).

42 Berkeley flyer quoted in "Campus Protest Against Slurs," *New York Times*, February 16, 1995, A22; Shelby Steele, "A Negative Vote on Affirmative Action," *New York Times Sunday Magazine*, May 13, 1990, 46–9, 73; Don Wycliff, "Blacks Debate the Costs of Affirmative Action," *New York Times*, June 10, 1990, E3 (Wilson); Jim Sleeper quoted in Steven A. Holmes, "Mulling the Idea of Affirmative Action for Poor Whites," *New York Times*, August 18, 1991, E3.

43 Terry H. Anderson, *Pursuit of Fairness*, 246.

44 David B. Wilkins and G. Mitu Gulati, "Why Are There So Few Lawyers in Corporate Law Firms? An Institutional Analysis," *California Law Review* 84 (May 1996): 554–64.

45 Stephen Steinberg, *Turning Back*, 86 (quotation), 143–6, 152–3; Ira Katznelson, *When Affirmative Action Was White: An Untold History of Racial Inequality in Twentieth-Century America* (New York: W. W. Norton & Company, 2005), x–xiii.

46 Terry H. Anderson, *Pursuit of Fairness*, 253–4, 267–71 (Supreme Court quoted on p. 271); MacLean, *Freedom Is Not Enough*, 314–20.

47 "Constitutional Scholars' Statement on Affirmative Action after *City of Richmond v. J. A. Croson Co.*," *Yale Law Journal* 98 (June 1989): 1712; Terry H. Anderson, *Pursuit of Fairness*, 260.

48 "Affirmative Action Foes Point to Obama," *Boston Globe*, March 18, 2008, A1; Peter Wallsten and David G. Savage, "Voting Rights Act Out of Date?" *Los Angeles Times*, March 18, 2009, A1.

CHAPTER 6: IS THIS AMERICA?

1 Maynard Jackson quoted in Mary R. Warner, *The Dilemma of Black Politics: A Report on Harassment of Black Elected Officials* (Sacramento, CA: National Association of Human Rights Workers, 1977), 106.

2 Testimony of Fannie Lou Hamer before the Credentials Committee of the Democratic National Convention, August 22, 1964, in *Sources of the African American Past: Primary Sources in American History*, 2nd edn., ed. Roy E. Finkenbine (New York: Pearson Education, 2004), 192.

3 U.S. Bureau of the Census, *1980 Statistical Abstract*, 514 (Table 849), U.S. Census Bureau website, accessed at: http://www.census.gov/compendia/statab/past_years.html

4 Marv [Rich] to Rochelle Horowitz, July 11, 1967, 1, file 14, box 19, Papers of the Scholarship, Education and Defense Fund for Racial Equality, State Historical Society of Wisconsin, Madison (SEDFRE Papers); Greta de Jong, "The Scholarship, Education and Defense Fund for Racial Equality and the Freedom Struggle in the Post-Civil Rights Era," paper presented at the 91st Annual Convention of the Association for the Study of African American Life and History, September 29, 2006.

5 Victor Ullman, "In Darkest America," *Nation*, September 4, 1967, 180; [Thomas G. Abernethy], "The Republican Party and Civil Rights," [1966], cons. with clippings from *Jackson Daily News*, April 18, 1966, file "Republican Party in Mississippi," box 194, Thomas G. Abernethy Papers, Archives and Special Collections, University of Mississippi, Oxford.

6 "You Gotta Love Me," *Newsweek*, August 2, 1971, 24; Black candidate in Mississippi quoted in Mary R. Warner, *Dilemma of Black Politics*, 31; U.S. Commission on Civil Rights, *The Voting Rights Act: Unfulfilled Goals* (Washington, DC: Government Printing Office, 1981), 23, 34.

7 Katherine Tate, *Black Faces in the Mirror: African Americans and Their Representatives in the U.S. Congress* (Princeton, NJ: Princeton University Press, 2003), 54; J. Morgan Kousser, *Colorblind Injustice: Minority Voting Rights and the Undoing of the Second Reconstruction* (Chapel Hill: University of North Carolina Press, 1999), 55; Frank R. Parker, *Black Votes Count: Political Empowerment in Mississippi after 1965* (Chapel Hill: University of North Carolina Press, 1990), 34–66 (Trenor and *Jackson Clarion-Ledger* quoted on p. 47).

8 J. Morgan Kousser, *Colorblind Injustice*, 55–6; Frank R. Parker, *Black Votes Count*, 95; U.S. Bureau of the Census, *2008 Statistical Abstract*, 255 (Table 402), U.S. Census Bureau website, accessed at: http://www.census.gov/compendia/statab/past_years.html.

9 Thomas R. Peake, *Keeping the Dream Alive: A History of the Southern Christian Leadership Conference from King to the Nineteen-Eighties* (New York: Peter Lang, 1987), 378–84.

10 U.S. Bureau of the Census, *2008 Statistical Abstract*, 251, 255 (Tables 394 and 402); Abigail M. Thernstrom, *Whose Votes Count? Affirmative Action and Minority Voting Rights* (Cambridge, MA: Harvard University Press, 1987), 3–9; "A Dinosaur Ruling," *New York Times*, June 30, 1993, A14; J. Morgan Kousser, *Colorblind Injustice*, 5, 245 (quotation), 384–5.

11 Jeffrey S. Adler, Introduction to *African-American Mayors: Race, Politics, and the American City*, eds. David R. Colburn and Jeffrey S. Adler (Urbana, IL: University of Illinois, 2001), 12; Katherine Tate, *Black Faces in the Mirror*, 66; David Lublin, *The Paradox of Representation: Racial Gerrymandering and Minority Interests in Congress* (Princeton, NJ: Princeton University Press, 1997), 41; JoAnn Wypijewski, "Postcards from Ohio," *Nation*, March 17, 2008, 14.

12 Jeffrey S. Adler, Introduction to *African-American Mayors*, ed. David R. Colburn and Jeffrey S. Adler, 10; Adolph Reed Jr., *Stirrings in the Jug: Black Politics in the Post-Segregation Era* (Minneapolis, MN: University of Minnesota Press, 1999), 168.

13 Heather Ann Thompson, "Rethinking the Collapse of Postwar Liberalism: The Rise of Mayor Coleman Young and the Politics of Race in Detroit," in *African-American Mayors*, ed. David R. Colburn and Jeffrey S. Adler, 229 (white resident quotation), 238–40; James B. Lane, "Black Political Power and Its Limits: Gary Mayor Richard G. Hatcher's Administration, 1968–87," in *African-American Mayors*, ed. David R. Colburn and Jeffrey S. Adler, 62–8.

14 Jeffrey S. Adler, Introduction to *African-American Mayors*, ed. David R. Colburn and Jeffrey S. Adler, 6; Roger Biles, "Mayor David Dinkins and the Politics of Race in New York City," *African-American Mayors*, ed. David R. Colburn and Jeffrey S. Adler, 139; James B. Lane, "Black Political Power and Its Limits," 64, 69.

15 SEDFRE, "Needs Assessment of Uniontown, Alabama," April 1973, 1, 4–6, encl. in Marvin Rich to Portia Smith, April 18, 1973, file "Scholarship, Education and Defense Fund, Inc., 1973–Aug. 1973," series 3, box 433, Rockefeller Brothers Fund Records, Rockefeller Archive Center, Sleepy Hollow,

NY; SEDFRE, "Andrew M. Hayden, The Mayor of Uniontown, Alabama," n.d. [1975], file 10, box 10, SEDFRE Papers.

16 Ronald H. Bayor, "African-American Mayors and Governance in Atlanta," in *African-American Mayors*, ed. David R. Colburn and Jeffrey S. Adler, 180; Adolph Reed Jr., *Stirrings in the Jug*, 168; Atlanta banker quoted in David R. Colburn, "Running for Office: African-American Mayors from 1967 to 1996," in *African-American Mayors*, ed. David R. Colburn and Jeffrey S. Adler, 40.

17 Ronald H. Bayor, "African-American Mayors and Governance," 181, 185–94 (Maynard Jackson quoted on p. 181); Adolph Reed Jr., *Stirrings in the Jug*, 4.

18 Andrew Young quoted in Ronald H. Bayor, "African-American Mayors and Governance," 189.

19 Mary R. Warner, *Dilemma of Black Politics*, 107–16 (Charles Freeman Joseph quoted on pp. 107 (white power structure), 108 (Chamber of Commerce), 109 (constant daily attack), 115–16 (no longer believe ... running our governments)).

20 Carl Stokes quoted in Mary R. Warner, *Dilemma of Black Politics*, 146.

21 Mary R. Warner, *Dilemma of Black Politics*, 124–7, 136; William L. Clay, *Just Permanent Interests: Black Americans in Congress, 1870–1991* (New York: Amistad Press, 1992), 319.

22 Mary R. Warner, *Dilemma of Black Politics*, 130 (Canty), 98 (*Winston County Journal* and Charles Evers quotations); William L. Clay, *Just Permanent Interests*, 316.

23 George Derek Musgrove, "The Harassment of Black Elected Officials: Race, Party Realignment, and State Power in the Post-Civil Rights United States," PhD dissertation, New York University, 2005, 2–18; Derek Musgrove to Greta de Jong, personal communication, April 2, 2009, in author's possession. A book based on this dissertation is forthcoming from the University of Georgia Press.

24 U.S. Bureau of the Census, *2008 Statistical Abstract*, 255 (Table 402); James B. Lane, "Black Political Power and Its Limits," 71; Adolph Reed Jr., *Stirrings in the Jug*, 97–8, 120.

25 William L. Clay, *Just Permanent Interests*, 198–9; Frank R. Parker, *Black Votes Count*, 131–4; Jesse Jackson quoted in "Black Candidate Urged," *Washington Post*, April 18, 1983, B3.

26 E. Lee Bernick and Charles L. Prysby, "Reactions to the Jackson Candidacy among Southern Black Democratic Party Activists," in *Blacks in Southern Politics*, eds. Laurence W. Moreland, Robert P. Steed, and Tod A. Baker, (New York: Praeger, 1987), 191; John J. McGlennon, "The Jackson Campaign in Virginia: Precinct and State-Level Activists," in *Blacks in Southern Politics*, eds. Laurence W. Moreland, Robert P. Steed and Tod A. Baker, 227; Jesse Jackson, "A Chance to Serve," presidential campaign announcement speech, Raleigh, NC, October 10, 1987, in *Keep Hope Alive: Jesse Jackson's 1988 Presidential Campaign*, eds. Frank Clemente and Frank Watkins (Boston, MA: South End Press, 1989), 27.

27 David O. Sears, Jack Citrin, and Rick Kosterman, "Jesse Jackson and the Southern White Electorate in 1984," in *Blacks in Southern Politics*, eds. Laurence W. Moreland, Robert P. Steed and Tod A. Baker, 219–223; Adolph

Reed Jr., *Stirrings in the Jug*, 212–215; Lawrence J. Hanks, "Pride and Pragmatism: Two Arguments for the Diversification of Party Interests," in *Black and Multiracial Politics in America*, eds. Yvette Alex-Assensoh and Lawrence J. Hanks (New York: New York University Press, 2000), 278–9 (stop Jesse quotation); Manning Marable, *The Crisis of Color and Democracy: Essays on Race, Class, and Power* (Monroe, ME: Common Courage Press, 1991), 161, 169.

28 Lani Guinier, *The Tyranny of the Majority: Fundamental Fairness and Representative Democracy* (New York: Free Press, 1994), 32–3; Pie-te Lien, "Who Votes in Multiracial America? An Analysis of Voting Registration and Turnout by Race and Ethnicity, 1990–1996," in *Black and Multiracial Politics*, eds. Yvette Alex-Assensoh and Lawrence J. Hanks, 201–3.

29 Lani Guinier, *Tyranny of the Majority*, 10–11.

30 Julious McGruder quoted in Lani Guinier, *Tyranny of the Majority*, 11.

31 Marc Mauer, *Race to Incarcerate*, 2nd edn. (New York: New Press, 2006), 205–6; Lani Guinier and Gerald Torres, *The Miner's Canary: Enlisting Race, Resisting Power, Transforming Democracy* (Cambridge, MA: Harvard University Press, 2003), 190–1, 265.

32 Paul Weyrich quoted in News Services, "TV Ads Attack Moral Majority, Other Groups for 'Intolerance,'" *Washington Post*, October 9, 1982, B6; Tracy Campbell, *Deliver the Vote: A History of Election Fraud, an American Political Tradition, 1742–2004* (New York: Carroll and Graf, 2005), 284.

33 "President Vetoes the 'Motor-Voter' Measure," *New York Times*, July 3, 1992, A14; "President Bush Impedes Democracy," *New York Times*, July 6, 1992, A12; Adam Clymer, "Voter Bill Passes in a G.O.P. Defeat," May 12, 1993, *New York Times*, A1.

34 Tracy Campbell, *Deliver the Vote*, xvi; Andrew Gumbel, *Steal This Vote: Dirty Elections and the Rotten History of Democracy in America* (New York: Nation Books, 2005), xiv.

35 "G.O.P. Memo Tells of Black Vote Cut," *New York Times*, October 25, 1986, 7; "The Measure of Republican 'Integrity,'" *New York Times*, November 1, 1986, 30. See also Tracy Campbell, *Deliver the Vote*, 293–294, 332–3; Andrew Gumbel, *Steal This Vote*, xv, 2–6, 28–9; and George Derek Musgrove, "Harassment of Black Elected Officials," 179–82, 192–5, 212–19, 228–32.

36 George Derek Musgrove, "Harassment of Black Elected Officials," 192–5.

37 Richard A. Cloward and Frances Fox Piven, "Trying to Break Down the Barriers," *Nation*, November 2, 1985, 433–7; Paul Bass, "Vote Drive an Issue Again in Bridgeport," *New York Times*, May 20, 1984, section 23, 1, 16.

38 Charles Sherrod quoted in Sharon Basco, "The Color of Money," *Nation*, February 1, 1999, 21–3; Glen Justice, "Even With Campaign Finance Law, Money Talks Louder Than Ever," *New York Times*, November 8, 2004, A16.

39 Robert Dreyfuss, "Till Earth and Heaven Ring," *Nation*, July 23/30, 2001, 11–16.

40 U.S. Commission on Civil Rights, *Voting Irregularities in Florida During the 2000 Presidential Election* (Washington, DC: Government Printing Office, 2001), 16, 25–8, 41–5, 56–77, 85, 95, 127.

41 U.S. Commission on Civil Rights, *Voting Irregularities in Florida*, iii (quotation), xii, 6–7, 12, 16, 27 (poll worker), 92; Tracy Campbell, *Deliver the Vote*, 311.

42 Allen Lichtman quoted in U.S. Commission on Civil Rights, *Voting Irregularities in Florida*, 12; CalTech/MIT Voting Technology Project, *Voting: What Is, What Could Be*, January 1, 2009, CalTech/MIT Voting Technology Project website, accessed at: http://vote.caltech.edu/drupal/node/10; Robert Pear, "Congress Passes Bill to Clean Up Election System," *New York Times*, October 17, 2002, A1.

43 Greg Palast, "Vanishing Votes," *Nation*, May 17, 2004, 6, 20; Tova Andrea Wang, "Identity Politics," *Nation*, August 16/23, 2004, 18; David Dill quoted in Melanie Warner, "Machine Politics in the Digital Age," *New York Times*, December 2, 2003, BU1, 11.

44 Lawyers' Committee, *Election Protection 2008: Helping Voters Today, Modernizing the System for Tomorrow: Preliminary Analysis of Voting Irregularities*, 5–6, Lawyers Committee for Civil Rights Under Law website, accessed at: http://www.lawyerscommittee.org/admin/voting_rights/documents/files/0017.pdf; John Nichols, "Just a T-Shirt Away," *Nation*, October 25, 2004, 4–5; JoAnn Wypijewski, "The Party's Over," *Nation*, November 22, 2004, 21–2; "Questions Still Lingering Over the Voting Process," *Talk of the Nation*, National Public Radio, November 8, 2004.

45 Mazie Butler Ferguson to Greta de Jong, personal communication, March 3, 2009, in author's possession.

46 Barack Obama, *Dreams From My Father: A Story of Race and Inheritance*, (New York: Random House, 2004), xiii–xvi, 74–87, 110–12; "Insights from the Campaign Trail," interview with Christopher Hayes, *Activate*, October 30, 2008, accessed at: http://activate.us/175731

47 "Transcript: Obama's Acceptance Speech," Yahoo News, November 5, 2008, accessed at: http://news.yahoo.com/s/ynews/ynews_pl135

CHAPTER 7: FIR$T CLA$$ CITIZEN$HIP

1 A. Philip Randolph quoted in Dona Cooper Hamilton and Charles V. Hamilton, *The Dual Agenda: Race and the Social Welfare Policies of Civil Rights Organizations* (New York: Columbia University Press, 1997), 127.

2 Key List Mailing No. 7, February 5, 1966, 5, item 2, reel 2, Mississippi Freedom Democratic Party Papers, State Historical Society of Wisconsin, Madison; "Government's 'No' to Squatters," *New York Times*, February 6, 1966, E2. For more on the Greenville protest, see James C. Cobb, " 'Somebody Done Nailed Us on the Cross': Federal Farm and Welfare Policy and the Civil Rights Movement in the Mississippi Delta," *Journal of American History* 77 (December 1990): 928–31 and John Dittmer, *Local People: The Struggle for Civil Rights in Mississippi* (Urbana, IL: University of Illinois Press, 1994), 366–8.

Studies of the black freedom movement that highlight the economic aspects of the struggle include Nan Elizabeth Woodruff, "African-American Struggles for Citizenship in the Arkansas and Mississippi Deltas in the Age of Jim Crow," *Radical History Review* 55 (winter 1993): 33–51; Dona Cooper Hamilton and Charles V. Hamilton, *Dual Agenda*; Greta de Jong, *A Different Day: African American Struggles for Justice in Rural Louisiana, 1900–1970* (Chapel Hill, NC: University of North Carolina Press, 2002); Nancy MacLean, *Freedom Is Not Enough: The Opening of the American Workplace* (New York: Russell Sage Foundation, 2006); Thomas F. Jackson, *From Civil Rights to Human Rights: Martin Luther King, Jr., and the Struggle for Racial Justice* (Philadelphia: University of Pennsylvania Press, 2007); and Glenda Elizabeth Gilmore, *Defying Dixie: The Radical Roots of Civil Rights* (New York: W. W. Norton & Company, 2009).

3 Miriam Feingold to Family, July 23, 1963, frame 0278, reel 1, Miriam Feingold Papers, State Historical Society of Wisconsin, Madison; Draft of notice, n.d. [1965], 3, file 8, box 1, Ferriday Freedom Movement Papers, State Historical Society of Wisconsin, Madison.

4 Martin Luther King Jr. quoted in Jackson, *From Civil Rights to Human Rights*, 342.

5 Martin Luther King Jr., *Where Do We Go from Here: Chaos or Community?* (New York: Harper & Row, 1967), 132.

6 Dona Cooper Hamilton and Charles V. Hamilton, *Dual Agenda*, 168–172 (PPC quoted on p. 171); "National Mobilization in Support of the Poor People's Campaign," pamphlet, n.d. [1968], file 14, box 28, Papers of the Scholarship, Education and Defense Fund for Racial Equality, State Historical Society of Wisconsin, Madison (SEDFRE Papers).

7 Augustus Hawkins, speech to the Annual Conference of the National Urban League, July 29, 1974, in National Urban League, *Full Employment as a National Goal: Proceedings of the 64th National Urban League Conference* (New York: National Urban League, 1975), 38–42 (quotation on p. 40).

8 Dona Cooper Hamilton and Charles V. Hamilton, *Dual Agenda*, 198–206; Michael B. Katz, Mark J. Stern and Jamie J. Fader, "The New African American Inequality," *Journal of American History* 92 (June 2005): 82; U.S. Bureau of the Census, *2008 Statistical Abstract*, 373 (Table 569), U.S. Census Bureau website, accessed at: http://www.census.gov/compendia/statab/past_years.html

9 Herbert Stein, "Full Employment at Last?" *Wall Street Journal*, September 14, 1977, 22; Arthur Okun quoted in Larry Martz, Rich Thomas and Pamela Lynn Abraham, "The Inflation Surge," *Newsweek*, May 29, 1978, 69.

10 Paul Volcker quoted in "Volcker Asserts U.S. Must Trim Living Standard," *New York Times*, October 18, 1979, A1; Christian Parenti, *Lockdown America: Police and Prisons in the Age of Crisis*, new ed. (London: Verso, 2008), 39; Robert K. Schaeffer, *Understanding Globalization: The Social Consequences of Political, Economic, and Environmental Change* (Lanham, MD: Rowman & Littlefield, 2003), 82.

11 U.S. Commission on Civil Rights, *A Time to Listen … a Time to Act: Voices from the Ghettos of the Nation's Cities* (Washington, DC: Government Printing Office, 1967), in *Welfare: A Documentary History of U.S. Policy and Politics*, eds. Gwendolyn Mink and Rickie Solinger (New York: New York University Press, 2003), 278.

12   Charlotte Devree to Ezra Levin et al., November 7, 1963, 2, file 1, box 7, Papers of the Scholarship, Education and Defense Fund for Racial Equality, State Historical Society of Wisconsin, Madison; "Mississippi: Short-Term Action," February 17, 1966, 5, encl. in Dudley Morris to Theodore M. Berry, memorandum, February 18, 1966, file "Administrative–Mississippi–1966 (2 of 2)," box 12, State Files, 1965–68, Records of the Director, Community Action Program Office, Office of Economic Opportunity, Record Group 381, National Archives, Washington, DC (RG 381).

13   Charles A. Reich, "Individual Rights and Social Welfare: The Emerging Legal Issues," *Yale Law Journal* 74 (June 1965): 1253–4, 1256; Johnnie Tillmon, "Welfare Is a Women's Issue," *Ms.*, spring 1972, 111.

14   U.S. Department of Health, Education, and Welfare, *A Constructive Public Welfare Program* (Washington, DC: Government Printing Office, 1965), 3; Walter Goodman, "The Case of Mrs. Sylvester Smith," *New York Times Sunday Magazine*, August 25, 1968, 28; Ronald A. Arundell, "Welfare Rights as Organizing Vehicle," in *The Mississippi Experience: Strategies for Welfare Rights Action*, ed. Paul A. Kurzman (New York: Association Press, 1971), 94 (Alabama statistics); David Zucchino, *Myth of the Welfare Queen* (New York: Scribner, 1997), 14; Inter-agency study quoted in Gareth Davies, *From Opportunity to Entitlement: The Transformation and Decline of Great Society Liberalism* (Lawrence: University Press of Kansas, 1996), 100.

15   Lawrence Neil Bailis, *Bread or Justice: Grassroots Organizing in the Welfare Rights Movement* (Lexington, MA.: D. C. Heath and Company, 1974), 11; Felicia Kornbluh, *The Battle for Welfare Rights: Politics and Poverty in Modern America* (Philadelphia: University of Pennsylvania Press, 2007), 25–9, 44–8, 64–6 (Sydelle Moore quoted on p. 47); George Wiley, Foreword to *Mississippi Experience*, ed. Paul A. Kurzman, 10–12; Annelise Orleck, *Storming Caesars Palace: How Black Mothers Fought their Own War on Poverty* (Boston, MA: Beacon Press, 2005), 98–116.

16   Lawrence Neil Bailis, *Bread or Justice*, 7–8; Felicia Kornbluh, *Battle for Welfare Rights*, 61 (Tillmon quotation).

17   Joyce Burson quoted in Felicia Kornbluh, *Battle for Welfare Rights*, 56; Joseph E. Paull, "Recipients Aroused: The New Welfare Rights Movement," *Social Work* 12 (April 1967): 102.

18   Felicia Kornbluh, *Battle for Welfare Rights*, 10, 17, 40, 75.

19   "*King v. Smith*," in *Welfare*, eds. Gwendolyn Mink and Rickie Solinger, 288.

20   "*Thompson v. Shapiro*" and "*Goldberg v. Kelly*," in *Welfare*, eds. Gwendolyn Mink and Rickie Solinger, 322 (Brennan); 327–30 (Alma Coldburn quoted on p. 328 and David Gilman on p. 329).

21   Charles A. Reich, "Individual Rights and Social Welfare," 1256; U.S. Department of Health, Education, and Welfare, *Welfare Myths vs. Facts* (Washington, DC: Government Printing Office, 1971), in *Welfare*, eds. Gwendolyn Mink and Rickie Solinger, 366; Premilla Nadasen, *Welfare Warriors: The Welfare Rights Movement in the United States* (New York: Routledge, 2005), xvi, 165–6; Beulah Sanders quoted in Felicia Kornbluh, *Battle for Welfare Rights*, 157.

22 Felicia Kornbluh, *Battle for Welfare Rights*, 15; HEW administrator quoted in Lawrence Neil Bailis, *Bread or Justice*, 144–145.

23 Felicia Kornbluh, *Battle for Welfare Rights*, 90–92; "Anti-NWRO Letters to Senator Russell Long," in *Welfare*, eds. Gwendolyn Mink and Rickie Solinger, 269.

24 Felicia Kornbluh, *Battle for Welfare Rights*, 96–97.

25 Dorcas Lenoir quoted in U.S. Commission on Civil Rights, *A Time to Listen*, 279.

26 Gareth Davies, *Opportunity to Entitlement*, 212–29; Felicia Kornbluh, *Battle for Welfare Rights*, 152–3; Dona Cooper Hamilton and Charles V. Hamilton, *Dual Agenda*, 182–91.

27 Premilla Nadasen, *Welfare Warriors*, 193–224; "1980s," and "Family Support Act of 1988," in *Welfare*, eds. Gwendolyn Mink and Rickie Solinger, 441, 525; Mimi Abramovitz, "Why Welfare Reform is a Sham," *Nation*, September 26, 1988, 237–41.

28 "1990–2002," in *Welfare*, eds. Gwendolyn Mink and Rickie Solinger, 535–7.

29 Alejandra Marchevsky and Jeanne Theoharis, *Not Working: Latina Immigrants, Low-wage Jobs, and the Failure of Welfare Reform* (New York: New York University Press, 2006) 6, 11; Frances Fox Piven, Foreword to *Welfare*, eds. Gwendolyn Mink and Rickie Solinger, xxi–ii; U.S. Bureau of the Census, *2009 Statistical Abstract*, 454 (Table 689).

30 "Economic Reality Bites," *New York Times*, August 28, 2004, A14; Applied Research Center, "Race and Recession," in *Welfare*, eds. Gwendolyn Mink and Rickie Solinger, 811.

31 Todd C. Shaw, "'We Refused to Lay Down Our Spears': The Persistence of Welfare Rights Activism, 1966–1996," in *Black Political Organizations in the Post-Civil Rights Era*, eds. Ollie A. Johnson III and Karin L. Stanford (New Brunswick, NJ: Rutgers University Press, 2002), 183–4, 188; Felicia Kornbluh, *Battle for Welfare Rights*, 178–9, 182; Cheri Honkala quoted in David Zucchino, *Myth of the Welfare Queen*, 217.

32 Todd C. Shaw, "We Refused to Lay Down Our Spears," 187; David Zucchino, *Myth of the Welfare Queen*, 47–50, 56, 93–8.

33 David Zucchino, *Myth of the Welfare Queen*, 293–4.

34 Welfare Warriors, "Shame on the Wisconsin Senate" in *Welfare*, eds. Gwendolyn Mink and Rickie Solinger, 640; Vanessa Tait, "Workers Just Like Anyone Else: Organizing Workfare Unions in New York City," in *Still Lifting, Still Climbing: Contemporary African American Women's Activism*, ed. Kimberly Springer (New York: New York University Press, 1999), 304–5; "Pataki on the Record: Excerpts from a Talk on Campaign Issues," *New York Times*, October 10, 1994, B4; Richard Schwartz quoted in Leslie Kaufman with Andrew Murr, "Welfare's Labor Pains," *Newsweek*, March 31, 1997, 39.

35 Vanessa Tait, "Workers Just Like Anyone Else," 310–16.

36 Peter Edelman, "Reforming Welfare – Take Two," *Nation*, February 4, 2002, 16–20; ACORN, "New Victories, 1995–2002," Association of Community

Organizations for Reform Now website, accessed at: http://www.acorn.org/index.php?id=2744

37 National Campaign for Jobs and Income Support to U.S. Department of Health and Human Services, November 29, 2001, in *Welfare*, eds. Gwendolyn Mink and Rickie Solinger, 762; Richard W. Stevenson, "Bush Urges Congress to Extend Welfare Law, With Changes," *New York Times*, January 15, 2003, A18; Robert Pear, "Defying Bush, Senate Increases Child Care Funds for the Poor," *New York Times*, March 31, 2004, A1, A19.

38 "The Quiet Revolution of a Parish Priest," *Ebony*, May 1968, 52–7; Thomas N. Bethell, *Sumter County Blues: The Ordeal of the Federation of Southern Cooperatives* (Washington, DC: National Committee in Support of Community Based Organizations, 1982), 4–5.

39 John Zippert, interview by author, tape recording, June 28, 1998, T. Harry Williams Center for Oral History, Louisiana State University, Baton Rouge; Federation of Southern Cooperatives, *Annual Report*, 1978, 5, file 13, box 83, Records of the Federation of Southern Cooperatives, Amistad Research Center, New Orleans, LA (FSCR).

40 William H. Peace III to Hubert H. Humphrey, August 23, 1971, 1, encl. in Gene Bradford to Carol Khosrovi, memorandum, September 10, 1971, file "Office of Program Development (1 of 3)," box 8, Deputy Director Subject files, 1966–73, Office of Economic Opportunity, RG 381; Thomas N. Bethell, *Sumter County Blues*, 2; Charles O. Prejean to Robert Smith, March 7, 1978, 2, file 18, box 15, FSCR.

41 Thomas N. Bethell, *Sumter County Blues*, 13–17; Charles O. Prejean to Carl Holman, August 5, 1980, 1, file 4, box 76, FSCR.

42 John Zippert to Jack Litzenberg, November 8, 1985, 1, file 3, box 47, FSCR; Federation of Southern Cooperatives–Land Assistance Fund website, accessed at: http://www.federationsoutherncoop.com; "The Federation/LAF's Katrina Disaster Relief and Recovery Project," *Federation of Southern Cooperatives-Land Assistance Fund Annual Report*, 2005–2006, 2–4, in author's possession.

43 "Introduction to the Black Panther Survival Programs," in *The Black Panther Party: Service to the People Programs*, ed. David Hilliard (Albuquerque, NM: University of New Mexico Press, 2008), 3.

44 Preface to *Black and Right: The Bold New Voice of Black Conservatives in America*, eds. Stan Faryna, Brad Stetson and Joseph G. Conti (Westport, CT: Praeger, 1997), xiii; Robert Woodson quoted in Marshall Ingwerson, "Forsyth County March Ignites Dreams and Doubts for Civil Rights," *Christian Science Monitor*, February 13, 1987, 5.

45 George Packer, "A Tale of Two Movements," *Nation*, December 14, 1998, 21–3.

46 Whitney M. Young Jr., "To Be Equal," in *Minority Group Politics: A Reader*, ed. Stephen J. Herzog (New York: Holt, Rinehart and Winston, 1971), 272–3; Robert C. Smith, *We Have No Leaders: African Americans in the Post-Civil Rights Era* (Albany, NY: State University of New York Press, 1996), 97; Thomas R. Peake, *Keeping the Dream Alive: A History of the Southern Christian Leadership Conference from King to the Nineteen-Eighties* (New

York: Peter Lang, 1987), 394; Joshua L. Weinstein, "Panel Stresses Religion to Help Avert Disturbances by Youths," *St. Petersburg Times*, May 5, 1987, 3B; Laura Sessions Stepp, "District is Snubbed by Antidrug Initiative," *Washington Post*, April 16, 1989, A22; "St. Petersburg is Site for SCLC Campaign," *St. Petersburg Times*, April 15, 1992, 3B; Manning Marable, "Black (Community) Power!" *Nation*, December 22, 1997, 21–4.

47 Deborah R. Grayson, "'Necessity Was the Midwife of Our Politics': Black Women's Health Activism in the Post-Civil Rights Era (1980–1996)," in *Still Lifting, Still Climbing*, ed. Kimberley Springer, 131–48.

48 Erica L. Gordon, "A Layin' On of Hands: Black Women's Community Work," in *Black Political Organizations*, eds. Ollie A. Johnson III and Karin L. Stanford, 69–76; Dorothy Height, *Open Wide the Freedom Gates: A Memoir* (New York: PublicAffairs, Perseus Books, 2003), 195–7, 188–9.

49 Height, *Open Wide the Freedom Gates*, 215–18 (quotations on pp. 216 and 218).

50 Adolph Reed Jr., *Stirrings in the Jug: Black Politics in the Post-Segregation Era* (Minneapolis, MN: University of Minnesota Press, 1999), 126; NCNW member quoted in Gordon, "A Layin' On of Hands," 74.

CHAPTER 8: ALL AROUND THE WORLD

1 Medha Patkar, "A River Comes to Prague," in *We Are Everywhere: The Irresistible Rise of Global Anticapitalism*, ed. Notes from Nowhere (London: Verso, 2003), 296.

2 Naomi Klein, *Fences and Windows: Dispatches from the Front Lines of the Globalization Debate* (New York: Picador USA, 2002), 130 (includes Pierre Pettigrew quotation); Ankie Hoogvelt, *Globalization and the Postcolonial World: The New Political Economy of Development*, 2nd edn. (Baltimore, MD: Johns Hopkins University Press, 2001) 5; Joseph Stiglitz, *Globalization and Its Discontents* (New York: W. W. Norton & Company, 2002), 73, 195, 208.

3 Joseph Stiglitz, *Globalization and Its Discontents*, 10–12; Robert K. Schaeffer, *Understanding Globalization: The Social Consequences of Political, Economic, and Environmental Change* (Lanham, MD: Rowman & Littlefield, 2003), 218.

4 Robert K. Schaeffer, *Understanding Globalization*, 53–6, 69.

5 Ankie Hoogvelt, *Globalization and the Postcolonial World*, 48–9; Robert K. Schaeffer, *Understanding Globalization*, 97–9.

6 Robert K. Schaeffer, *Understanding Globalization*, 104–10.

7 Robert K. Schaeffer, *Understanding Globalization*, 6 (Sutherland quotation), 218–25.

8 Jeff Faux, "A Global Strategy for Labour," in *Another World Is Possible: Popular Alternatives to Globalization at the World Social Forum*, eds. William F. Fisher and Thomas Ponniah (London: Zed Books, 2003), 78; Joseph Stiglitz, *Globalization and Its Discontents*, 207–8; Jay R. Mandle, *Globalization and the Poor* (Cambridge, UK: Cambridge University Press, 2003), 45, 61, 106–7, 126–7; Andrew L. Barlow, *Between Fear and Hope: Globalization and Race in the United States* (Lanham, MD: Rowman & Littlefield, 2003), 72–4.

9 Robert K. Schaeffer, *Understanding Globalization*, 130–35; Joseph Stiglitz, *Globalization and Its Discontents*, 17; Ankie Hoogvelt, *Globalization and the Postcolonial World*, 135, 187–8.

10 Dilip Ratha and Zhimei Xu, comp., *Migration and Remittances Factbook 2008* [2008], accessed at: http://siteresources.worldbank.org/INTPROSPECTS/Resources/334934-1199807908806/World.pdf

11 Manning Marable, *The Crisis of Color and Democracy: Essays on Race, Class, and Power* (Monroe, ME: Common Courage Press, 1991), 128–9; Howard Winant, *The World Is a Ghetto: Race and Democracy Since World War II* (New York: Basic Books, 2001), 269–71; Andrew L. Barlow, *Between Fear and Hope*, 145.

12 U.S. Bureau of the Census, *2008 Statistical Abstract*, 44 (Table 44) and 45 (Table 46), U.S. Census Bureau website, accessed at: http://www.census.gov/compendia/statab/past_years.html; Thomas Byrne Edsall with Mary D. Edsall, *Chain Reaction: The Impact of Race, Rights, and Taxes on American Politics* (New York: W. W. Norton & Company, 1992), 109; Patrick J. Buchanan, *The Death of the West: How Dying Populations and Immigrant Invasions Imperil Our Country and Civilization* (New York: Thomas Dunne Books, St. Martin's Press, 2002), 97, 142, 228; Evelyn Hu-DeHart, "Race, Civil Rights, and the New Immigrants: Nativism and the New World Order," in *Civil Rights and Race Relations in the Post Reagan-Bush Era*, ed. Samuel L. Myers Jr. (Westport, CT: Greenwood Publishing Group, 1997), 19.

13 Akwasi B. Assensoh, "Conflict or Cooperation? Africans and African Americans in Multiracial America," in *Black and Multiracial Politics in America*, eds. Yvette Alex-Assensoh and Lawrence J. Hanks (New York: New York University Press, 2000), 125; Christine Evans, John Lantigua, Christine Stapleton and Jane Daugherty, "Harvest Yields Loss of Lives and Money," *Palm Beach Post* (Fla.), December 7, 2003, accessed at: http://www.palmbeachpost.com/moderndayslavery/content/moderndayslavery/reports/day1_main1207.html; Christian Parenti, *Lockdown America: Police and Prisons in the Age of Crisis*, new edn. (London: Verso, 2008), 150–2.

14 Stephen Steinberg, *Turning Back: The Retreat from Racial Justice in American Thought and Policy* (Boston, MA: Beacon Press, 1995), 188, 193–5.

15 Michael Jones-Correa, "Immigrants, Blacks, and Cities," in *Black and Multicultural Politics*, eds. Yvettee Alex-Assensoh and Lawrence J. Hanks, 142–4, 150.

16 "Black-Korean Tension Still Exists in L.A.," *All Things Considered*, National Public Radio, April 20, 1993.

17 Heather K. Parker, "Tom Bradley and the Politics of Race," in *African-American Mayors: Race, Politics, and the American City*, eds. David R. Colburn and Jeffrey S. Adler (Urbana, IL: University of Illinois, 2001), 165; Yvette Alex-Assensoh, Introduction to *Black and Multicultural Politics*, eds. Yvettee Alex-Assensoh and Lawrence J. Hanks, 3; Martin F. Nolan, "Old World Curse Tests Americans," *Boston Globe*, May 4, 1992, 6.

18 "Black-Korean Alliance of LA Disbanding," *All Things Considered*, National Public Radio, December 24, 1992 (Chu); Roberto Lovato, "The Smog of Race War in LA," *Nation*, April 2, 2007, 23–4.

19 Ermína Maricato, "Cities, Urban Population Conference Synthesis," in *Another World Is Possible*, eds. William F. Fisher and Thomas Ponniah, 173–9; Ankie Hoogvelt, *Globalization and the Postcolonial World*, 176, 187–91.
20 W. E. B. Du Bois, *Black Reconstruction in America: An Essay Toward a History of the Part Which Black Folk Played in the Attempt to Reconstruct Democracy in America, 1860–1880* (New York: Russell & Russell, 1962; 1935), 15; Akwasi B. Assensoh, "Conflict or Cooperation?," 115–19.
21 Stokely Carmichael and Charles V. Hamilton, *Black Power: The Politics of Liberation in America* (New York: Random House, 1967), 2–32; Kristin Anderson-Bricker, "'Triple Jeopardy': Feminist Consciousness in SNCC, 1964–1975," in *Still Lifting, Still Climbing: Contemporary African American Women's Activism*, ed. Kimberly Springer (New York: New York University Press, 1999), 50–63.
22 Dorothy Height, *Open Wide the Freedom Gates: A Memoir* (New York: PublicAffairs, Perseus Books, 2003), 232.
23 ACORN Fair Housing, *The Impending Rate Shock: A Study of Home Mortgages in 130 American Cities* (Washington, DC: Association of Community Organizations for Reform Now, 2006), 1; Jesse Jackson, "A Chance to Serve," presidential campaign announcement speech, Raleigh, NC, October 10, 1987, in *Keep Hope Alive: Jesse Jackson's 1988 Presidential Campaign*, eds. Frank Clemente and Frank Watkins (Boston, MA: South End Press, 1989), 30; Karin L. Stanford, "Reverend Jesse Jackson and the Rainbow/PUSH Coalition," in *Black Political Organizations in the Post-Civil Rights Era*, eds. Ollie A. Johnson III and Karin L. Stanford (New Brunswick, NJ: Rutgers University Press, 2002), 162; Robert D. Bullard, *Dumping in Dixie: Race, Class, and Environmental Quality*, 3rd edn. (Boulder, CO: Westview Press, 2000), 155–6.
24 Howard Winant, *World Is a Ghetto*, 186–204.
25 Michel Marriott and Martin Weil, "S. Africa Protest Continues," *Washington Post*, November 27, 1984, B1; Barbara Gamarekian, "Apartheid Protest Takes Page from 60's History," *New York Times*, November 30, 1984, A13; William L. Clay, *Just Permanent Interests: Black Americans in Congress, 1870–1991* (New York: Amistad Press, 1992), 280–2; Howard Winant, *World Is a Ghetto*, 203, 205–7.
26 Andrew Kopkind, "Warning and Hope," *Nation*, November 22, 1986, 538.
27 Robert K. Schaeffer, *Understanding Globalization*, 111–12; Joseph Stiglitz, *Globalization and Its Discontents*, 97.
28 Valentine M. Moghadam, "Gender and Globalization: Female Labor and Women's Mobilization," in *Global Social Change: Historical and Comparative Perspectives*, eds. Christopher Chase-Dunn and Salvatore J. Babones (Baltimore, MD: Johns Hopkins University Press, 2006), 243–61.
29 Naomi Klein, *Fences and Windows*, 215; Zapatistas quoted in "Peasant Guerrilla Army in Chiapas State Declares War on Federal Government," *BBC Summary of World Broadcasts*, January 3, 1994.
30 Tod Robberson, "Zapatista Rebels Reject Mexico's Peace Program," *Washington Post*, June 13, 1994, A1; Tim Weiner, "Mexico's New Leader Swiftly Seeks Peace in Chiapas," *New York Times*, December 4, 2000, A10; Naomi Klein, *Fences and Windows*, 216–18 (quotation on p. 217).

31 Jay R. Mandle, *Globalization and the Poor*, 31; "Newsmaker," Cable News Network, August 28, 1993 (Lowery and Lewis).

32 Frederick H. Buttel and Kenneth A. Gould, "Environmentalism and the Trajectory of the Anti-Corporate Globalization Movement," in *Global Social Change*, eds. Christopher Chase-Dunn and Salvatore J. Babones, 273; Robert K. Schaeffer, *Understanding Globalization*, 227–34; Anthony DePalma, "NAFTA's Powerful Little Secret," *New York Times*, March 11, 2001, BU1, 13 (quotation on p. 13).

33 Joseph Stiglitz, *Globalization and Its Discontents*, 19, 225.

34 Joseph Stiglitz, *Globalization and Its Discontents*, 226–7; Helmut Schmidt quoted in Robert D. Putnam and Nicholas Bayne, *Hanging Together: The Seven-Power Summits* (Cambridge, MA: Harvard University Press, 1984), 17.

35 "Global Day of Action: Party and Protest against 'Free Trade' and the WTO, May 1998" in *We Are Everywhere*, ed. Notes from Nowhere, 102–5 (quotations on p. 103).

36 "Global Day of Action, November 30th, 1999," in *We Are Everywhere*, ed. Notes from Nowhere, 204–8; Joseph Kahn and David E. Sanger, "Trade Obstacles Unmoved, Seattle Talks End in Failure," *New York Times*, December 4, 1999, A6; Jonathan Peterson, "Inside, Outside Forces Change WTO Forever," *Los Angeles Times*, December 5, 1999, 1.

37 John Drake and Gerald Mizejewski, "D.C. Police Arrest Hundreds, Then Free Many," *Washington Post*, April 16, 2000, C1; "Global Day of Action, 26 September 2000," in *We Are Everywhere*, ed. Notes from Nowhere, 286.

38 Naomi Klein, *Fences and Windows*, 149; "Global Day of Action, November 9th, 2001," in *We Are Everywhere*, ed. Notes from Nowhere, 418.

39 Michael Moore quoted in Sam Howe Verhovek and Steven Greenhouse, "National Guard is Called to Quell Trade-Talk Protests," *New York Times*, December 1, 1999, A1; Stanley Fischer quoted in Peter Morton, "IMF, World Bank Are Misunderstood Say Their Leaders," *National Post* (Canada), April 14, 2000, C12; "Smashing Starbucks' Windows Won't Free World's Oppressed," *USA Today*, December 2, 1999, 14A; Michael Medved, "Battle in Seattle," *USA Today*, December 7, 1999, 19A; William R. Macklin, "From the Fringes onto the Front Page," *Philadelphia Inquirer*, December 5, 1999, D1.

40 Naomi Klein, *Fences and Windows*, 9; "Global Day of Action, September 26th, 2000" and "Global Day of Action, November 9th, 2001," in *We Are Everywhere*, ed. Notes from Nowhere, 286–9, 421.

41 "Durban Social Forum Declaration," in *We Are Everywhere*, ed. Notes from Nowhere, 400; "Between the Broken and the Built," interview with Ashwin Desai by Holly Wren Spaulding, in *We Are Everywhere*, ed. Notes from Nowhere, 486–97 (quotation on p. 496).

42 Grey Filastine, "Not in Service," in *We Are Everywhere*, ed. Notes from Nowhere, 211–13.

43 Jeff Faux, "Global Strategy for Labor," 83; Vandana Shiva, "Environment and Sustainability: The Living Democracy Movement: Alternatives to the Bankruptcy of Globalization," in *Another World Is Possible*, eds. William F. Fisher and Thomas Ponniah, 115.

44 Naomi Klein, *Fences and Windows*, 17; Joshua Karliner and Karolo Aparicio, "Transnational Corporations: Issues and Proposals," in *Another World Is Possible*, eds. William F. Fisher and Thomas Ponniah, 59; Congress of South African Trade Unions, "A Strategic Perspective on the International Trade Union Movement for the Twenty-first Century," in *Another World Is Possible*, eds. William F. Fisher and Thomas Ponniah, 69; "Social Movements Manifesto," in *Another World Is Possible*, eds. William F. Fisher and Thomas Ponniah, 346.

45 Ankie Hoogvelt, *Globalization and the Post-colonial World*, xiii, 91; Gary Burtless, Robert Z. Lawrence, Robert E. Litan and Robert J. Shapiro, *Globaphobia: Confronting Fears about Open Trade* (Washington, DC: Brookings Institution Press, 1998), 132; Naomi Klein, *Fences and Windows*, 11, 61–3.

46 Naomi Klein, *Fences and Windows*, 11; James Wolfensohn quoted in Jeff Faux, "Global Strategy for Labor," 79; Joseph Stiglitz, *Globalization and Its Discontents*, 250, 255; Frederick H. Buttel and Kenneth A. Gould, "Environmentalism and the Trajectory," 279; Joseph Stiglitz, *Globalization and Its Discontents*, 215, 226; Colin Bradford, Johannes Linn, and Paul Martin, "Global Governance Breakthrough: The G20 Summit and the Future Agenda," Brookings Institution Policy Brief No. 168, December 2008, 1–2, 4, accessed at: http://www.brookings.edu/papers/2008/12_g20_summit_bradford_linn.aspx.

47 "Job Losses, Economic Realities Hit Home in Indiana City," *The News Hour*, Public Broadcasting Service, March 6, 2009, accessed at: http://www.pbs.org/newshour/bb/business/jan-june09/elkhart_03-06.html

INDEX

Abernathy, Ralph 78
abolitionists 16, 17, 18
Abramovitz, Mimi 158–9
ACORN *see* Association of
    Community Organizations for
    Reform Now
Addonizio, Hugh 37
Adidas Corporation 179
AFDC (Aid to Families with
    Dependent Children) 151–3, 155,
    158–9, 161
affirmative action
    activism 101, 103–4, 117–19
    Clinton administration 121
    court cases 110–12, 116–17, 121
    effectiveness 100, 112–13, 114–15,
        122, 136
    goals and timetables 100, 101,
        105–7, 109, 114, 115
    Johnson administration 104–6
    limits 101, 108–9, 119–20, 122–3
    Nixon administration 106–9,
        113–14
    opposition 79, 100–1, 102, 109–10,
        113–17, 119–20
    origins 4, 100, 101–6
    rationale 78, 104, 107, 110, 112,
        121–2
    Reagan administration 96, 114–16
    support 115, 117, 120–2
Africa
    Atlantic slave trade 9
    cooperation with African Americans
        178–9

decolonization 28, 171
global justice protests 188
migration 9, 175
racist perceptions 17
Africa, Ramona 86
African Americans
    colonial era 9–14
    criminal justice system 20, 30, 54,
        65–71, 78, 84–8, 130, 177–8
    disfranchisement 1, 15, 20, 21, 29,
        69, 77, 125, 127, 138–40, 142–4
    early republic 14–17
    economic advances after 1965 4, 54,
        112–13
    economic disparities 1, 24–7, 30–3,
        54–61, 64–5, 114–15, 138–9
    education 3, 4, 20–1, 24, 26, 27,
        30, 34, 39–41, 54, 60, 61–5, 77,
        81, 87–92, 112–13, 166
    employment discrimination 16, 20,
        21, 27, 30, 54, 100–4, 117–19,
        120–1
    health problems 61, 81, 83, 166–7
    housing segregation 21, 23–8, 30,
        39, 41, 54, 55, 56–8, 65, 81,
        92–5
    Hurricane Katrina 73–5
    Jim Crow era 1, 3, 6, 7, 17–29, 33,
        36, 41, 49, 52, 56, 58, 63, 65, 70,
        71, 115, 153, 180
    mass incarceration 66–71, 85–6,
        139
    media portrayals 74–5, 76, 80, 134,
        135, 167

middle class 4, 18, 23, 50, 81, 91, 113, 117, 121
migration 26, 28, 31–2, 35–6, 80
political participation 4, 15, 18, 20, 28, 29, 35, 36, 79, 80, 81, 83, 88, 124–46, 148, 163, 164; see also black elected officials
Reconstruction era 17–18
self-help efforts 5, 75, 78, 80, 148, 165–8
social welfare system 7, 22–3, 37–8, 45, 47, 48–9, 51, 52, 79, 148, 151–63
unemployment 26, 29, 54, 55, 81, 92, 101–2, 107, 108, 133, 147, 150, 176–7
African National Congress (ANC) 180, 181
Aid to Families with Dependent Children (AFDC) 151–3, 155, 158–9, 161
Alabama
affirmative action 101, 110
civil rights activism 28, 76, 80, 84, 131–2, 87–8
Hurricane Katrina 73
politics 42, 65, 141
public assistance programs 153, 155
racism 2, 35, 38, 43, 59, 62, 65, 84, 87–8, 93, 113, 131–2, 164
Allen v. State Board of Elections (1969) 128
American Bar Association 86
American Enterprise Institute 150
American Revolution 14–15
ANC (African National Congress) 180, 181
anti-apartheid activism 180–2
Anti-Drug Abuse Act (1986) 67
anti-immigrant sentiment 174–5, 184
antitax sentiment
business leaders 19, 31, 46, 130–1, 174
impact on public services 26, 41, 60–1, 65, 73–4, 77, 87, 88, 92, 130–1, 174
political leaders 19, 47–8, 49–50, 193

property owners 35, 37, 38, 41–2, 47, 48, 50, 65, 72, 126, 193
tax cuts 46, 49–50, 51, 60–1, 74, 170
Aparicio, Karolo 190
apartheid 180–2
Arizona 43, 122
Arkansas 51, 63, 138–9, 141
Arnwine, Barbara 74
Asia 17, 28, 46, 171, 175, 188
Asian Americans 176–8, 179
Association of Citizens' Councils of Mississippi 35
Association of Community Organizations for Reform Now (ACORN)
fair housing activism 96–8
founding 80, 160
social justice activism 146, 161–2, 179
voting rights activism 141–2, 145
Asuza Christian Community 166
AT&T Corporation 174
Atkins, Thomas 89
Atlanta (Georgia) 72, 98–9, 130, 132–3
Atomic Safety and Licensing Board 83
Atwater, Lee 48
Austin, Richard 130
Avery, Billye 166

Bacon, Nathaniel 11
Bailey, Thomas Pearce 21
Baker, Ella 146
Bakke, Allen 111–12, 113
Baltimore (Maryland) 37
banks
deregulation 51, 97–9, 173
global economy 172, 180, 185, 189, 192
political influence 132, 169, 193
racist lending practices 25, 57, 58, 93, 96–9, 133
Baptista, John 10
Barbados 183
Barlow, Andrew 68
Baton Rouge (Louisiana) 59
Batson, Ruth 89
Belafonte, Harry 181 (Fig. 8.1)

Benezet, Anthony 13
Bensonhurst (New York) 39
Benton Harbor (Michigan) 133–4
Berkeley (California) 186
Berlin, Ira 9
Birmingham (Alabama) 2, 101, 110
black elected officials
  achievements 136
  corruption charges 134–5
  increase in number 79, 83, 88,
    128–9, 135, 146
  problems 4, 124–5, 126, 130–6, 171
  white hostility 126, 129, 130–2,
    133–4
Black Family Reunion 167
Black Family Summit 166
Black-Korean Alliance 177
Black Liberation Front 165
black middle class 4, 18, 23, 50, 81,
  91, 113, 117, 121
Black Panther Party 165
black power movement 62–3, 79, 165
black self-help 5, 75, 78, 80, 148,
  165–8
Black Women's Alliance 178–9
Blackmun, Harry 56
Blackwell, Unita 36
*Board of Education of Oklahoma v.
  Dowell* (1991) 64
Boeing Corporation 71
Bolivia 191
Bond, Julian 2, 79, 110
Bophal (India) 60
Boston (Massachusetts) 39, 40, 62,
  88–90, 131, 153, 166
boycotts 4, 24, 28, 29, 62, 76, 80, 85,
  88, 117–19, 180–1
Braithewaite, Ann 26
Braithewaite, Jim 26
Brazil 183
Brennan, William 155
Bretton Woods Conference (1944)
  170–1
Bridgeport (Connecticut) 142
Brookings Institution 190–1
Brooklyn (New York) 154
Brooks, J. R. 164
Broward County (Florida) 143
Brown, Luther 82

*Brown v. Board of Education of
  Topeka, Kansas* (1954) 28, 39,
  61, 63, 87, 91
Buchanan, Pat 45, 175
Buenos Aires (Argentina) 188
Bullard, Robert 81, 83
Burden, Jackie 53
Burger, Warren 56
Burmeister, James 53
Burnham, Rowland 9
Burson, Joyce 154
Bush, George H. W. 117, 135, 138,
  140
Bush, George W. 51, 74, 85, 94,
  142–3, 159, 163, 164
busing 39–40, 44, 47, 48, 62, 63, 64,
  89–90

California
  activism 84, 118, 119, 120, 162,
    186
  affirmative action 111–12, 118, 119
  immigrants 175, 176, 177–8
  prisons 71, 86
  Proposition 13 41
  Proposition 187 175
  racism 30, 70, 82, 84, 119
Campbell, Tracy 140
Canada 170, 173, 179, 184, 185
Cancer Alley (Louisiana) 59
Canty, Henrietta 135
capitalism
  free market *see* free market
    capitalism
  global *see* globalization
  government intervention 22, 35,
    48, 170, 179, 184, 189, 190–1,
    192–3
  industrial 16, 22
  postindustrial *see* deindustrialization
  racism and 2, 8–16, 18, 19–22, 31,
    178–9
CAPs (Community Action Programs)
  33–4, 36, 38, 45
Carey, Gordon 101
Caribbean 175, 176
Carmichael, Stokely 2, 63
Carter, Jimmy 50, 93, 116, 140,
  150–1, 164

CDGM (Child Development Group of Mississippi) 34, 36
Celeste, Richard 96
Charlotte (North Carolina) 62
Chemical Waste Management Corporation 60–1
Chicago (Illinois) 39, 47, 48, 80, 93, 95, 118, 131, 154, 162
Chicago Housing Authority 49
Child Development Group of Mississippi (CDGM) 34, 36
Chile 83
Chisholm, Shirley 134
Chu, Marsha 177
Cicero (Illinois) 93
Cisneros, Henry 99
Citizens United for the Rehabilitation of Errants 86
City of Mobile v. Bolden (1980) 128
City of Richmond v. J. A. Croson (1989) 116–17
Civil Rights Act (1866) 17
Civil Rights Act (1964)
    enforcement 4, 39, 81, 102–6, 109
    limits 5, 30, 100, 147
    opposition 43
    passage 29
    Title VII 102–4, 106, 109, 111, 114
Civil Rights Act (1991) 117
civil rights activism 4, 28–9, 66, 76–99
    criminal justice system 84–7
    environmental justice 4, 80–4, 179
    equal education 28, 87–92
    equal employment opportunities 4, 101, 103–4, 110–12, 116, 117–19, 121–2
    fair housing 24, 92–8
    South African apartheid 180–1
    voting rights 125–6, 128–9, 141–6
civil rights enforcement
    criminal justice 85
    environmental justice 82–3
    equal employment opportunities 100, 102–8, 110–12, 116–17, 121–2
    fair housing 56–8, 93–6

    ineffective 21, 45, 51, 55–6, 57–8, 63–5, 76, 91, 95–6, 99, 103–4, 105–6, 116–17, 120–1, 126–7
    resistance 38–42, 44, 52, 87–90, 94–6
    school desegregation 39–40, 63–5, 87–8, 92
    voting rights 127–9
civil rights legislation
    enforcement 4, 31, 42, 76, 82–3, 87–8, 96, 102–4, 107, 146
    limits 1, 4, 30, 53, 77, 124–5, 144, 147
    opposition 31, 42
    passage 6, 17, 29, 57, 117, 144
civil rights movement
    achievements 6, 28–9, 76, 79, 119, 146
    economic component 6, 31–4, 148, 152
    influence 189–90
    limits 77
    opposition 7, 48, 73, 135
    origins 28–9
Civil War 2, 17, 19, 20
Claiborne Parish (Louisiana) 83
Clark County Welfare Rights Organization 153
Clay, William 135
Cleaver, Emanuel 119
Cleveland (Ohio) 130, 134, 151
Clinton, Bill 50, 51, 70, 82, 85, 96, 98, 121, 140, 159, 187
Clinton, Hillary 129
Clotfelter, Charles 62
Coahoma County (Mississippi) 35
Cobb, Charles 81
Cobbs, Hamner 35
Coca Cola Company 118, 132
cocaine 67, 69
Colbert, Stephen 1
Cold War 28, 174
Coldburn, Alma 155
Coleman, William 115
Coles, Robert 34
Colmer, William 113
Colonial Heights (Virginia) 94–5
colonialism 8–9, 171, 178

colorblind policies
  perpetuate racism 1–2, 20, 43,
    56, 72, 76, 77–8, 99, 101, 104,
    114
  supporters 4, 38–9, 43, 77, 109,
    114, 116, 119, 122, 129
Commission for Racial Justice (CRJ)
    59, 81
Commission on Technology,
    Automation and Economic
    Progress 108
Community Action Programs (CAPs)
    33–4, 36, 38, 45
Community Reinvestment Act (1977)
    93, 96–7
Congress of Racial Equality (CORE)
    28, 78–80, 101, 125, 145, 148,
    152, 154, 163, 189
Congress of South African Trade
    Unions 190
Congressional Black Caucus 81
Connecticut 66, 85, 142
Connerly, Ward 72, 122
Connor, Bull 73
construction industry 80, 105–6, 107,
    108, 110, 116–17
consumerism 27, 32, 46, 66, 155
Contractors Association of Eastern
    Pennsylvania v. Secretary of Labor
    (1971) 111
Cook, Carl 110
cooperatives 5, 37, 80, 148, 163–5,
    179, 183
CORE (Congress of Racial Equality)
    28, 78–80, 101, 125, 145, 148,
    151, 154, 189
corporations
  affirmative action 107, 113, 115–16,
    117–19
  employment discrimination 117–19,
    121
  global economy 45–6, 83, 137, 169,
    173–4, 180, 184–5, 189, 191
  government subsidies 149, 161
  political influence 19, 22, 46–7, 49,
    60–1, 109, 132, 133–4
Council for a Black Economic Agenda
    165
Crescent City (California) 71

criminal justice system 20, 30, 65–71,
    78, 84–7, 88, 130, 139–40, 177–8
CRJ (Commission for Racial Justice)
    59, 81
Crosson, Everett 104
cultural racism 54, 71–2, 77–8, 89,
    121, 177, 192
Czech Republic 187

Dailey, James 60–1
Daley, Richard 93
Dan River Mills 103
de Klerk, F. W. 181
deindustrialization
  cause of unemployment 156, 173–4
  causes 45–7, 137, 173–4
  impact on African Americans 26,
    54, 55, 71, 108, 120, 148, 176–8
  problem for black elected officials
    131
  white workers' anxiety 100, 109,
    192
Democratic Leadership Council (DLC)
    50–1, 138
Democratic National Committee 50
Democratic Party
  African Americans 80, 124, 135,
    136–8, 140–1, 142, 146
  defections from in 1960s 43, 48–9
  free market policies 3, 19, 50–1, 159
  New Deal coalition 22, 31, 34, 45,
    108, 113, 119, 135
  racism 16, 18, 19–20, 33, 42, 43,
    49, 129
  support for freedom struggle 29, 48,
    56–7, 114, 140–1, 157–8
Denton, Nancy 56
Desai, Ashwin 188–9
Detroit (Michigan) 63, 130, 131, 165
developing nations 5, 169, 171–2,
    173–4, 175, 178–9, 182–3, 188–9,
    191, 192
Development Alternatives with Women
    for a New Era 183
Dill, David 144
Dinkins, David 131
direct action
  anti-apartheid 180–1
  civil rights 29, 66–7, 76, 80

equal employment opportunity
117–19
environmental justice 81
fair housing 94–5, 96
global justice 186–7, 190
police brutality 84
school desegregation 88, 89
racial violence 165
voting rights 141–2
welfare rights 153, 154, 160–1,
165
disfranchisement 1, 20, 21, 29, 69, 77,
125, 127, 138–40, 142–4
Disney Corporation 161
District of Columbia 67
diversity initiatives 112, 119, 121–2;
see also affirmative action
DLC (Democratic Leadership Council)
50–1, 138
Doha (Qatar) 187
domestic workers 21, 23, 136, 153,
157
Dominican Republic 179
Donahue, Dan 48–9
Dowd, Maureen 79
D'Souza, Dinesh 72, 77
Du Bois, W. E. B. 178
Du, Soon Ja 177
Dukakis, Michael 138
Duke Power Company 111
Dymally, Mervyn 30

early voting 145
Eastland, James 126
economic deregulation 3, 5, 46, 47,
96–9, 171–4, 179, 182–5, 191
economic inequality 22, 28, 47,
49–50, 51–2, 148–9, 173, 190
Economic Opportunity Act (1964)
32–4, 35
Edsall, Mary 49–50
Edsall, Thomas Byrne 49–50
education 18, 60, 107; *see also* African
Americans; schools
EEOC (Equal Employment
Opportunity Commission) 102–4,
105, 107, 116
Egypt 187
Ehrlichman, John 108

Eisner, Michael 161
Election Protection Program 144–5
elections 4, 79, 124, 125, 127–9,
138–9, 140–1, 142–5
electoral politics 4, 79, 124–46
dilution of black votes 127–8
early voting 145
influence of money 132–4, 142
minority-majority districts 128–9
obstacles to black participation
124–5, 126–9, 136–41
racial bloc voting 127–8, 129
redistricting plans 127–9
reforms 140, 144–5
Elkhart (Indiana) 192
Ella Baker Center for Human Rights
84
Ellender, Allen 102
emancipation 17
Emanuel Downing 14
Emelle (Alabama) 60–1
Emergency Land Fund 164
employment discrimination 20, 21, 27,
30, 54, 100–4, 117, 118–19,
120–1
England 8, 11, 12
Enlightenment 2, 14–15
Enron Corporation 191
environmental justice movement 80–4,
170, 179, 185, 188, 189, 191
Environmental Protection Agency
(EPA) 58, 82
environmental racism 3, 4, 58–61,
80–4
EPA (Environmental Protection
Agency) 58, 82
Equal Employment Opportunity Act
(1972) 107
Equal Employment Opportunity
Commission (EEOC) 102–4, 105,
107, 116
Europe
colonizing efforts 9, 14, 17, 171
ethnic conflict 174–5, 177
global economy 46, 169, 173, 177,
185, 188, 192
Evers, Charles 135
Executive Order 11246 104, 115
Executive Order 12898 82–3

Fair Housing Act (1968) 57, 93, 99
fair housing activism 24, 92–8
Fair Housing Amendments Act (1988) 94
fair trade 164, 184, 190, 191
Family Assistance Plan (FAP) 158
Family Support Act (1988) 158
FAP (Family Assistance Plan) 158
Farmers Home Administration 113
Faux, Jeff 173, 189
Fayette (Mississippi) 135
Fayetteville (North Carolina) 53
federal government
    complicity in racism 7, 21, 23–6, 28, 30, 58
    crime policies 67–8
    housing policies 23–6, 56–8, 93–4, 96–9, 160
    social programs 22–6, 42, 45, 46, 47, 48, 49, 51, 65, 67, 70, 78, 121
    see also social welfare system; war on poverty
    subsidization of white middle class 23, 25–6, 27–8, 42, 121, 149, 157, 161
    see also civil rights enforcement
Federal Housing Administration (FHA) 25, 57
Federal Reserve Board 151, 172
Federation of Southern Cooperatives (FSC) 80, 163–5
Federation of Southern Cooperatives-Land Assistance Fund (FSC-LAF) 164
Feingold, Miriam 148
Fellner, William 150
felony disfranchisement laws 69, 139–40
Ferguson, Mazie Butler 145
FHA (Federal Housing Administration) 25, 57
Fields, Mamie Garvin 20
Fifteenth Amendment 18
Filastine, Grey 189
Fischer, Stanley 188
Fitzgibbons, Mark 4
Fleming, Cynthia 87
Fletcher, Arthur 107

Florida 44, 47, 68, 85, 142–4, 144, 166, 176
Ford, Sibble 10
Fort Bragg (North Carolina) 53
Fourteenth Amendment 17, 128, 155
Fourth Amendment 152
France 174, 175, 185
free black people 12–13, 15
free labor 8, 10, 18
free market capitalism
    critiques 178–9, 182–5, 188–90
    failures 22, 49–52, 60, 74–5, 133, 137, 182–91, 192
    ideological dominance 47–52, 133, 149–51
    impact on African Americans 74–5, 97–9
    impact on United States 46–7, 49–52, 96–9, 192
    perpetuates racism 1, 3, 31, 35–6, 74–5
    supporters 43, 46, 48, 79
    see also globalization
free trade 5, 46, 51, 169–74, 179, 183–5, 190–1
freedom of choice plans (in school integration) 39, 87–8
Freeman v. Pitts (1992) 64
Freund, David 28
FSC (Federation of Southern Cooperatives) 80, 163–5
FSC-LAF (Federation of Southern Cooperatives-Land Assistance Fund) 164
Full Employment and Balanced Growth Act (1978) 150
full employment policies 32, 102, 108, 148–51, 159, 170
Fuller, Robert 95

G8 187; see also Group of Seven; G20
G20 191; see also Group of Seven; G8
Gadsen (Alabama) 84
Gadsen County (Florida) 144
GAO (General Accounting Office) 58, 106
Garrity, W. Arthur 89–90
Gary (Indiana) 130–1, 136, 157

GATT (General Agreement on Tariffs and Trade) 171, 172–3
General Accounting Office (GAO) 58, 106
General Agreement on Tariffs and Trade (GATT) 171, 172–3
Geneva (Switzerland) 185–6
Genoa (Italy) 187
Georgia
  politics 14, 50, 130, 132–3, 135
  racism 13, 43, 72, 98–9, 159–60, 165
Georgia State Conference of NAACP Branches 142
Germany 28, 174, 175, 185
gerrymandering 127, 128–9
GI Bill 25, 42, 121
Gibbes, Robert W. 17
Gilman, David 155
Ginsberg, Mitchell 156
Giuliani, Carlo 187
Giuliani, Rudolph 85, 162
Glen Park (Indiana) 130
global justice movement
  achievements 187, 190–1
  arguments and philosophy 5, 182–5, 88–90
  black participation 83–4, 164, 169, 178–81
  influence of black freedom movement 189–90
  interracialism 188–90
  origins 181–3
global South see developing nations
globalization
  black responses 83–4, 168, 178–81
  critiques 5, 182–5, 88–91
  defenses 187–8
  ethnic conflict 173–8
  financial crises 97–9, 172, 182, 191
  impact 3, 31, 46–7, 97–9, 100, 121, 173–8, 182–3
  origins 45–7, 170–3
  undemocratic aspects 174, 178, 184–5, 186, 187
Goldberg v. Kelly (1970) 155
Goldfield, Michael 109
Goldwater, Barry 43–4, 45
Gooch, William 12

Gore, Albert 142
Great Depression 22, 52, 170
Green Collar Jobs Campaign 84
Green factors (in school integration) 39, 64
Green for All 84
Green v. County School Board of New Kent County (1968) 39
Greenpeace 82
Greenville (Mississippi) 147
Group of Seven (G7) 185; see also G8; G20
Grutter v. Bollinger (2003) 121
Guinier, Lani 138
Gulati, Mitu 120
Gulf Coast 59, 73, 75, 165
Gumbel, Andrew 140
Gwinnet County (Georgia) 72

Hamer, Fannie Lou 124
Hamilton, Charles 2, 63
Harlins, Latasha 177
Harris, Roy 43
Haselden, Kyle 102
Hatch, Orrin 115
Hatcher, Richard 79, 130–1, 136
HAVA (Help America Vote Act) 144
Hawaii 146
Hawkins, Augustus 108, 149–50
Hayden, Andrew 131
Hayes, Christopher 146
Head Start 33 (Fig. 2.1), 34, 35, 38
Height, Dorothy 73, 167, 179
Helms, Jesse 180
Help America Vote Act (HAVA) 144
Henson, James 110
HEW (US Department of Health, Education and Welfare) 39, 61, 107, 153, 156–7
Hill, Jim 90
Hillsborough (North Carolina) 103
Hillson, Jon 89
Hinds County Welfare Rights Movement 153
Hitler, Adolf 53
Hodges, Leah 74, 75
Holmes, Robert Earl 113
Home Owners Loan Corporation 25
home ownership 23, 58, 96–9, 167

homelessness 49, 80, 96, 131, 137, 149, 160, 179
Honkala, Cheri 160–1
Hoogvelt, Ankie 178, 190
Hopwood v. University of Texas Law School (1996) 121
housing segregation 21, 23–8, 30, 39, 41, 54, 55, 56–8, 65, 81, 83, 92–5
Houston (Texas) 58, 61, 81, 82, 122
Houston, Charles 23
Howard University 104
Hu-DeHart, Evelyn 175
HUD (US Department of Housing and Urban Development) 57, 94, 96, 99
human rights 78, 83, 149, 179, 191
Humphrey, Hubert 102, 150
Hurricane Hugo 96
Hurricane Katrina 73–5, 164

Illinois
  activism 80, 91, 93, 118, 154, 162
  deindustrialization 131
  politics 43, 47, 69
  racism 39, 91, 93
  resistance to black freedom struggle 48–9, 93, 95
IMF (International Monetary Fund) 171–91 *passim*
immigrants 174–8
Immigration and Naturalization Service (INS) 176
indentured servants 8, 9–10, 14
India 60, 178, 179, 183, 185, 187, 188, 189
Indiana 115, 130–1, 136, 157, 192
Indianapolis (Indiana) 115
Indonesia 146, 174, 182
industrialization 16, 22
inflation 46, 47, 50, 149–51, 157
Innis, Roy 79
INS (Immigration and Naturalization Service) 176
Institute (West Virginia) 60
Institutional Revolutionary Party (Mexico) 183
integration
  employment 103–4, 111, 118–19
  housing 55, 56–8

schools 39–41, 61–5, 87–92
social programs 35
resistance 35, 39–41, 43–4, 48, 52, 55–8, 61–5, 79, 87–92, 103–4, 111, 118–19
International Bank for Reconstruction and Development (World Bank) 171–91 *passim*
international financial institutions 170–91 *passim*
International Monetary Fund (IMF) 171–91 *passim*
interracial cooperation
  civil rights era 38
  colonial era 9, 10, 11, 13
  early republic 16
  Jim Crow era 21, 23–4
  Reconstruction era 18–20
  post-civil rights era 80, 82, 84, 119, 122, 124, 126, 137, 148–9, 154, 188–90
Iraq 75
IRS (US Internal Revenue Service) 134–5
Italy 185

J. P. Stevens and Company 103
Jackson, Jesse 80, 118, 136–8, 179
Jackson, Maynard 132
James, Michael 53
Japan 82, 185
Jefferson, Thomas 14
Jennings, Josephine 103
Jim Crow system
  emergence after Reconstruction 7, 17–22,
  lingering effects 1–3, 6, 52, 56, 114–15
  parallels in post-civil rights era 41, 49, 63, 65, 70, 71, 153, 180
  reinforced in New Deal era 23–7
  undermined after World War II 28–9, 33
Johannesburg (South Africa) 188
Johnson, Lyndon B.
  affirmative action 104–6
  civil rights enforcement 29, 30, 44, 55, 56–7, 124

economic policies 32–4, 108, 147,
   158
election 43
Johnson, Paul 36
Jones, Van 84
Joseph, Charles Freeman 133–4

Kansas City (Missouri) 65
Karliner, Joshua 190
Katznelson, Ira 121
Kelly, Guy 88
Kemp, Jack 96, 99
Kennedy, Anthony 56, 86
Kennedy, John F. 29, 56, 102
Kensington Welfare Rights Union
   (KWRU) 160–1
Kentucky 62, 90, 92
Key, Elizabeth 10, 12
Key, V. O., Jr. 21
Keynes, John Maynard 170
King v. Smith (1968) 155
King, Martin Luther, Jr.
   assassination 57, 148
   civil rights leadership 28, 76, 80,
      146, 190
   fair housing activism 93
   March on Washington speech 77,
      114
   social justice activism 108, 148
   support for affirmative action 77–8,
      117–18
King, Rodney 70, 177
Kirk, Paul, Jr. 50
Klein, Naomi 170, 183, 187,
   188
Kopkind, Andrew 182
Kornbluh, Felicia 155
Kousser, J. Morgan 129
Kramer, Marian 160
Kruse, Kevin 41
Ku Klux Klan 18, 38, 78, 165
KWRU (Kensington Welfare Rights
   Union) 160–1

labor unions
   efforts to undermine 19, 21, 46,
      108, 151, 161, 179
   exclusion of African Americans 16,
      105–6, 107, 110

global justice activism 173, 180,
   184, 185, 188
participation in freedom struggle 83,
   84, 141, 149, 162
strengthened in New Deal era 22,
   109
Lambert, Thomas 10
Lanier, Bob 122
Lassiter, Matthew 42
Latin America 9, 175, 188
Latinos 58, 90, 96, 128, 143, 154,
   159, 176–8, 179
law and order rhetoric 42, 43, 45, 55,
   70, 130
Lawrence, Ellett 35
lawsuits
   affirmative action 110–12, 116, 117
   criminal justice 85
   environmental justice 81, 82,
   equal education 87, 89
   equal employment opportunity 105,
      106, 107
   essential to civil rights enforcement
      4, 29
   fair housing 24, 93, 94
   voting rights 127–9, 141, 142
   welfare rights 155, 160
Lawyers' Committee (Lawyers'
   Committee for Civil Rights Under
   Law) 74, 78, 128
Lawyers' Committee for Civil Rights
   Under Law (Lawyers' Committee)
   74, 78, 128
LDF (NAACP Legal Defense and
   Education Fund) 78
Leon County (Florida) 144
LeSage (Louisiana) 83
Lewis, John 79, 184
Lichtman, Allen 144
Little Rock (Arkansas) 63
living wage ordinances 162
Lockheed Martin Corporation 161
Long, Russell 41, 61
Los Angeles (California) 30, 70, 177–8
Louima, Abner 85
Louisiana
   activism 37, 148, 163
   environmental racism 59, 60, 82,
      83, 179

Louisiana (*cont'd*)
  Hurricane Katrina 73–5
  resistance to black freedom struggle
    37, 39–40, 41–2, 43, 61, 90, 102,
    141
Louisiana Association of Business and
  Industry 60
Louisville (Kentucky) 62, 90
Lovato, Roberto 177
Lowery, Joseph 78, 184
Lowndes County (Alabama) 38
Lowndes, William 37
Lublin, David 129
Luckett, Semmes 35–6
lynching 20, 70; *see also* racial
  violence

MacLean, Nancy 113
Macomb County (Michigan) 49
Malaysia 182
Mandela, Nelson 180, 181
Manila (Philippines) 188
Marable, Manning 80
March on Washington for Jobs and
  Freedom (1963) 32, 77
Marine Mammal Protection Act (1972)
  184
Marshall Plan 101, 104, 166
Maryland 10, 11, 37, 85, 134, 160
Massachusetts 39, 40, 62, 88–90, 131,
  133, 138, 156, 160, 166
Massachusetts Welfare Rights
  Organization 160
Massey, Douglas 56
Matsuda, Mari 91–2
McCain-Feingold Act (2002) 142
McCain, John 129, 145
McGruder, Julious 139
McKeldin, Theodore 37
McKissick, Floyd 79, 80
McKnight, Albert J. 163
McLean, Paul Gene 103
mechanization 28, 31, 35
Merrillville (Indiana) 130
Metcalfe, Ralph 134
Mexico 173, 183, 184
Miami (Florida) 44
Michigan 49, 130, 131, 133–4, 165
Microsoft Corporation 71

migration
  black 26, 28, 31–2, 35–6, 80
  international 169, 174–5, 192
Milliken v. Bradley (1974) 63
Milliken v. Bradley II (1977) 63
Minchin, Timothy 103
Minneapolis (Minnesota) 162
Minnesota 162
Mississippi
  activism 34, 124, 125, 128, 142,
    147, 167
  environmental racism 59
  Hurricane Katrina 73
  politics 35–6, 126, 136, 141, 148
  public assistance programs 152, 153
  resistance to black freedom struggle
    7, 35–6, 38, 93, 113, 126–7, 135
Mississippi Council on Human
  Relations 43
Mississippi Freedom Democratic Party
  124
Missouri 65, 101, 105, 122
Missouri v. Jenkins (1995) 64
Mitchell, Clarence 134
Mitchell, George 98–9
Mitchell, John 55, 106
Model Cities program 136
Montgomery (Alabama) 28, 76, 80,
  101
Montgomery bus boycott 28, 76, 80
Moore, Michael 187
Moore, Sydelle 153
Morash, Evelyn 90
Morgan, Edmund 10, 14
Morocco 183
Morton, Samuel 17
Moss Point (Mississippi) 126–7
Mothers for Adequate Welfare 153
Motor Voter Act (National Voter
  Registration Act) 140
Moynihan, Daniel Patrick 104
Muhammad, Ishmael 75
Mumbai (India) 188
Murray, Charles 72
Musgrove, Derek 135

NAACP *see* National Association for
  the Advancement of Colored
  People

NAACP Legal Defense and Education
Fund (LDF) 78
NAFTA (North American Free Trade
Agreement) 173, 183, 184, 185
National Advisory Commission on
Civil Disorders 37, 108
National Association for the
Advancement of Colored People
(NAACP)
continuation after 1965 78, 79
criminal justice activism 85
equal education activism 28–9, 89
equal employment opportunity
activism 103, 118–19
fair housing activism 24
social justice activism 108, 158, 166
voting rights activism 141–2, 145
National Association of Human Rights
Workers 134
National Association of Manufacturers
115
National Association of Real Estate
Brokers 24
National Black Conference of Mayors
119
National Black Women's Health
Project 166–7
National Campaign for Jobs and
Income Support 162
National Committee Against
Discrimination in Housing
(NCDH) 93–4
National Coordinating Committee of
Welfare Rights Groups 154
National Council of Negro Women
(NCNW) 167, 168, 179
National Environmental Justice
Advisory Council 82
National Fair Housing Alliance
(NFHA) 94
National Front (France) 175
National People of Color
Environmental Leadership Summit
83–4
National Urban League (NUL) 29, 32,
78, 101, 118–19, 158, 166
National Voter Fund 142
National Voter Registration ("Motor
Voter") Act 140

National Welfare Rights Organization
(NWRO) 154, 156, 157, 158,
160
National Welfare Rights Union
(NWRU) 160, 161
Nationalist Party (South Africa) 180
Native Americans 8, 179
nativism 174–5, 184
Nazism 28
NCDH (National Committee Against
Discrimination in Housing) 93–4
NCNW (National Council of Negro
Women) 167, 168, 179
neo-fascism 174–5
neo-Nazism 53, 95
Netherlands 175
Nettles, Larry 87
Neufeldt, Ed 192
Nevada 153
New Deal 2, 7, 22–7, 31, 34, 45, 46,
48, 121
New England 8, 14
New Hampshire 170
New Haven (Connecticut) 66
New Jersey 34, 37, 67, 92, 111
New Jersey State Police Department 85
New Orleans (Louisiana) 23, 59, 73–5
New York City (New York) 68, 85,
90, 97, 131, 142, 153, 154, 155,
156, 161–2, 176
New York City Department of Social
Services 155
New York State 16, 39, 140, 153,
154, 160
Newark (New Jersey) 34, 37, 67, 111
NFHA (National Fair Housing
Alliance) 94
Nicholas, Francis 11
Nichols, Bill 65
Nigeria 179
Nike Corporation 179, 191
Nixon, Richard
abuses of power 135
affirmative action 113–14, 117
civil rights enforcement 45, 55–6,
57, 61–2
economic policies 45, 158, 171
law and order rhetoric 66–7
southern strategy 44–5, 51

Nolan, Martin 177
nonviolence 28, 79
Norco (Louisiana) 179
Norfolk (Virginia) 63–4
North America 2, 8–14, 171, 180,
184, 192
North American Free Trade Agreement
(NAFTA) 173, 183, 184, 185
North Carolina 53, 58, 62, 81–2, 85,
103, 111, 129, 145, 180
Northeast Community Action Group
81
Northwood Manor (Texas) 81
Novak, Robert 43
NRC (US Nuclear Regulatory
Commission) 83
NUL (National Urban League) 29, 32,
78, 101, 118–19, 158, 166
Nunn, Sam 50
NWRO (National Welfare Rights
Organization) 154, 156, 157, 158,
160
NWRU (National Welfare Rights
Union) 160, 161

Oakland (California) 84, 162
Obama, Barack 4, 79, 84, 122, 129,
145–6, 192–3
O'Connor, Sandra Day 56, 116–17
OEO (Office of Economic
Opportunity) 33–4, 36, 45, 152,
163
OFCC (Office of Federal Contract
Compliance) 105–6
OFCCP (Office of Federal Contract
Compliance Program) 116
Office of Economic Opportunity
(OEO) 33–4, 36, 45, 152,
163
Office of Environmental Equity 82
Office of Environmental Justice 82
Office of Federal Contract Compliance
(OFCC) 105–6
Office of Federal Contract Compliance
Programs (OFCCP) 116
Ohio 96, 129, 130, 134, 151
Ohio Northern University 93
Okun, Arthur 150
Omnibus Crime Act (1994) 70

Omnibus Crime Control and Safe
Streets Act (1968) 67
OPEC (Organization of Petroleum
Exporting Countries) 46, 171
Operation Breadbasket 117–18
Operation PUSH (People United to
Serve Humanity) 80, 118–19, 179
Orfield, Gary 64
Organization of Petroleum Exporting
Countries (OPEC) 46, 171

Palast, Greg 144
Panama 182
Parenti, Christian 176
Paris, Wendell 60
Pataki, George 161
Paull, Joseph 154
Peace, William H., III 164
Pennsylvania 26, 85, 110, 131, 160–1
People's Party 19–20
Percy, Charles 43–4
Personal Responsibility and Work
Opportunity Reconciliation Act
(1996) 159
Peru 179
Petersburg (Virginia) 95
petrochemical industry 59–61, 82
Pettigrew, Pierre 170
Pew Center 66, 86
Philadelphia (Pennsylvania) 26, 110,
131, 160–1
Philadelphia Plan 106, 108, 109,
111
Philippines 176, 185–6
Phillips County (Arkansas) 138–9
Phillips, Kevin 43
Pinnix, Ramona 103
Pittsburgh (Pennsylvania) 85
plantation system 8, 9–14, 16, 18, 19,
20–1, 23, 28, 31, 35, 59–60, 126,
133, 147, 149, 153
Plessy v. Ferguson (1896) 21
Polaroid Corporation 180
police brutality 30, 70, 78, 84–5, 88,
130, 186–7
Poor People's Campaign (PPC) 148–9
popular culture 21–2, 24, 74–5, 134,
135, 167
Populism 19–20

Port Gibson (Mississippi) 127
Porto Alegre (Brazil) 189
poverty
  antipoverty programs 22–3, 31–3, 80, 147–9
  causes 5, 8, 11, 22, 29, 30–1, 122, 147–9, 151–6, 158–63, 191, 171, 174
  global 171, 174, 179, 191
  incidence in black communities 26, 29, 30, 50, 54, 58, 61, 65–6, 74, 92, 133, 151–2, 165
  see also global justice movement; social justice activism; war on poverty; welfare rights movement
Poverty/Rights Action Center 80, 154
Powell, Lewis 56
Powledge, Fred 76
PPC (Poor People's Campaign) 148–9
Prague (Czech Republic) 187
Prejean, Charles 163, 164
Preston, Richard 10
prison-industrial complex 65–71
prisoners' rights movement 85–6
privatization 8, 50, 51, 169, 178, 188
property rights 14–15, 38–9, 42, 57, 149
Proposition 13 (California, 1978) 41
Proposition 187 (California, 1994) 175
public assistance programs see social welfare system
public housing 26, 27, 41, 48, 49, 58, 69, 74, 93, 166
Puerto Rico 83
Punch, John 9
PUSH (People United to Serve Humanity) 80, 118–19, 137–8, 179

Quarles v. Philip Morris (1968) 110–11

racial profiling 68, 84, 85
racial violence
  Jim Crow era 1, 20, 33, 38, 77
  civil rights era 29, 77, 124
  post-civil rights era 39, 53, 62, 78, 87, 89, 93, 126–7, 134, 175, 176–7

racism
  capitalism and 2, 10–14, 15–16, 20–2, 31, 54, 71, 77–8, 178–9
  class structure and 2, 6, 13–14, 15, 22, 26, 38, 39–40, 48, 50, 68–9, 77–8, 119, 120, 138–9, 142–4
  collective responsibility to end 3, 31, 41–2, 91–2
  economic and political uses 7, 16, 19–21, 35–8, 42–5, 47–9, 108, 113–14
  as individual prejudice 2, 7, 13, 23, 25, 28, 53, 55–6, 90, 93, 96, 99, 100, 105, 110, 114, 116, 121–2
  as institutional and systemic 2–3, 4, 6, 7, 13–14, 22–7, 28, 30, 52, 53–6, 64–5, 72–3, 77–8, 90, 91–2, 93, 95–9, 100, 105–6, 110–11, 114–15, 116, 121–2, 136–41
  invisibility after 1965 1, 54, 71–3, 77
  as labor control 2, 12, 21, 28, 54, 71, 171, 178
  opportunities for eliminating 17–20, 28, 31
  origins 2, 8–14
  persistence after 1965 1–2, 4, 53–75, 76, 81–3, 84–92, 93, 94–6, 98–9, 101–4, 105–6, 124, 126–35, 138–40, 152, 157, 159–60, 164, 165, 167, 192
  as public policy 2–3, 7, 12–13, 19, 20–1, 23–6, 28, 30, 37, 39, 41, 57, 58–61, 80–4, 88, 89
  redistributive policies needed to end 1, 18, 35, 51, 72, 77–8, 100–1, 110, 114–15
  white Americans' stake in 2, 7, 11, 13–15, 21, 38–9, 110–11, 120
  see also African Americans; banks; colorblind policies, criminal justice system; cultural racism; electoral politics; employment discrimination; environmental racism; housing segregation; popular culture; property rights; schools; scientific racism
Rainbow Coalition 80, 137–8
Rainbow/PUSH Coalition 80
Randolph, A. Philip 102

Rathke, Wade 160
Ray, Dolores 62
Ray, James Earl 57
Reagan, Ronald
  abuses of power 135
  affirmative action 114–16
  civil rights enforcement 55–6, 64,
    94, 95–6, 117, 181
  crime policies 67
  economic policies 49–50, 72, 137,
    158–9, 164
  election victories 139–40
  free market ideology 44, 47–9, 79,
    165, 172
Reconstruction 17–18, 28, 126
Reddick, Antoine 66
redlining 25, 57, 93
Reed, Adolph, Jr. 130, 136, 167
Regents of the University of California
  v. Bakke (1978) 111–12, 113
Rehnquist, William 56
Reich, Charles 152, 156
Republic of New Afrika 165
Republican National Committee 141
Republican Party
  affirmative action 114–16
  African Americans 22, 133
  free market policies 3, 31, 158,
    159–61, 192
  hostility to freedom struggle 33, 43,
    56, 135, 136, 140–1
  political dominance 141, 143, 145
  southern strategy 42–5, 47–9, 108,
    137
  support for freedom struggle 16, 18
republicanism 15–16
residential segregation see housing
  segregation
restrictive covenants 24, 25
Reynolds, William Bradford 55, 64,
  95–6, 116
Ribicoff, Abraham 156
Rich, Marvin 126
Richmond (Virginia) 116–17, 142
riots 8, 30, 57, 66–7, 70, 177, 182, 191
Rivers, Eugene 166
Rockefeller, Nelson 44
Rockford (Illinois) 91
Romney, George 57

Roosevelt, Franklin D. 22
Rovere, Richard 43
Royal African Company 12
Russia 187
Rustin, Bayard 32, 102
Rwanda 178

Samson, Roger 41
Sanders, Beulah 156, 160
Sayon, Ernest 85
Scalia, Antonin 56
Schmidt, Helmut 185
Scholarship, Education and Defense
  Fund for Racial Equality (SEDFRE)
  79, 125–6, 132, 145, 146
schools
  integration 28, 39–41, 61–2, 87–92
  private 39–41, 65, 88, 91
  public 18, 24, 26, 28, 38–41, 44,
    45, 60, 61–5, 73, 87–92, 131,
    176, 177
  segregation 20–1, 26, 27, 30, 39,
    79, 61–5, 87–9, 90–1
  tracking 90–1
Schwartz, Richard 161
scientific racism 17, 22, 71, 72
SCLC (Southern Christian Leadership
  Conference) 28, 78, 79, 80, 81,
  84, 93, 94–5, 117–18, 148–9,
  166, 184
Seattle (Washington) 186–7, 188, 189
SEDFRE (Scholarship, Education and
  Defense Fund for Racial Equality)
  79, 125–6, 132, 145, 146
segregation
  Jim Crow era 1, 20–2, 23–6, 28, 29,
    30, 32, 77, 101
  post-civil rights era 1, 38, 56–8,
    61–5, 87–9, 90–2, 92–5, 114, 133
segregationists
  civil rights era 3, 7, 31, 35–41, 102,
    124, 152, 154
  Jim Crow era 20–1, 24
  post-civil rights era 47–8, 61–2,
    103–4, 126–7
Sellers, Barney 61–2
Sentencing Reform Act (1984) 67
September 11, 2001 terrorist attacks
  51, 187

Servicemen's Readjustment Act (GI Bill) (1944) 25, 42, 121
sharecropping 18, 20, 26, 153
Sharpeville (South Africa) 180
Shaw v. Reno (1993) 129
Shell Oil Company 179
Shepard, Peggy Morrow 83
Sherrill, Robert 35
Sherrod, Charles 142
Shintech Corporation 82
Shiva, Vandana 189
Shulman, Stephen 104
Shultz, George 106, 107, 109
Sierra Club 82
Sierra Leone 178
Simmons, William J. 7
Singapore 174
slave trade 8–9, 11–12, 15
slavery
  abolition 16, 18
  impact on American Revolution 14–15,
  lingering effects 1–3, 101, 110, 114
  emergence in colonial era 7–14
  parallels in post-civil rights era 49, 70, 140, 176, 192
Sleeper, Jim 119
slums *see* urban problems
Smedley, Audrey 17
Smith, J. Clay, Jr. 116
Smith, Jennifer E. 70
Smith, Shanna 94
Smith, Sylvester (Mrs) 155
Smith, William French 116
Smyka, Willie 103
SNCC (Student Nonviolent Coordinating Committee) 29, 78–9, 80, 125, 148, 178–9, 189
social justice activism 5–6, 30–4, 36, 60, 78, 80, 83, 84, 96–7, 137–8, 146, 147–68, 178–9, 181–91
Social Security Act (1935) 23, 157–8
social welfare system
  inadequacies 5, 66, 69, 151–3, 155, 157–63
  opposition 37–8, 42, 47, 48–9, 72, 79, 148, 157–9
  racism 7, 22–3, 152, 156, 157, 159–60

reforms (1960s) 32–3, 154–7
reforms (post-1960s) 158–60, 161–3
workfare programs 161–2
see also welfare rights movement
Solman, Paul 192
Somalia 178
South Africa 180–2, 188–9, 190
South Boston High School 62, 89
South Carolina 13, 14, 19, 20, 37, 43, 48, 96, 141
South Korea 182
Southern Center for Human Rights 86
Southern Christian Leadership Conference (SCLC) 28, 78, 79, 80, 81, 84, 93, 94–5, 117–18, 148–9, 166, 184
Southern Independent School Association 40
Soviet Union 28, 177
Spencer, Nicholas 12
Springfield (Ohio) 129
St. James Citizens for Jobs and the Environment 82
St. James Parish (Louisiana) 60, 82
St. John the Baptist Parish (Louisiana) 82
St. Louis (Missouri) 101, 105
St. Petersburg (Florida) 166
Staats, Elmer 106
Stanford University 144
Starbucks Corporation 191
Starkville (Mississippi) 41
states' rights 15, 23, 34, 44, 45, 48, 159–60
Steele, Shelby 72, 119
Stein, Herbert 150
Steinberg, Stephen 120, 176
Stennis, John 36
Stewart, T. McCants 19
Stiglitz, Joseph 182, 185, 191
Stokes, Carl 130, 134
structural adjustment programs 172, 174, 178, 182, 183, 188–9, 190
student activism 29, 83, 85, 87–8, 141, 154, 162, 185
Student Nonviolent Coordinating Committee (SNCC) 29, 78–9, 80, 125, 148, 178–9, 189

suburbs
  complicity in racism 3, 38–9, 41–2, 63, 65, 72
  exclusion of African Americans 25–6, 31, 39–40, 41, 57, 58, 63, 66, 75, 93, 94–5, 121
  racial disparities 61, 66, 68, 69, 92
  subsidization by federal government 25–6, 42, 121, 149
  white flight 41, 62, 91, 130–1, 133, 136
Sumter County (Alabama) 164
Sunflower County (Mississippi) 126
Sutherland, Peter 173
Sylvester, Edward 105

TANF (Temporary Assistance to Needy Families) 159–60, 162–3
taxes see antitax sentiment
Taylor, Linda 47
Tellep, Daniel 161
Temporary Assistance to Needy Families (TANF) 159–60, 162–3
Tennessee 141
Texaco Corporation 118–19
Texas 39, 58, 59, 61, 81, 82, 86, 122
textile industry 103–4
Thailand 174, 182
Thernstrom, Abigail 72, 129
Thernstrom, Stephan 72
Third World Women's Alliance 179
Thomas, Clarence 116
Thomas, George 113
Thompson v. Shapiro (1969) 155
Threadgill, Sheryl 62
three-fifths clause (of US Constitution) 15, 140
Thurmond, Strom 37, 43, 48
Tillmon, Johnnie 152, 154
Tinnin, Annie Belle 103
tracking (in schools) 90–1
Trenor, Odie 127
Tunisia 183

UCC (United Community Corporation) 34, 37
Ullman, Victor 126
unemployment
  causes 3, 26, 30, 46–7, 51, 77–8, 150–1, 156, 174, 177, 192
  black responses 31–2, 137, 148–9, 151–65
  impact on African Americans 26, 29, 54, 50, 55, 66–7, 69, 71, 81, 92, 101–2, 107, 108, 133, 147, 150, 176–7
  policy makers' responses 30–2, 36–7, 66–71, 96, 108, 122, 149–51
  statistics 30, 54, 149–50
Union Carbide Corporation 60
unions see labor unions
Uniontown (Alabama) 131–2
United Community Corporation (UCC) 34, 37
United Kingdom 170, 174, 175, 185
United Nations Commission on Human Rights 179
United Parcel Service 185
United States Student Association 142
universities 107, 111–12, 113, 120, 121
University of California 111–12, 119, 120
University of Michigan 121
University of Texas 121
urban problems
  black responses 78, 80, 91–2, 96, 148–9, 165–6
  causes 24–7, 30, 41–2, 54, 55, 58, 65–6, 91–2, 131, 149, 174, 176–7
  impact on African Americans 33, 54, 65–6, 68, 69–70, 96–9, 140, 151–2
  policy makers' responses 30–2, 36–7, 66–71, 96, 108
urban renewal 26, 132
urban uprisings 30, 57, 66–7, 70, 177, 191
US Bureau of Labor Statistics 158
US Commission on Civil Rights 40, 96, 127, 143, 151
US Congress
  civil rights legislation 29, 56–7, 93, 94, 106, 108, 117, 128, 140, 144, 180–1
  crime legislation 67, 70
  free trade legislation 184
  slaveholders' influence 15
  social legislation 23, 32–3, 150, 157–8, 159, 162–3, 193

US Constitution 15, 17–18, 44, 56, 142
US Department of Health and Human Services 162
US Department of Health, Education and Welfare (HEW) 39, 61, 107, 153, 156–7
US Department of Housing and Urban Development (HUD) 57, 94, 96, 99
US Department of Justice 55–6, 57, 61, 64, 85, 87, 106, 115, 116, 125, 127, 134
US Department of Labor 105, 106, 107, 116, 149
US Internal Revenue Service (IRS) 134–5
US Nuclear Regulatory Commission (NRC) 83
US Steel Corporation 130–1
US Supreme Court
  decisions hostile to freedom struggle 21, 63, 64, 112, 113, 116–17, 128–9
  decisions supporting freedom struggle 24, 28, 39, 41, 66, 86, 111–12, 121, 128, 155
  strict constructionism after 1965 44, 45, 56
US Treasury 151

Vaden, Frances 95
veterans 25
Veterans Administration 25
Vietnam War 46, 66, 95
Viguerie, Richard 4
Virginia 8–13 passim, 63–4, 94–5, 103, 110, 116–17, 128, 142
Virginia Assembly 10, 12
Virginia State University (VSU) 95
Vivian, C. T. 96
Volcker, Paul 151
Volunteers in Service to America 88
voter fraud 140–1
voter registration 29, 42, 80, 124, 125, 127, 138–9, 140–2, 144–5, 146, 148, 163
voting rights
  court cases 127–9
  extension to African Americans 18

opposition 15, 126–7, 139, 140–1
  see also disfranchisement; voter registration; Voting Rights Act
Voting Rights Act (1965) 4, 5, 29, 30, 79, 96, 124–5, 128–9, 145, 147
VSU (Virginia State University) 95

Wacquant, Loïc 70
Wallace, George 42, 43, 45, 66
war on drugs 67–70, 86
war on poverty 3, 30–8, 45, 52, 54, 149
Wards Cove Packing Co. v. Antonio (1989) 117
Warner, Mary 134
Warren County (North Carolina) 58, 81–2
Washington Parish (Louisiana) 90
Washington State 186–7, 188, 189
Washington, DC 83, 85, 91, 96, 148–9, 154, 157, 161, 167, 180, 181, 187, 191
Washington, George 14
Watergate scandal 135
Watson, Tom 19
Watts (California) 30, 67, 177
Welfare Recipients' League 153
welfare rights movement 5, 80, 151–63
  achievements 153–7
  arguments and philosophy 152, 154, 155, 156, 157–9, 160, 161–2
  continuation after 1960s 160–3
  opposition 157–8
  origins 151–4
Welfare Warriors 160, 161
West Virginia 60
West, John 10
Westside Mothers 160
Weyrich, Paul 140
Whirlpool Corporation 133
White Citizens' Council 7, 35, 37, 40, 43, 113
white flight 41, 62, 91, 130, 136; see also suburbs
White House Council on Environmental Quality 84
white supremacy see racism
White v. Regester (1973) 128
Whitmire, John 86–7

Wilcox Academy 88
Wilcox County (Alabama) 62, 87–8
Wilcox County High School 62, 87
Wiley, George 79, 154
Wilkins, David 120
Wilkins, Robert 85
Wilkins, Roy 108
Williams, Clifford 91
Williams, Patricia 99
Wilson, Pete 118
Wilson, William Julius 119
Wisconsin 161
Wolfensohn, James 191
women 12, 15, 69, 103, 106, 122,
    137, 151–2, 154, 156, 157,
    166–7, 179, 182–3
Women's International Committee for
    Economic Justice 183
Women's International League for
    Peace and Freedom 161
Woodson, Robert 165
Woodward, C. Vann 19
World Bank (International Bank for
    Reconstruction and Development)
    171–91 passim
World Research Group 71
World Social Forum 189–90

World Trade Organization (WTO)
    173, 184, 185–7, 189, 191
World War II 2, 25, 26, 28, 31, 41,
    46, 56, 101, 121, 171, 180
Wright, Beverly 60
Wright, Malcolm 53
WTO (World Trade Organization)
    173, 184, 185–7, 189, 191
Wyman, Hastings, Jr. 48
Wypijewski, JoAnn 129

xenophobia 174–5

Young Republicans 43
Young, Andrew 79, 133
Young, Coleman 130
Young, Whitney 32–3, 101, 104, 166
Younge, Gary 5
Yugoslavia 177
Yuill, Kevin 108

Zapatista National Liberation Army
    183
Zippert, John 163
zoning 24, 39, 57, 58, 64, 81, 84, 88,
    89
Zucchino, David 160